A Global Agenda

Issues Before the United Nations
2009-2010

Edited by Dulcie Leimbach
With an introduction by Sir Brian Urquhart

Published by the United Nations Association of the United States of America, New York, New York
Production of "A Global Agenda" was made possible by a generous grant from Kyung Hee University

UNITED NATIONS ASSOCIATION, USA Inc.

Published in the United States of America
by the United Nations Association of the United States of America.
801 Second Avenue, New York, N.Y. 10017

ISBN 978-0-615-29719-4

Cover photos courtesy of UN Photo, from left: David Manyua, Eskinder Debebe
and Sebastian Rich

Back cover photo: UN/DPI

Printed in the United States of America

Advisory Board: Steven A. Dimoff, Nahela Hadi, Euiyoung Kim, Yersu Kim, William H. Luers,
Stephen Schlesinger, Courtney Smith, Sir Brian Urquhart

Consulting Editor: Barbara Crossette

Editor: Dulcie Leimbach
Policy Editor: Ayca Ariyoruk

Articles Editors: Betsy Wade and Charles McEwen

Senior Researcher: Simon Minching
Appendices Researcher: Max McGowen
Associate Researchers: Ulrika Haglund, Asa Horner
and Tendai Musakwa

Photo Researchers: Anastasiya Bardunova, Kimberly Chin and Ulrika Haglund

Indexer: Simon Minching

Design: Laurie Baker, Cohoe Baker Design cohoebaker@nyc.rr.com

Contents

continued

continued

About UNA-USA

The United Nations Association of the United States of America is a non-profit membership organization dedicated to building understanding of and support for the ideals and vital work of the United Nations among American people. Its educational and humanitarian campaigns, including teaching students in urban schools, clearing minefields and providing school-based support for children in African communities that have been hurt by HIV/AIDS, allow people to have a strong influence at a local level.

In addition, UNA-USA's highly regarded policy and advocacy programs stress the importance of nations working together and the need for American leadership at the United Nations. UNA-USA's publications department produces a biweekly e-newsletter, the Global Bulletin, and a quarterly magazine, The InterDependent. The association is affiliated with the World Federation of United Nations Associations, which was established in 1946 as a public movement for the UN.

Our Mission

We are dedicated to educating, inspiring and mobilizing Americans to support the principles and vital work of the UN, strengthening the UN system, promoting constructive United States leadership in that system and achieving the goals of the UN Charter. ∎

About Kyung Hee University

Kyung Hee University has taken a leading role in the academic mission to realize a peaceful world by establishing a proud tradition through its founding spirit of "promoting universal values for human society." During the last 59 years, Kyung Hee has relentlessly struggled to build a better society by pursuing a creative academic synthesis of research, education and practice. During these years, Kyung Hee has developed a center of academic excellence through its integrated campuses: Seoul Campus, Global Campus and Kwangnung Campus. The university has contributed to the universal development of many academic disciplines, including the humanities, natural sciences, social sciences, medicine, the arts and physical education. It has helped develop the study of so-called third medicine, which represents a synthesis of Eastern and Western medical traditions. At the same time, Kyung Hee has devoted unremitting efforts to pursue a mission of social responsibility beyond its campuses by promoting world peace and advancement of humanity through its International Association of University Presidents, by inspiring the adoption of the United Nations International Day and Year of Peace, by publishing The World Encyclopedia of Peace, by holding the 1999 Seoul International Conference of NGOs and by undertaking the construction of the UN Peace Park and Global NGO Complex. The university's principals are **Euiyoung Kim**, dean of the Office of International Affairs, professor of political science and chairman of the steering committee of the World Civic Forum; and **Yersu Kim**, director of the Global Academy for Future Civilizations. ∎

Contributors

Irwin Arieff is a writer and editor who worked for Reuters for 23 years in New York, Washington and Paris before leaving daily journalism in 2007. He served in the Reuters UN bureau for seven years, and other postings included chief US political correspondent, White House correspondent and science and medicine correspondent. Arieff has a master's degree in journalism from Northwestern University and a B.A. from the University of Pennsylvania. He also served in the Peace Corps, specializing in rural development in Senegal and Mauritania.

Ayca Ariyoruk is a senior policy associate at UNA-USA, where she is promoting renewal of the UN and is on a task force promoting human rights. Before joining UNA-USA, Ariyoruk worked at Newsweek and was a research fellow at the Center for UN Reform Education, where she founded UN ReformWatch, a print and electronic publication. In 2002, Ariyoruk was named the Marcia Robbins-Wilf International Young Scholar and Research Assistant at the Washington Institute for Near East Policy, where she studied issues concerning US engagement with Turkey and Israel. Ariyoruk received her M.A. from the John C. Whitehead School of Diplomacy and International Relations at Seton Hall University and her B.A. in political science from the University of Nebraska.

Rosemary Banks has been New Zealand's ambassador to the UN since 2005. She previously served as deputy high commissioner to the Solomon Islands and Australia. In her first 10 years of government service, Banks held various positions at the Ministry of Foreign Affairs and Trade. She was also posted to the New Zealand Mission to the United Nations in Geneva and New York. Banks has an M.A. in Russian from the University of Canterbury in New Zealand and an M.S. from the London School of Economics.

Anastasiya Bardunova is a publications intern at UNA-USA. As a recipient of a Global Undergraduate Exchange Fellowship from the International Research and Exchanges Board, she is studying international relations at

Columbia University for the 2008-2009 academic year. She is working toward a bachelor's degree in her home country of Belarus in intercultural studies.

Damiano Beltrami is a multimedia international reporter who is currently a Fulbright scholar pursuing a master's degree at the City University of New York Graduate School of Journalism. He has previously reported for the Italian economic daily Il Sole-24Ore from northern India, Eastern Europe and the Baltic region. He earned a master's of philosophy in English and applied linguistics from Cambridge University. Beltrami is also preparing an interactive project on Iraqi refugees in Jordan through a New York Foreign Press Association scholarship. He contributes regularly to the UNA-USA e-newsletter.

Eriks Berzins is a researcher for UNA-USA in the policy department, specializing in nuclear nonproliferation and Middle East security issues. At the UN Department for Disarmament Affairs, he wrote policy briefings for the under-secretary-general on weapons issues and reported on the First Committee of the General Assembly. Berzins is a former Ford Foundation fellow and graduated with highest honors from Occidental College with a bachelor's degree in diplomacy and world affairs.

Arnav Chakravarty was an intern in UNA-USA's publication department in 2008. He is a sophomore at New York University majoring in economics. He was a regular contributor to UNA-USA's e-newsletter, covering such topics as peacekeeping and UN reform.

Isabelle Marie Chevrier is a professor in the School of Economic, Political and Policy Sciences at the University of Texas, Dallas, where she is the director of the master's program in public policy and political economy. She teaches courses on negotiations and conflict resolution in the public sector, international negotiations and conflict and peacemaking in the public policy, political economy, political science and public affairs programs. Her primary areas of research are in the negotiations to ban the possession and use of biological and chemical weapons, their impact on proliferation and the threat of bioterrorism. In 2004, she received a Fulbright fellowship to teach at the Nelson Mandela Center for Peace and Conflict Resolution at Jamia Millia Islamia University in New Delhi. She is also a member and former chair of the scientists working group on biological and chemical weapons at the Center for Arms Control and Nonproliferation in Washington, D.C., and chair of the board of directors of the Biological Weapons Prevention Project in Geneva. Chevrier has a Ph.D. in public policy from Harvard.

Kimberly Chin is a publications intern at UNA-USA. She is a junior at Hofstra University studying journalism and political science. She has worked on the school's newspaper and radio station and is the editor in chief of a newsletter for the Center for Civic Engagement, a campus organization.

Roger A. Coate is the Paul D. Coverdell Chair of Public Policy at Georgia College and State University in Milledgeville and a distinguished professor emeritus of political science at the University of South Carolina in Columbia. He has written many books on UN affairs, including, most recently, as a co-author, "United Nations Politics: International Organization in a Divided World" and "The United Nations and Changing World Politics." Coate received a Ph.D. from Ohio State University and an M.A. from the Johns Hopkins School of Advanced International Studies.

James Cockayne is a senior associate at the International Peace Institute in New York, where he helps manage a multimillion-dollar Coping With Crisis research and policy-development program. He is an expert on the UN Security Council, peace operations, organized crime, private security, war crimes and international law. Trained as a lawyer, Cockayne's research straddles international relations and international law. Before joining the Peace Institute, he was director of the transnational crime and extradition units for the Australian attorney general, where he oversaw Australian international criminal law policy and practice and received an official commendation for his work on Afghanistan and Iraq. He has also worked on war-crimes trials at the International Criminal Tribunal for Rwanda and in Sierra Leone and in private legal practice in Sydney and Paris. In addition, Cockayne was chairman of the editorial committee of the Journal of International Criminal Justice in 2007-2008 and was a 2005 Mellon Fellow in security and humanitarian action. He has degrees from New York University (LLM, international legal studies) and the University of Sydney (LLB Hons I, BA Hons I, University Medal). He has contributed regularly to broadcasts and the press in the US, Britain and Australia.

Barbara Crossette is the editor of UNA-USA's quarterly magazine, The InterDependent, and a regular contributor to the e-newsletter. She is also the UN correspondent for The Nation and was the New York Times UN bureau chief from 1994 to 2001. Before that she was the Times's chief correspondent in Southeast Asia and South Asia as well as a diplomatic reporter in Washington. She is the author of "So Close to Heaven: The Vanishing Buddhist Kingdoms of the Himalayas"; "The Great Hill Stations of Asia"; and a Foreign Policy Association study, "India: Old Civilizations in a New World." Crossette won a George Polk award for her coverage in India of the assassination of Rajiv Gandhi in 1991 and won an Interaction award in 1998 for reporting international humanitarian issues. She is a member of the Council on Foreign Relations and is on the board of the Carnegie Council on Ethics in Foreign Affairs.

Emily Davila is the assistant director at the Lutheran Office for World Community, which represents the Lutheran World Federation at the UN in New York. Davila is also the chair of Ecumenical Women, a coalition and blog that advocates for women's human rights at the UN and in church institutions. She has led projects on youth development and peacebuilding in Rwanda, Kenya and Gambia and is a co-founder of the Global Youth Coalition on AIDS. Davila has a master's degree in strategic communications from Columbia University.

Jayantha Dhanapala is currently the president of the Nobel Peace Prize-winning Pugwash Conferences on Science and World Affairs; a member of the governing board of the Stockholm International Peace Research Institute, the UN University Council and other advisory boards. He is a former UN under-secretary-general for disarmament affairs and a former ambassador of Sri Lanka to the US and to the UN office in Geneva. As a Sri Lankan diplomat, Dhanapala also served in London, Beijing, Washington, D.C., New Delhi and Geneva. He was chairman of the Nonproliferation Treaty Review and Extension Conference of 1995 and director of the UN Institute for Disarmament Research from 1987 to 1992. Dhanapala has received many international awards and honorary doctorates and has written four books and several articles in international journals and has lectured widely. He speaks Sinhala, English, Chinese and French and lives in Sri Lanka.

Steven A. Dimoff (adviser) is vice president of UNA-USA's Washington office, responsible for monitoring a range of policy issues, including US financing of the UN system, US ratification of international human rights treaties and trends in foreign assistance programs. Dimoff joined UNA-USA after serving as a legislative assistant on foreign policy in the House of Representatives. He has a B.A. in American government from Ohio University, an M.A. from the Johns Hopkins School of Advanced International Studies and an M.A. from the University of Nancy, France, with a specialization in European political and economic integration.

Jacques Fomerand joined the UN Secretariat in 1977, where he followed economic, social and coordination questions in the Department of Economic and Social Affairs. From 1992 to 2003, he was director of the UN University office in North America. He now teaches at John Jay College of the City University of New York, Seton Hall University and Occidental College and has published widely on matters related to the UN. His latest book is "A Dictionary of the United Nations." He is completing a study on the practice of human rights.

Karen Freeman is a freelance journalist and journalism educator who has worked with nongovernmental organizations in Eastern Europe. She was also the night editor for the Editorial desk of The New York Times, working with the editorial writers and the op-ed columnists. Before The Times, she was the science editor at The St. Louis Post-Dispatch and worked as an associate professor of journalism at Pennsylvania State University. Freeman was a Knight International Journalism fellow in Moldova in 2006. She now lives in Dublin.

Richard Gowan is the associate director for multilateral diplomacy and conflict prevention at the Center on International Cooperation at New York University. He is also the UN policy fellow at the European Council on Foreign Relations. From 2005 to 2007, he was the first coordinator of the Center on International Cooperation's Annual Review of Global Peace Operations, the most comprehensive publication of data and analysis on peacekeeping in the public domain. Gowan studied history and international relations at Cambridge University.

Nahela Hadi (adviser) is the chief operating officer and senior vice president of UNA-USA. Hadi joined the organization in 1999 as the marketing consultant for the new Adopt-A-Minefield campaign. She then became the deputy director and developed and implemented a marketing strategy for the program. As the program's executive director, she expanded the campaign, developing partnerships with national and international mine action organizations. In 2005, Hadi's portfolio grew with the creation of UNA-USA's Humanitarian Campaigns department and the inclusion of HERO: A UNA-USA Campaign, which provides school-based support to orphans and other children in HIV/AIDS-affected communities in Africa. Before joining UNA-USA, Hadi worked in Washington in the public interest and social marketing fields. Born in Kabul, Afghanistan, Hadi is a member of the country's former ruling family. She attended Hampshire College in Amherst, Mass.

Ulrika Haglund is a publications intern with UNA-USA. While living in New York, she is studying French in a program through the University of Lund in Sweden.

Jessica Hartl has been the coordinator for the Council of Organizations division of UNA-USA since July 2005, managing a network of nongovernmental organizations to promote public awareness about global issues and to strengthen the US-UN relationship. Previously, Hartl worked for international nonprofit organizations, developing an expertise in program coordination and management, event planning, fund-raising, public relations and educational advocacy. Hartl received a bachelor's degree in French from Pomona College and has a master's degree in international peace and conflict resolution from Arcadia University in Philadelphia.

William D. Hartung is the director of the Arms and Security Initiative at the New America Foundation, a nonprofit institute started in 1999 and based in Washington, DC. The foundation is a resource for journalists, policy makers and citizens' groups on weapons proliferation, the economics of military spending and alternative approaches to national security strategy. Before coming to New America, Hartung worked for 15 years as director of the Arms Trade Resource Center at the World Policy Institute at the New School in New York City. He was also a policy analyst and speechwriter for New York State Attorney General Robert Abrams and a project director at the New York-based Council on Economic Priorities. An expert on weapons proliferation and the politics and economics of military spending, regional security and national security strategy, Hartung is the editor, with Miriam Pemberton, of "Lessons From Iraq: Avoiding the Next War."

Matthew Heaphy has been the deputy convener of the American Nongovernmental Organizations Coalition for the International Criminal Court since July 2006. Before joining the coalition, Heaphy worked as an associate legal officer in Trial Chamber I at the International Criminal Tribunal for the former Yugoslavia in The Hague and interned as a law clerk to Judge Anita Usacka at the International Criminal Court. He also worked as an antitrust litigation lawyer in San Francisco. During law school, Heaphy clerked in the litigation department of a Brazilian law firm and represented human rights advocates as a Frank C. Newman intern at the 59th Session of the UN Commission on Human Rights. A graduate of Wesleyan University and the University of San Francisco School of Law cum laude, Heaphy has been a member of the State Bar of California since December 2003.

Asa Horner is a publications intern with UNA-USA. He is a junior at Bard College, majoring in political studies with a focus on American foreign policy and modern Chinese history.

Paul Kavanagh is the permanent representative of Ireland to the UN. From 2006 to 2007, he served in Geneva as the permanent representative to the UN, World Trade Organization and international offices. From 2004 to 2006, he was the Irish ambassador to the European Union's Political and Security Committee in Brussels. He has also worked in Ireland's Department of Foreign Affairs and in numerous posts representing Ireland at the UN. He has a bachelor's degree in modern history and French from University College Dublin.

Dulcie Leimbach is the publications director of UNA-USA and worked on the 2004-05 issue of "A Global Agenda." She oversees the editing and writing for the UNA e-newsletter and the organization's quarterly magazine, The InterDependent. Before joining UNA-USA in 2008, Leimbach worked for The New York Times as a freelance editor and writer for more than 20 years, publishing articles in most sections of the paper, including the Sunday Magazine, Op-Ed and Book Review. She also helped edit the paper's op-ed columnists and editorials and worked on the Business, Education, Metro, National and Week in Review desks. Leimbach has taught journalism at

Hofstra University and has a B.S. in journalism from the University of Colorado and an M.F.A. from Warren Wilson College.

William H. Luers (adviser) is president of UNA-USA. Before joining the organization in 1999, Luers was president of the Metropolitan Museum of Art for 13 years and had a 31-year career in the Foreign Service. He served as US ambassador to Czechoslovakia from 1983 to 1986 and to Venezuela from 1978 to 1982 and held numerous posts in Italy, Germany, Russia and in the State Department, where he was the deputy assistant secretary of state for Europe and for Inter-American Affairs. Luers has been a visiting lecturer at the Woodrow Wilson School of Public and International Affairs at Princeton University, at George Washington University in Washington and at the Johns Hopkins School of Advanced International Studies. Luers received a B.A. from Hamilton College and an M.A. from Columbia University after four years in the US Navy. He did graduate work in philosophy at Northwestern University and holds honorary doctorate degrees from Hamilton College and Marlboro College.

Charles McEwen retired in 2008 after working 27 years as a copy editor at The New York Times. He has degrees from the Graduate School of Journalism at Columbia University and from Davidson College.

Max McGowen is a junior at George Washington University majoring in political science. He was a publications intern at UNA-USA in 2008. Previously, he worked for the Institute for Politics, Democracy and the Internet at George Washington's Graduate School of Political Management.

Alistair Millar is the director of the Center on Global Counterterrorism Cooperation, a project of the Fourth Freedom Forum, a research and policy institute that works to improve coordination of the international community's response to terrorism. Millar also teaches graduate courses on counterterrorism and US foreign policy at Johns Hopkins University and George Washington University. He has written numerous chapters, articles and reports on international counterterrorism efforts, sanctions regimes and non-proliferation. With Eric Rosand (see below), he wrote "Allied Against Terrorism: What's Needed to Strengthen Worldwide Commitment." Millar, who is based in the center's Washington office, has an M.A. from Leeds University in Britain and is a Ph.D. candidate at the University of Bradford in Britain.

Simon Minching is a researcher for UNA-USA in the publications department, with special interests in US foreign policy in the Middle East and democracy studies. Formerly an intern in the policy department, Minching graduated with highest honors from St. John's University, receiving a B.S. in government and politics.

Tendai Musakwa is a publications intern with UNA-USA. He is a senior at Vassar College, majoring in Chinese and political science and works as a press assistant in Vassar's college relations office. Musakwa, who is from Zimbabwe, plans to attend Oxford University for graduate school, focusing on Chinese studies.

Roger Nokes is the coordinator of chapter relations in the Membership Department of UNA-USA. He has a B.A. in history and political science from Kean University in New Jersey and will receive an M.A. in diplomacy and international relations in May 2009 from the John C. Whitehead School of Diplomacy and International Relations at Seton Hall University.

Ana Gomez Rojo is an intern with the American Nongovernmental Organizations Coalition for the International Criminal Court, a UNA-USA program. She graduated from the Universidad Pontificia de Comillas in Madrid with a degree in law and international relations.

Eric Rosand is a senior fellow at the Center on Global Counterterrorism Cooperation and a nonresident fellow at New York University's Center on International Cooperation. He was previously chief of the multilateral affairs unit in the Office of the Coordinator for Counterterrorism at the US State Department. Before that, he served as the US Mission to the UN's counter-terrorism expert. He has published numerous articles and book chapters and lectured widely on the role of multilateral institutions in the fight against terrorism. He has a B.A. from Haverford College, a J.D. from Columbia University Law School and an LLM in international law from Cambridge University. He is based in the center's New York office.

Nikolina Saso was a policy intern at UNA-USA in 2008 and is from Serbia. She has worked as a translator and program coordinator for the Organization for Security and Cooperation in Europe.

Stephen Schlesinger (adviser) is an adjunct fellow at the Century Foundation in New York City and a former director of the World Policy Institute at the New School. In the early 1970s, he edited and published The New Democrat Magazine. Thereafter, he was a staff writer at Time Magazine, served as Gov. Mario Cuomo's speechwriter and foreign policy adviser and worked at the United Nations at Habitat. He is a co-editor of "Journals 1952-2000 by Arthur Schlesinger Jr." and the author of three books: "Act of Creation: The Founding of the United Nations," which won the 2004 Harry S. Truman Book Award; "Bitter Fruit: The Story of the U.S. Coup in Guatemala" (with Stephen Kinzer), which was listed as a New York Times notable book for 1982 and has sold over 100,000 copies; and "The New Reformers." Schlesinger is a frequent contributor to magazines and newspapers, including The Washington Post, The Los Angeles Times, The Nation and The New York Observer.

Courtney B. Smith (adviser) is associate dean of the John C. Whitehead School of Diplomacy and International Relations at Seton Hall University, where he is also an associate professor and director of the UN Intensive Summer Study Program. His teaching and scholarship focus on international organizations, specifically the UN. Smith has published articles or book chapters on global consensus building, Security Council reform, the secretary-general, peacekeeping, the US-UN relationship, the UN Year of Dialogue Among Civilizations, peacebuilding, human rights and teaching about the UN. His book, "Politics and Process at the United Nations: The Global Dance," has been honored by the Academic Council on the United Nations System and Choice: Current Reviews for Academic Libraries. Smith earned his Ph.D. at Ohio State University.

Lydia Swart has been the executive director of the Center for UN Reform Education since June 2006. She previously worked at nongovernmental organizations like Amnesty International in London, the Animal Welfare Institute, the Environmental Investigation Agency, the Academy for Educational Development in Washington, the Coalition for the International Criminal Court and the Hague Appeal for Peace 1999 (of which she was a founding board member) both in New York and the Netherlands. In 2004 and 2005, Swart worked for the Secretariat of the Assembly of States Parties to the International Criminal Court in The Hague.

Christopher J. Tangney is the communications assistant at UNA-USA, responsible for producing the e-newsletter, called the Global Bulletin, as well as editing and writing articles for the biweekly publication. He has also contributed articles to UNA's magazine, The InterDependent. Previously, he was an editor and writer at IAG Research and worked in various editorial positions at The Boston Globe. He has a B.A. in political science and an M.A. in applied sociology from the University of Massachusetts, Boston.

Mark Turner was the UN correspondent for the Financial Times from 2002 to 2007, during which he was posted to Iraq in 2004. He was Africa correspondent, based in Nairobi, from 1998 to 2002, covering economic and political developments across the continent. In 2002, he worked in Afghanistan covering the deployment of British troops. He also wrote about European Union foreign policy in Brussels for the Economist publication, European Voice. He has an M.A. in social and political sciences from Cambridge University.

Sir Brian Urquhart (adviser) was the second person to be recruited for the Secretariat of the Preparatory Commission of the UN after six years of wartime service in the British Army. He was personal assistant to Gladwyn Jebb, the executive secretary of the Preparatory Commission and then to Trygve Lie, the first secretary-general. From 1954 to 1971, he worked with

Ralph Bunche on conflict control, including the organization and direction of peacekeeping operations in the Middle East, Kashmir, Cyprus, Lebanon, Congo and elsewhere. He was also involved in organizing the first and second International Conferences on the Peaceful Uses of Atomic Energy and in setting up the International Atomic Energy Agency. In 1972, Sir Brian succeeded Ralph Bunche as under-secretary-general for special political affairs. He retired from the UN in 1986, and until 1995 was scholar in residence with the international affairs program of the Ford Foundation. His books include "Hammarskjold," "Ralph Bunche: An American Odyssey" and "A Life in Peace and War" (a memoir).

Georgianna Vaughan is a policy intern with UNA-USA. She graduated in 2008 from Cambridge University with a degree in history, specializing in migration and cultural assimilation.

Betsy Wade is a freelance editor who formerly ran the New York Times foreign copy desk, was a news editor in the Times's UN bureau and wrote the paper's Practical Traveler column.

Shelly Walden is an international program officer with the Government Accountability Project and has monitored internal justice issues in the UN system for the last two years. Walden is an expert on the establishment and operation of ethics offices at intergovernmental organizations and has written extensively on the strengthening and harmonizing of UN whistleblower protection policies. Before joining the Government Accountability Project in 2004, Walden was a freelance reporter. She also worked in Bolivia with Save the Children in collaboration with the Foundation for Sustainable Development. Walden graduated from the University of North Carolina at Chapel Hill with a B.A. in journalism and international studies. ▪

Prologue

It is with great pleasure that I announce the publication of "A Global Agenda" in 2009, a book that presents the world's most pressing issues to the public and, specifically, those before the United Nations. With a generous grant from Kyung Hee University in Seoul, the revival of this comprehensive guide, revived after a few years' hiatus, is meant not only to stimulate discussion but to also help set agendas and determine policies at the UN and at nongovernmental organizations and in academia.

The chapters are composed of essays and reports written by journalists, policy experts and scholars whose contributions reflect their deep understanding of the UN and the important matters at hand—international security, peacekeeping, climate change, humanitarian and development aid, human rights, international justice and UN reform. Some of the events mentioned in the essays may have already been superseded by the time you read about them here, but the arguments made for causes and programs will certainly still hold. The texts are enhanced with photographs and an appendix that provides data on the inner workings of the UN. The introduction, written by Sir Brian Urquhart, is an eloquent plea for the UN to reinvent itself and for readers to continue to take the basic tenets of the organization to heart as a primary tool for change throughout the world.

In putting the book together, from last fall to early spring, I became more and more aware of the vast range and reach of the UN's activities. Just when I thought I had grasped the magnitude of its work, I discovered yet another agency or department toiling away, making me realize how impossible it was to fully know the UN—a testament to the ambitious goals of this highly complex institution. Alleviating human suffering is everyone's problem, but for the UN, it is a reason for being, whether the organization likes the job or not. Along with compiling mind-numbing facts and figures that reveal the world's gross and grotesque inequities, the UN also acts, stepping in to try to relieve so much hurt and despair that one can't help feeling optimistic about the charges under its care.

Is there any other international institution, for example, that not only delivers food to people in far-flung corners at the drop of an anchor but also prescribes sophisticated economic plans to countries in need, mines abstruse scientific data on the environment, sets up electoral processes in war-torn countries, devises international counterterrorism measures, monitors nuclear-weapons proliferation, offers literacy classes, immunizes children from deadly diseases, advocates for women's rights and generally promotes peace wherever it can? If there is a rival, it is hiding in the UN's shadows. Let's not forget the number of Nobel Peace Prizes the UN and people affiliated with the organization have garnered over the decades as well: 11 to be exact.

It has also become apparent that the problems facing our enormous, messy globe loom larger than ever now that the financial crisis has left its mark, only adding to the woes most of humanity encounters on a daily basis. The book captures such mind-boggling facts that you wince while reading them. Take Roger A. Coate's chapter on protecting the environment, in which he states that nearly 50 percent of the population in southern Asia has no sanitation facilities, putting people in direct contact with human waste. Something as simple as a toilet is lacking, creating havoc on health and well-being. Or read Jayantha Dhanapala's essay in Chapter 1 on security, and find out that military expenditures in 2007 across the globe were estimated at $1.3 trillion, or 2.5 percent of the world's gross domestic product; in other words, about $202 a person. That's enough to buy many toilets. In terms of hunger, 65 percent of the 923 million people who are deemed undernourished live in just seven countries: India, China, Congo, Bangladesh, Indonesia, Pakistan and Ethiopia. Irwin Arieff boils such information down in Chapter 4, on humanitarian assistance and development aid.

Despite the myriad facts that tumble out of the book, there are bright spots that act as reminders that change is possible if not inevitable—one hopes, of course, for the better. The International Criminal Court, detailed in Chapter 6, once again by Irwin Arieff, started its first trial this year: the defendant, Thomas Lubanga, the leader of an ethnic militia in Congo, is accused of recruiting child soldiers. In March 2009, the court also took a major step by issuing an arrest warrant for a sitting head of state, President Omar al-Bashir of Sudan, who has been charged with war crimes committed in Darfur.

Universal primary education has also made strides as one of the Millennium Development Goals, with 8 of the 10 regions falling under the MDG umbrella attaining primary-school enrollment rates of more than 90 percent. The number of children not attending primary school, Roger A. Coate writes in Chapter 4, declined from 103 million in 1990 to 73 million in 2006. The UN's role in eradicating diseases is a behemoth undertaking, as its UNAIDS agency fights HIV/AIDS, tuberculosis and malaria. Irwin Arieff writes that by the end of 2008, some two million people with AIDS were being treated with lifesaving antiretroviral drugs through UN-supported programs. That is 43 percent more people being treated than in December

2007. Antimalaria programs that the UN supports had distributed 70 million insecticide-treated bed nets in 2008, and more than 4.6 million people were being treated with tuberculosis drugs under UN auspices.

Peacekeeping efforts, as laid out in geographical detail in Chapter 2, may keep falling into UN hands, but without the organization's "blue helmets," as the peacekeeping forces are called, there surely would be more blood marring the landscape. The scope of the agency's work—whether it is "truce supervision" in the Middle East or "observer groups" in Pakistan and India or actual peacekeeping missions in Congo, maintaining calm and order in places that might otherwise be anything but is a Herculean assignment no one country can generally manage. Imperfections may abound in peacekeeping processes, though the UN continues to be called on to swoop in and do the policing.

As Mark Turner, who wrote the overview for this chapter, said, "Citizens facing crises in the world's fragile frontiers increasingly find themselves with nowhere to turn but to an overstretched, understaffed UN." Can the peacekeeping forces manage another year—six months?—in their hyperstressed capacity? The people on the ground may want to say no even as they receive a go-ahead to send more officers to troubled spots.

Guaranteeing human rights is another category deserving a chapter of its own. Jacques Fomerand analyzes the behind-the-scenes details and nuances of the Human Rights Council and its complicated job of ensuring such rights to every individual in every country. Despite the challenges inherent in such labors—trying to establish standards and enforcing them among hundreds of countries and heads of states—and the criticism lodged against the council, discussions prevail on ways to improve its work and structure, as if to stop navigating these shoals would mean defeat in protecting innocent civilians.

Reforming the UN merits Chapter 7, not last because of relevance but because fixing flaws from within could very well be the toughest test for any institution. As Rosemary Banks writes in her essay about the 2005 World Summit and the reaffirmation to strengthen the UN, "reform was seen as a means to make the UN better able to respond to rising expectations and growing demands." The more abstract the UN's role becomes, the more it seems to grow unwieldy. The notion of reform, however, implies positive outcomes, and so the advocates march on. The organization may suffer from bloat, yet the visionaries do not stop trying to overhaul its worst practices while making models of its best ones.

As editor of "A Global Agenda," I was fortunate to be guided by a group of smart, helpful advisers and privileged to work under the patient tutelage of Barbara Crossette, a journalist who has covered the UN for many years and a foreign correspondent who has crisscrossed time zones for even longer. Ayca Ariyoruk, a UNA-USA policy expert, put together the table of contents brilliantly. Two additional highly competent editors, Betsy Wade and Charles McEwen, ensured that the book was readable and consistent, working round the clock. And Laurie Baker created a sparkling clean look to lighten the tough subjects. So it is with gratitude that I send "A Global Agenda," with the help of all the editors, researchers, writers, advisers and the designer who took part in it, out to educate and enlighten and even inspire people to come up with more ways to solve our global ills.

My thanks go to William H. Luers, the president of UNA-USA, for securing the grant from Kyung Hee University to publish the book and for entrusting me with this project. I also want to express appreciation to Nahela Hadi, UNA-USA's chief operating officer, for allowing me the time to work on the book uninterrupted, and to the advisers who responded agreeably to urgent e-mails and offered consultation on every aspect of the contents. I could not forget to thank all the UNA-USA interns—Simon Minching, Max McGowen, Tendai Musakwa, Asa Horner, Ulrika Haglund, Anastasiya Bardunova, Georgianna Vaughan, Kimberly Chin and Damiano Beltrami—who wrote their essays with energy and passion, while also handling fact-checking and research at breakneck speed.

At first we did not think there was enough time—only four months—to produce a complete guide of such breadth and depth. There seemed hardly enough daylight hours to cover just one topic. But we aimed to get the book done for Kyung Hee University's World Civic Forum in May, so that the essays could be discussed in earnest by students, scholars and others. Now that we know that a small group of people can indeed create a book from scratch in this short amount of time, it is clear that such determined focus can be used to solve bigger problems. ■ *–Dulcie Leimbach, March 15, 2009*

Introduction

"We the peoples . . . "
The United Nations, Its General Assembly And Some Suggestions

Sir Brian Urquhart

The first session of the United Nations General Assembly took place in Central Hall, Westminster, in the freezing English January of 1946. Although London was gray and dilapidated and most people were war-weary, the fledgling UN was a thrilling place, and the press and public galleries were jammed. In those days, there was much less electronic amplification, more brilliant speakers and a few great orators. People actually listened to debates. The General Assembly was the center of world attention and was meticulously covered by the world's newspapers and radio. Almost everyone, including the public lining up outside, still remembered clearly what war was like, and the UN was going to make war a thing of the past. It was the most promising and important organization in the world. The UN had 51 members. The phrase "global problems" did not exist. Sixty-three years later, inevitably, the situation is rather different.

The General Assembly has had many dramatic moments, including some that were historic without being dramatic. The adoption of the Universal Declaration of Human Rights in 1948 was historically a supremely important achievement. The furious demand by Chairman Nikita S. Khrushchev of the Soviet Union, during the Congo crisis, that Dag Hammarskjold resign as secretary-general, Hammarskjold's reply and the standing ovation that greeted it was certainly dramatic.

The approval of the plan for the first UN peacekeeping force, in Egypt, was both historically important and an anomaly, resulting from the distorting effect of the cold war on the UN.

In the early years the Soviet Union could, and did, use its veto often to block action in the Security Council. In the General Assembly, the Western countries had a safe majority. The United States therefore put through the assembly the Uniting for Peace Resolution, otherwise known as the Acheson

Plan, which allowed questions of peace and security, if blocked by veto in the Security Council, to be transferred to the General Assembly. This transparent device to get around its veto was strongly denounced as illegal by the Soviet Union. Ironically, it was first used in 1956 to get around British and French vetoes over Suez, when, for the first and only time, the assembly authorized a peacekeeping force.

The assembly reflects the international trends of the time. The period of decolonization from 1947, during which the assembly acted as an important catalyst, produced a flood of new members. This changed both the voting balance and the main emphasis of the agenda of the assembly, eliminating the West's safe majority. In the 1970s, the new members went further, putting through initiatives—the New World Economic Order and the Zionism is Racism resolution, for example—which, although they had no binding legal force, shocked and dismayed the Western members. These actions provoked a hostility to the UN itself that still survives in some corners of political opinion. (The Zionism resolution was rescinded by the assembly in 1991.)

The General Assembly has given the world many important documents, of which perhaps the most famous is the Universal Declaration of Human Rights. Such authoritative statements open up major fields of activity for nongovernmental organizations as well as governments. The assembly takes on new global problems as they arise—the environment, for example, in the 1970s, or climate change in our time. The assembly has also provided the launching point for new international initiatives like President Eisenhower's 1954 Atoms for Peace proposal, which gave birth to the International Atomic Energy Agency and the first great international conferences on the peaceful uses of atomic energy.

The function of preventing important issues from being forgotten has been an essential, if not always popular, function of the General Assembly. The problems of South-West Africa (Namibia) and apartheid in South Africa were on its agenda for almost 40 years before they were finally resolved. General and Complete Disarmament has been on it for 49 years, and Palestine, in one form or another, for more than 60.

The assembly has also been the place where new concepts of human and international behavior can be formulated, approved and start to play an effective role in the life of our planet. Of these, the most historic example is the Universal Declaration of Human Rights. A more recent principle is the Responsibility to Protect, which was approved in the 60th anniversary session in 2005. Responsibility to Protect—R2P—states that countries and the international community have a duty to protect civilians from mass atrocities and that the international community has a responsibility to act when governments fail to protect their own population from such crimes.

Responsibility to Protect brings me to the question of leadership. Kofi Annan, secretary-general at the time, urged the need for formulating such a concept in a speech to the assembly in 1999. It was taken up by Canada, among others, and was eventually worked into the text that was adopted in 2005. Without leadership of this kind, even the best ideas will go nowhere.

No serious person can doubt the importance of the main subjects on the assembly's agenda. Nuclear disarmament and nonproliferation remain one of the issues on which the future of human—and, indeed animal—life on this planet may well depend. Much of the impetus and initiative for action on this literally vital subject hovers just outside the scope of the General Assembly, but that in no way excludes it from strongly expressing its views and suggestions. Ironically, virtually all current casualties of conflict are caused by relatively simple conventional weapons, so there is no excuse for relaxing the assembly's perennial efforts to deal with them, either.

Another major item on the assembly's agenda is keeping and building peace. Peacekeeping, although it is not mentioned in the Charter and started as an improvisation, has become what The New York Times recently called the UN's "flagship mission." With 18 operations and 113,000 personnel worldwide, however, peacekeeping has become far more complex and sometimes less effective than the original, and much simpler, peacekeeping operations. The Security Council periodically fails to resist the temptation to throw peacekeeping forces into critical situations where there is "no peace to keep," as in Bosnia in the early 1990s or currently in Darfur or Congo. This is not the only problem. There is now a critical difficulty in raising the personnel and the necessary technical equipment, particularly helicopters and sophisticated communications equipment, to staff and equip so many operations.

I have for some years urged that the concept of a standing, specially trained, specifically UN peacekeeping establishment, or at least a basis for it in some kind of UN peacekeeping reserve system, should be seriously considered. I have learned that the vast majority of governments don't want to hear about such an idea, let alone act on it. A basic objection to a standing UN peacekeeping group is that it might be an infringement of national sovereignty. Only a steadfast group of nongovernmental organizations are working hard to keep this idea alive. Sooner rather than later the choice will have to be made between a steady deterioration of UN peacekeeping and a new way of recruiting, maintaining and commanding respect for UN peacekeeping operations. A serious debate in the assembly might help to start this process.

There is an overarching but seldom discussed issue that deeply affects the future and effectiveness not only of peacekeeping, but also of many other areas of UN activity, like humanitarian action or human rights. That issue is how to develop a working balance between national sovereignty, the basic building block of the Charter, and active international responsibility, which the public constantly expects the UN to provide. It is one thing to approve in principle a concept like the Responsibility to Protect; it is quite another to put such a concept into effect in Darfur, or in suffering Zimbabwe, or even in the relief of a catastrophic natural disaster in Myanmar. Whatever their understandable reservations about discussing this highly sensitive problem, it is surely time for the members of the UN, who constantly discuss the need to improve its performance, to have a frank and serious discussion of the organization's greatest basic problem and contradiction.

The overall achievement of the General Assembly is far more impressive than is now widely recognized. In the mind of the public, the assembly is a 192-member body that meets inexorably for three months every fall and is characterized by long speeches, often to very sparse audiences. The deliberations of its committees, meeting mostly underground at the UN Headquarters, are unintelligible to the average outsider and put a major strain on national foreign services, especially those of the smaller member states. The assembly produces a vast volume of documents in six official languages. Its head-of state-meetings are often noted more for their disruption of New York traffic than for the importance of their content. The assembly is widely believed to be incapable of agreeing on the solution to important political problems, even those directly relating to the UN, like the reform of the now-anachronistic membership of the Security Council.

The 59-year-old UN building on the East River in New York is now being gutted and modernized. Perhaps some attention might also be given to modernizing what many see as the incurably archaic and deadening procedures of the UN's most important deliberative body. No one, however, should underestimate the difficulty of streamlining a representative body of 192 sovereign states, working in six languages on a vast range of subjects, many of them controversial.

Finally, is a purely intergovernmental body still sufficiently representative of our globalized, instantly communicating world? This is not a popular subject. But the first three words of the Charter are "We the peoples ... " although they are never mentioned again in that document. Other intergovernmental bodies, the European Union for one, have a parliamentary body elected directly by the people. In 1945, one of the hardest-headed pragmatists of the time, Ernest Bevin, British foreign secretary, called for a study of such a world parliamentary body in the House of Commons. It is not a new idea.

Of course such an addition could be developed only gradually and with the approval of the General Assembly, but might it not be an enlivening partner for that much-maligned and disregarded body? Might it also counter a widespread popular feeling that the UN is some foreign entity that does not really concern people, and therefore doesn't interest them as much as it should? International political institutions must advance with the times and maintain a popular base if their deliberations and decisions are to be understood and acted on. And we know all too well that success in dealing with at least some of the global problems that will determine our future requires universal and active support from the people as well as from their governments. ▪

For the peacekeepers

"Knotted Gun" by Carl Frederik Reutersward, a Swede, was a gift from Luxembourg to the United Nations in 1988. The sculpture is internationally recognized as a symbol of nonviolence and stands in front of UN headquarters.

Maintaining International Security

The Moment to Remake A Plan Is Now

William D. Hartung

The first decade of the 21st century has been marked by growing concerns about terrorism and major military interventions in Iraq and Afghanistan, which have been justified as responses to threats of terrorism and the spread of weapons of mass destruction. The United Nations has been a central actor in addressing these security challenges. From encouraging member states to adopt the legal instruments needed to combat the terrorist threat effectively to serving as a forum for efforts to eliminate weapons of mass destruction, the UN has played a critical leadership role in finding solutions to the most pressing problems of the era.

Unfortunately, not all roads to peace and security have been pursued through the kinds of cooperative action that the UN can facilitate. For example, the Bush administration set the tone for what it described as the "global war on terror" with its declaration of a new doctrine of preventive war, characterized by a commitment to address "gathering threats" before they have "fully formed."

The new doctrine was applied most vigorously in Iraq, where allegations that Saddam Hussein's regime was racing to acquire nuclear, chemical or biological weapons were used as the rationale for a US-led intervention. It has since been established, in significant part by efforts of UN inspectors, that Iraq had no weapons of mass destruction, and no major programs for producing them, when the US moved. In short, a war that has cost hundreds of thousands of lives and nearly $1 trillion in budgetary expenditures need not have been fought.

Nontraditional Threats

The failure in Iraq and the advent of new leadership in Washington and in other major capitals sets the stage for a new approach to security, placing conflict prevention at the center of global approaches to security. There is an emerging consensus across the political spectrum that military force should truly be a last resort in addressing threats to peace, with nonmilitary tools like diplomacy, sharing of intelligence, law enforcement and economic assistance claiming greater emphasis and more resources.

But the needed change in emphasis must go beyond rearranging the tools in the security kit. The idea of what constitutes a security threat needs to be redefined to include not only terrorism but also nonmilitary threats like climate change, epidemics of disease and entrenched poverty and inequality. Not only do these nontraditional threats pose a greater risk to human life, but also, over the long run, addressing them is most likely to reduce the incidence of war and terrorism.

With this in mind, some of the $1.3 trillion now devoted to military spending worldwide should be devoted to a security shift that puts more resources into fighting all-encompassing threats like climate change. For example, some of the funds freed up by reducing military spending could be invested in more efficient forms of transportation, clean energy sources, the creation of "green buildings" (both through new construction and retrofitting existing structures) and other products and processes meant to reduce the world's so-called carbon footprint.

Besides the urgent need to head off the worst consequences of threats like climate change and epidemics, there are geopolitical benefits to tackling these problems—they can be successfully dealt with only through genuine global cooperation. Cooperation in these spheres can in turn help establish the basis for negotiation rather than confrontation in the reduction of traditional threats like terrorism, ethnic and territorial strife and competition over energy resources. A cooperative approach to peace and security is not merely an option, it is a necessity if the world is to survive and thrive in this century and beyond.

What It Will Take

Carrying out this new security paradigm will require considerable political will and extensive public education. But there is no question that the time is ripe for such a shift, as the old approaches prove increasingly ineffective and new, more complex security challenges come to the fore. As global leaders increasingly commit themselves to cooperative efforts on everything from curbing climate change to eliminating nuclear weapons, it will be up to civil society to ensure that concrete steps are taken to fulfill these promises. The one institution that creates a common platform for bringing together the concerns of governments and other organizations on these issues of pressing international concern is the UN. Citizens' groups and government leaders should use the full potential of the organization to usher in a new era in security affairs. ■

Creating a Legal Foundation And a Strategy to Combat Terrorism

Eric Rosand and Alistair Millar

Soon after the 9/11 attacks in 2001, Kofi Annan, the United Nations secretary-general at the time, reminded the Security Council that if countries were going to take action, the global struggle against terrorism had to be seen "as necessary and legitimate by their peoples—and that such universal legitimacy is something the United Nations can do much to confer."

As evidenced by its rush to the UN in the immediate aftermath of the 9/11 attacks, the United States saw the value and need to have the UN's backing in its response to the attacks. In most parts of the world it is easier to convince a country to take action if one can point to a UN resolution or treaty calling for such efforts, rather than relying exclusively on bilateral or informal group pressure.

To its credit, the UN has delivered in this area. As a result of a series of resolutions and treaties adopted by a range of UN bodies, the UN system has played a significant role in building a legal foundation and producing a global strategy to fight terrorism. Starting in the early 1960s, the General Assembly and specialized agencies began developing this framework, which now includes 16 international instruments that criminalize nearly every imaginable terrorist offense and facilitate international legal cooperation. These instruments have laid important foundations in numerous counterterrorism-related fields, allowing the UN system to create a broad framework of international criminal law.

(Negotiations on a 17th instrument, the comprehensive convention against international terrorism, remain deadlocked over differences on the definition of terrorism. A list of the conventions and protocols is available at www.un.org/terrorism/instruments.shtml.)

Antiterrorism Tools

Since the 9/11 attacks, there has been a striking increase in the number of countries joining and carrying out these treaties; for example, those that have ratified the 12 instruments that were in force before 9/11 have risen from two (Botswana and Britain) to more than 100 as of December 2008. This willingness to participate in the effort is attributable to various factors, but perhaps the most important reason is the technical assistance that the UN's Terrorism Prevention Branch has provided. More than 6,700 criminal justice officials in 150 countries have made use of the help, according to a report from the secretary-general's office issued in July 2008.

Training activities include helping countries to draft national laws to better address terrorism; advising officials on how to speed up the legal process and achieve compliance with international standards; and providing judges and prosecutors with information on how to put new laws into practice and to cooperate with their counterparts in other countries. Partly as a result of this training, 21 countries have adopted new or amended counterterrorism laws, including Afghanistan, Argentina, Burundi, Colombia, Niger and Tunisia.

In addition to the universal treaties, the Security Council has adopted a number of resolutions, most of them under Chapter VII of the UN Charter and most since 9/11, imposing a range of often complex obligations on all UN member states and focusing on security-related and other preventive aspects of counterterrorism.

For example, the council has required states to criminalize the financing of terrorism, strengthen border controls to prevent terrorists from entering and prosecute or extradite suspected terrorists (Resolution 1373, 2001); to freeze the assets of Al Qaeda, Taliban and associated groups (Resolution 1390, 2002; Resolution 1455, 2003; Resolution 1617, 2005; Resolution 1735, 2006; and Resolution 1822, 2008); and ensure that weapons of mass destruction and related materials do not fall into the hands of terrorists (Resolution 1540, 2004).

The capstone of the rule-setting counterterrorism effort was laid in September 2006, when the General Assembly adopted the first-ever global counterterrorism strategy, called, aptly, the UN Global Counter-Terrorism Strategy (GA Resolution 60/288, 2006). It pulls together all pre-existing UN counterterrorism resolutions and treaties into a single, coherent and universally adopted framework supported by the entire UN membership.

The strategy also incorporates long-term efforts to address conditions conducive to the spread of terrorism, thus moving beyond the council's emphasis on law enforcement and other security measures, and it underscores the need for all states to respect human rights and promote the rule of law while fighting terrorism. It also acknowledges the wide range of stakeholders, beyond states, that have a role to play in its effectiveness, like regional bodies, the private sector and civil society. It is, in fact, the first UN document on counterterrorism to include a role for civil society.

With this framework of global consensus in place, attention needs to turn to ensuring that the UN has the necessary resources, expertise and intergovernmental institutions to support national and regional efforts. ■

Disarmament and Arms Proliferation

Jayantha Dhanapala

History records the invention, proliferation and use of weapons. It also records efforts to reduce arsenals and regulate the spread and use of weapons. This corresponds to humankind's contradictory propensities for war and peace. With the evolution of technology, weapons have become more lethal and have increased civilian casualties. With widening global trade, weapons have been exported and imported like any other commodity at increasing costs, including opportunity costs. According to the Stockholm International Peace Research Institute, world military expenditure in 2007 is estimated at $1.339 trillion, or 2.5 percent of the world's gross domestic product—about $202 for every person. The United States alone accounted for 45 percent of this amount. Global arms exports are estimated at $45.6 billion in 2006. They fueled 14 major armed conflicts in 2007.

The emergence in the 20th century of chemical, biological and nuclear weapons as distinct from conventional weapons marked a watershed. These weapons of mass destruction were shown to be vastly more devastating to human life and material property than earlier weapons, causing long-lasting environmental and genetic effects. Thus the elimination or control of such weapons became the priority of the United Nations and the international community.

The 1972 Biological Weapons Convention, with 162 subscribing countries, and the 1993 Chemical Weapons Convention, with 186, banned these two categories of weapons. The only category not subject to a universal ban is the nuclear weapon. Treaties between the two largest holders of nuclear weapons—the US and Russia, which have 95 percent of them—and multilateral treaties banning nuclear tests and the spread of these weapons to additional countries have sought to regulate their increase within countries as well as their horizontal spread. It is estimated that today there are more than 25,000 nuclear warheads in the world, with the US, Russia, Britain, France, China, India, Pakistan and Israel possessing almost 10,300 ready to be launched within minutes.

One Solution With Two Gates

The structure for controlling all weapons has two aspects. One is to seek disarmament through universal bans on inhumane weapons or particular categories of weapons for humanitarian reasons. The other is to seek to control levels of arsenals or to prevent new possessors.

Disarmament requires verifiable destruction of existing weapons and cessation of production, sale, storage, transfer or acquisition. Thus total disarmament (as distinct from limitation) of biological weapons, chemical weapons, antipersonnel land mines, cluster munitions, laser weapons and other categories has been achieved globally, even though the treaties negotiated for these purposes may not be universal and verification not reliable. General and complete disarmament has been the agreed goal of the UN. Whether disarmament brings security or security must precede disarmament remains disputed.

Agreed disarmament goals are set in place through a web of many-sided or two-way treaties. Multilateral treaties, those expected to have many adherents, are negotiated in the Geneva-based Conference on Disarmament, which is the sole multilateral negotiating body, and are carried out within the UN framework. Treaties involving more than two nations, but not a large number, can be concluded regionally or among other groups of countries, as with nuclear-weapon-free zones.

Although the Geneva conference and its predecessor bodies have negotiated many treaties, including the Chemical Weapons Convention and the Comprehensive Test-Ban Treaty, its procedures, requiring a consensus among all its members, have led to a stalemate for over a decade.

'Ottawa' and 'Oslo' Bring Results

Existing treaties can be amended or receive new protocols through conferences of the subscribing countries. This process also requires procedures that can be obstructed, especially by the major powers. Because of this, like-minded countries, encouraged by dedicated nongovernmental organizations, have adopted innovative treaty-making procedures like the "Ottawa process," which led to the antipersonnel mine convention. This was signed in 1997 outside the UN structure, but thereafter brought within the bounds of the organization. It has 156 subscribing countries, although major powers like China, Russia and the US remain outside. By the same technique, the "Oslo process" resulted in the Convention on Cluster Munitions in 2008.

The one treaty that aims to combine disarmament and arms control is the Treaty on the Non-Proliferation of Nuclear Weapons, which is the world's most widely subscribed-to arms treaty. This pact is carried out through the UN, which organizes review conferences and serves as its secretariat.

The treaty openly accepts two categories of nations: nuclear-weapon states and nonnuclear-weapon states. In terms of the disarmament approach, countries with nuclear weapons are exhorted only to negotiate reduction and elimination of their weapons, whereas those without are forbidden to acquire them. The International Atomic Energy Agency, an independent arm of the UN based in Vienna, is empowered to enter into arrangements with nonnuclear countries when peaceful uses are involved, to verify there is no diversion for other purposes.

As far as arms control is concerned, holders of nuclear weapons are allowed to retain them with the restraints that apply through other treaties. Nonnuclear countries are not only subject to the absolute prohibition against acquisition but can also have nuclear energy subject only to safeguards of the International Atomic Energy Agency. The agency reports to the Security Council on nonproliferation issues and otherwise to the General Assembly.

Ambivalence and Tensions

The presence in this agreement of two categories of countries that are treated differently has caused tensions, which have only increased over the 40 years of the treaty. Strains on the treaty have risen further with the emergence of Israel, India and Pakistan as nuclear countries outside the frame of the treaty—proliferations known to have been assisted by the nuclear countries defined in the treaty—and the recent grant of benefits to India that were hitherto confined to nonnuclear countries defined in the treaty. A review conference scheduled for 2010 is therefore in jeopardy, especially after the failure of a 2005 review.

The discovery of Iraq's clandestine nuclear weapon program in the early 1990s; the withdrawal of North Korea from the treaty and its subsequent nuclear test; the acknowledgment and rectification of Libya's noncompliance; and the continuing questions over Iran have seriously weakened the treaty as a means to reduce nuclear spread. With the ambiguity of the treaty's approach, regional conflicts breed insecurity and therefore give rise to development and hoarding of nuclear weapons. For others, nuclear weapons are a badge of great-power status.

Rejoining Is Essential

At this juncture, only a rejoining of the disarmament approach and a nonproliferation approach seem capable of saving the treaty. This is an urgent issue, because climate change is driving many countries toward use of nuclear energy in a "nuclear renaissance." However, the technologies of peaceful use and weapons use can no longer be kept in sealed compartments.

The threat of nuclear terrorism is also real. In the US, op-ed articles in The Wall Street Journal in January 2007 and 2008 called for a world free of nuclear weapons. These were signed by four elder statesmen, George P. Shultz, former US secretary of state; Henry A. Kissinger, also a former secretary of state; Sam Nunn, former head of the US Senate Armed Services Committee; and William J. Perry, former secretary of defense. These calls for the end of nuclear deterrence theory have been echoed by similar sentiments in Britain, Italy and Germany. They were also endorsed by President Barack Obama in his election campaign.

The translation of those campaign promises into policy will lead the world to the only viable way in dealing with weapons of mass destruction: universal elimination under strict verification. ■

Controlling Chemical and Biological Weapons And Other Arms

Marie Isabelle Chevrier

Article XI of the United Nations Charter gives the General Assembly responsibility to consider principles governing disarmament and the regulation of arms. Thus, the UN has been involved with arms control and disarmament since it began. One of the earliest tasks of the new UN was to grapple with weapons of mass destruction. General Assembly resolutions in 1946 called for disarmament of atomic and other weapons of mass destruction. In 1948 the Commission for Conventional Armaments included biological weapons in its definition of "weapons of mass destruction."

Biological Weapons

The 1972 Biological and Toxin Weapons Convention was the first international agreement to outlaw acquisition, development and production of an entire class of weapons. Brought into force in 1975, this convention has withstood an egregious violation of its provisions by Russia and a failed effort from 1995-2001 to strengthen its effectiveness and improve its implementation. As of December 2008, the convention had 163 signers. The convention has undergone six review conferences, occurring every five years, since the first in 1981. After the fifth in 2002, the parties to the convention have had yearly expert and governmental meetings to discuss specific topics relating to the convention, including national implementation, education, awareness-raising, codes of conduct and other topics.

These yearly meetings will continue at least until the seventh review in 2011. The convention has an implementation support staff in Geneva under the auspices of the Department of Disarmament Affairs. Means of verifying convention provisions, including declarations by signers and on-site activities at relevant facilities, remains a topic of significant disagreement. A 1994 mandate to develop legally binding measures to strengthen its effectiveness and improve its implementation remains in force, but no meetings have taken place since 2001.

Chemical Weapons

The 1993 Chemical Weapons Convention outlaws the development and possession of chemical weapons and contains a long annex about verifying the destruction of production facilities, chemical-weapon stocks and other provisions of the convention. The Organization for the Prevention of Chemical Weapons, an independent, autonomous international organization that has a working relationship with the UN, is responsible for carrying out the convention. The organization includes the Conference of States Parties and the Executive Council, which are the decision-making bodies, and the Technical Secretariat, which is responsible for administration, operations—including inspections—and other areas of treaty completion efforts. Of the 186 states that have signed the convention, six have declared that they possess chemical weapons.

As of December 2008, 41 percent of the declared stockpiles have been destroyed. Most of the original, as well as the remaining, chemical stockpiles, are located in the US and Russia.

Destruction of stockpiles has taken more time and been more expensive than anticipated. Although two states, Albania and South Korea, have completed destruction of their chemical weapon stockpiles, remaining states have not met destruction deadlines as set forth in the convention. Nevertheless, steady progress continues.

There has also been major progress in the destruction of production facilities; 61 of 65 of these have now been destroyed. While recognizing that the convention has made enormous progress in the first decade or so of its operation, major challenges remain. Some countries that are not party to the convention are thought to possess chemical weapon stockpiles. Making the convention truly universal, therefore, remains a high priority.

The US, Russia and the other countries that are in the process of destroying stockpiles must sustain a political and financial commitment to completing the process. The status of so-called incapacitating chemical weapons, which are banned under most interpretations of the convention, should be unambiguously affirmed as weapons whose development and production are outlawed.

Resolutions in the General Assembly in 1982 (designated 35/98D) and 1987 (designated 42/37C) and in the Security Council in 1988 (S/620) requested that the secretary-general investigate charges of use of chemical, biological or toxin weapons and asked the secretary-general to develop technical guidelines and procedures for such investigations. The secretary-general made several investigations of chemical weapon use between 1982 and 1992. From 1986 through 1988, investigations concluded that Iraq used chemical weapons against Iran. Security Council Resolution 1540 (adopted in 2004) established a committee to ensure that countries passed legislation and took other steps to prevent the proliferation of nuclear, chemical and biological weapons to countries not party to the conventions. The committee issued reports in 2006 and 2008.

Conventional Weapons and Small Arms

The UN has provided leadership and support to many efforts to ban certain conventional weapons, limit or restrict the trade in other conventional weapons and promote transparency in the weapons trade. One example to promote transparency is the UN Register of Conventional Arms, established by a General Assembly Resolution in 1991. The register lists arms imports and exports noted in reports from countries.

The Convention on Certain Conventional Weapons, also known as the Inhumane Weapons Convention, is an umbrella agreement with protocols banning certain weapons that are inhumane or cause undue suffering. As of 2008, the convention carried five protocols; these prohibit weapons with non-detectable fragments, incendiary weapons, blinding lasers, mines, booby traps, other devices and explosive remnants of war. The most recent protocol, on the explosive remnants of war, is the first multilaterally negotiated instrument to deal with the problem of unexploded and abandoned ordnance. It is intended to eradicate the daily threat that such leftovers pose to populations.

In 2001 the UN sponsored a conference to establish a program of action to prevent, combat and eradicate the illicit trade in small arms and light weapons. The program encourages countries to enact laws to combat illicit trade, to destroy confiscated weapons and to cooperate in identifying and tracing illicit arms and light weapons. The UN Department of Disarmament Affairs has provided support for this effort.

The most recently negotiated convention, on cluster munitions, prohibits all use, stockpiling, production and transfer of cluster munitions. It was completed in Dublin in May 2008. It also calls for assistance to victims, clearance of contaminated areas and destruction of stockpiles. The treaty will enter into force six months after 30 countries have ratified it. Ninety-four countries signed by the end of 2008.

The General Assembly, the Security Council and the Department of Disarmament Affairs have all made persistent, important contributions to disarmament and arms control. In contrast to 1946, norms regarding the possession, development and acquisition, as well as the use, of abhorrent weapons have become embedded in international law. The leadership of people and institutions of the UN has been critical in this regard. ■

UN Photo/David Manyua

Peacekeeping forces from the joint African Union-United Nations Mission in Darfur, Sudan, guarding a supply convoy in January 2008.

Efforts for Peace

Doing the Work: An Overview of UN Missions

Mark Turner

In the final days of 2008, as a new American president prepared to take office with a platform of renewed global responsibility, the US Congressional watchdog issued a little-noticed but prescient assessment of the state of United Nations peacekeeping.

Upon a request from the Senate Committee on Foreign Relations, the Government Accountability Office tackled an interesting question: given the dramatic rise in UN peacekeeping over the last decade, what might the UN's next mission look like, and does the organization have the necessary tools?

Its conclusions: "A potential new operation would likely be large and complex, take place in sub-Saharan Africa, and . . . require member states to contribute 21,000 troops and military observers."

The accountability office estimated that such a mission would require engineers, aviation specialists and units to deter international terrorist threats. It would need significant intelligence resources, as well as special units to deal with improvised explosive devices. And it would most likely require 1,500 police officers, 5,000 civilian staff and helicopter support 24 hours a day every day.

In other words, this potential operation was most likely to be very significant indeed, with an assignment of multiple complex tasks—from the restoration of law to election support to the protection of hundreds of thousands of refugees. Any one of these would, on its own, pose a large challenge even for a well-equipped force sent from the developed world.

The assessment was a measure of the extraordinary recent surge in UN peacekeeping and underlined an expectation of continued growth, especially in Africa, requiring even more troops and capacity than today's historic levels.

A Wider Net and Explosive Need

The independent assessment from Washington was matched in January 2009 by one from a UN official. "In 2000, a new surge in peacekeeping saw deployment figures leap from less than 14,000 personnel to nearly 40,000," said Alain Le Roy, head of UN peacekeeping, in a speech to the Security Council. "This has turned out to be a sustained surge that continues until today, exactly a decade later, with 112,000 deployed and many more to come." He continued, "Today, we are larger and spread more widely than ever before, with mandates that are more complex and robust than ever."

One might be tempted to interpret this growth, and predictions of more to come, as a mark of confidence in the institution's effectiveness. But the Government Accountability Office's conclusions, echoing repeated warnings by UN peacekeepers, offered a striking note of caution.

"The UN would likely face difficulty in obtaining the troops, specialized military units, police and civilians it would need," the report said.

The organization already has fewer forces deployed than are authorized: a 20 percent shortage of deployed troops, a 34 percent shortage in deployed police and 22 percent in civilian staff. It is becoming harder to fill the gap as time goes on. There is a dwindling reserve of forces able to do the job, with troops already overwhelmingly drawn from the developing world. In numerous cases, they are struggling to live up to requirements.

Furthermore, the accountability office said, "Even if the UN were to obtain the needed personnel, it would face logistics challenges." This might include the construction of accommodations for 10,000 people, starting from the ground up, the rebuilding of a decrepit or nonexistent road networks and large-scale overseas procurement.

Under Enormous Strain

In practice, it is almost inevitable that this theoretical new mission would face long delays in deployment, even as the newspapers and television screens fill up with images of people fleeing violence, warlords running amok, children dying of dysentery.

So what is going on? Experts are increasingly concerned that the UN's peacekeeping department is under severe and mounting strain. The same experts predict that the department will continue to receive even more complex and sensitive tasks.

It is little wonder, then, that an increasing number of peacekeeping officials, diplomats and analysts are worried that UN peacekeeping may be near a breaking point. A department that was thought all but moribund in the early to mid-90s, in the wake of disasters in Rwanda, Somalia and Bosnia, has now exceeded all expectations of growth. The UN peacekeeping department oversees more than 110,000 personnel, serving in 18 peace operations or directing peacebuilding projects.

Many of these operations are highly complex, playing roles far beyond the traditional concept of peacekeeping, which was essentially meant to be a force placed between two countries working through a peace agreement.

As a tool originally designed only for times where there was a peace to keep, peacekeeping operations now find themselves engaged in active conflicts, battling slum ganglords in Haiti, fighting rebels in the eastern Congo or confronting a bewildering array of militias in Darfur's conflict.

The trend is not universally upward. Several peacekeeping missions have wound down over recent years, including Burundi and Sierra Leone, amid evidence of some success. In 2008 the Eritrea/Ethiopia mission also ended, although that case was wrapped up because of obstacles placed by the contending parties, rather than any resolution.

No End in Sight

Overall, however, the trend has been to call for increasing numbers of missions given increasing numbers of tasks.

With the US and NATO heavily invested in Iraq and Afghanistan, peacekeepers today are being asked to tackle even the world's most high-profile conflicts, with thousands of new troops deployed, for example, on the Israel-Lebanon border after the 2006 conflict.

Renewed fighting in the Middle East has prompted calls for a UN force to monitor the Egypt-Gaza border. In addition, piracy in the Gulf of Aden throughout 2008 and into this year, including the hijacking of an oil tanker and the collapse of a legitimate government in Somalia, led to demands for new UN, or UN-led, operations. On Jan. 16, 2009, the Security Council passed Resolution 1863, renewing the authorization of the African Union mission in Somalia and expressing the intent to create a UN force to replace it.

It was also notable that the European Union declined to send a rapid-reaction force in Congo's recent upheaval, leaving it to an overwhelmed UN contingent.

As a result, citizens facing crises in the world's fragile frontiers increasingly find themselves with nowhere to turn but to an overstretched, understaffed UN. "United Nations peacekeeping is clearly overstretched," Le Roy warned. "We face operational overstretch and, I would argue, political overstretch, too. With 18 operations deployed in 5 continents, with 78,000 military, 11,500 police and 23,500 civilians deployed, the operational challenge of maintaining full support to all our missions and mounting new ones is far beyond" what was envisioned in a report on reforms prepared in 2000.

"I believe 2009 is a pivotal year for peacekeeping. A number of our missions face risks that are so significant that there is a potential for mission failure, with terrible consequences for the United Nations."

Voices are rising to bemoan the tendency of powerful nations to drop the political ball after authorizing a UN mission, on the apparent assumption that the peacekeepers will be enough. Many practitioners and academics warn that more emphasis must be placed on tackling underlying problems. While a peacekeeping mission might buy time, they say, it is unlikely to solve a fundamental conflict and may only push the problems down the road.

Many missions, Le Roy noted, "are fundamentally political operations supporting complex transitions to peace within deeply divided countries. Even with well-crafted mandates, these missions need continuous and concerted international support as they manage constant tactical, political adjustments on the ground. Yet for many of our missions, there is no consensus in the international community regarding the optimal political direction."

Meanwhile, at headquarters, the UN peacekeeping command has undergone a significant restructuring exercise.

Ban Ki-moon, the secretary-general, decided early in his tenure that peacekeeping would be his first major reform. Overcoming considerable resistance from within, he split the department into two: operations and field support. Many officials, already stretched, worked long hours to make it happen. The consequences of the decision are still being worked out.

This chapter will survey a range of UN missions, from Congo, which saw a dramatic rise in violence in late 2008, and Darfur, where the UN is still struggling to reach strength amid continued ethnic violence, to equally crucial operations in Georgia and Haiti, not to mention peace efforts overall in the Middle East.

It will also examine a range of other UN interventions, from Afghanistan to Iraq, where the main security work has been left to separate organizations, but ones in which the UN has played a broker role.

Is Peacekeeping Enough?

Underlying all these cases, however, remains a similar set of questions, many explicitly asked by the UN itself. Le Roy gives voice to some of these:

"Is peacekeeping being deployed beyond its capabilities? Is the current model of peacekeeping up to the challenges of these new mandates? Does it have the right resources? Are there sufficient troops of requisite capabilities? Can we find the air assets essential to meet these robust mandates with mobility and deterrence? In too many cases, the answer is no."

Furthermore, is the UN properly configured to manage the complexity of the peacebuilding challenges at the heart of resolving internal conflict and civil war? And are the political and regional dimensions driving a crisis being adequately addressed, and is peacekeeping the right tool? Peacekeeping, however well resourced, will simply not be sufficient where the parties are not willing to achieve peace.

The new millennium has opened with a highly dramatic first decade, and recent events suggest there is little chance it will calm down soon. It also seems likely that UN peacekeeping will continue to play an important part in unfolding events. Whether that is for the good or leads to disaster may well depend on governments' readiness to face up to what they have created.

"Too often in the history of human endeavor," Le Roy said, "change in attitude and change in action come only after a crisis. It is my deep hope that this time we will not need a new generation of reports full of regretful lessons.

"Success requires both clarity of vision on the instrument of UN peacekeeping and global consensus to support it."

Without that clarity, governments may face a time of reckoning sooner than they imagine. ∎

The Largest Force, Barely Holding Congo Together

Mark Turner

The people of the Democratic Republic of the Congo, formerly Zaire, have faced one of the most protracted, large-scale and devastating periods of conflict in modern history.

The second Congo war, which began in 1998, and which at its height involved eight African nations, has, 10 years later, directly or indirectly contributed to the deaths of at least 5.4 million people, according to the International Rescue Committee. That would make it the most costly conflict, in terms of human life, since World War II.

One of its fundamental problems—an apparently intractable struggle between ethnic Hutus and Tutsis, the central drama of the 1994 Rwandan genocide—remains unresolved.

The second Congo war officially ended in mid-2003, with the creation of a transitional government, and in 2006 the country held its first democratic elections. But political instability and widespread violence continued to plague the eastern part of the country, leading to vast misery, most often untold and unrecorded.

The UN peacekeeping operation there, known as Monuc for its French title, Mission des Nations Unies en République Démocratique du Congo, has grown from what was initially a limited-duration observer force to the largest UN peacekeeping project in the world, engaged in its most active conflict, and with no end in sight.

Laurent Nkunda

The eastern conflict erupted dramatically once more in late October 2008, when a renegade Tutsi general came close to toppling the eastern city of Goma. Government troops all but melted away, and the UN force was effectively all that stood between some semblance of a political process and a new war.

Laurent Nkunda, the renegade general, stepped back from the brink, and the Congo government subsequently made a deal with Rwanda, which had backed Nkunda. As of late January 2009 the general was under arrest, reportedly held in Rwanda, and Rwandan forces had been allowed to hunt down continued detachments of Hutu rebels in the Congo.

But there were mounting questions as to how long the Rwandans should stay and about the consequences of what was perceived as yet another occupation by foreign forces. The International Crisis Group, a nonprofit organization, warned in early 2009 that the deal "risks a new escalation of combat in the eastern Congo and an even greater humanitarian crisis, without assurances that it will solve the region's political and security problems."

UN peacekeepers, who came under growing criticism during Nkunda's advance because they failed to adequately safeguard civilians adequately, say they find themselves in a highly fragile situation. On the one hand they do have a significant force, with almost 20,000 military personnel currently authorized, including more than 4,000 Indians, as well as helicopter support, observers and police units. But the size of the territory and scope of the challenge means everything is spread thin.

By UN standards, the Congo force is a large mission, with over 17,000 military personnel, Alain Le Roy, the peacekeeping head, said in a December 2008 article in The Washington Post. "However," he continued, "compared with the tasks it is assigned and the extent of the Congo—roughly the size of the US east of the Mississippi and virtually without infrastructure—this number is actually rather small. In Kosovo, for example, NATO deployed 40,000 highly trained and well equipped troops to an area 200 times smaller than the DRC."

Making matters worse, when the crisis hit in late October, it became apparent that no one else was willing to help. Appeals to the European Union to send a force, or for any country to lead a powerful multinational force, were rebuffed. That marked a worrying shift. In 2003, during a flare-up in the northeastern Ituri region, France did send troops to bring order. Some thought that might prove a model for future times. But five years later, it became clear that kind of support was no longer on offer, at least not for a conflict of such apparently low political priority as the eastern Congo.

Meanwhile, as with most of UN peacekeeping today, the overwhelming majority of troops are from the developing world and have a mixed record. On the one hand, Indian and other soldiers have proved ready to stand firm before aggression and to hunt down militia members in some of the most robust operations the UN has going. Despite its failure to prevent many atrocities against civilians, the Congo force can legitimately claim to have saved thousands of lives.

On the other hand, the mission has been rocked by a procession of scandals, including findings of widespread sexual abuse and charges of arms- and gold-trading. Indian and Pakistani soldiers were among those accused of either trading in gold and ivory or of providing armed protection for smugglers. There were reports in the international media of peacekeepers' supplying arms to militias.

The UN, stung by accusations that it was exploiting the very people it had been sent to protect, has undertaken an ambitious but slow process, riddled with setbacks, of improving discipline and accountability. This is a process that troop contributors resist. Officials at the UN say that the Congo is a vivid example of the limitations of peacekeeping missions. Expectations are high, as UN peacekeeping is the only possibility, but in practice the UN is almost always one step behind the situation on the ground and can ultimately do little in the absence of a genuine political process.

Worse, peacekeepers are handed a paradoxical mandate. On one level, they are meant to be neutral guardians of a peace process. On the other, they are asked to join forces with the Congo government in hunting down rebels. These tasks can be at dangerous cross-purposes.

Le Roy made his position clear in December 2008 when he said: "Monuc forces cannot serve as a substitute for the Congolese army to fight a war or impose peace. The UN peacekeepers are not an expeditionary or counter-insurgency force. It is difficult to overstate the challenges facing peacekeepers in such circumstances, where irregular combatants in mixed uniforms or civilian clothing trade heavy-weapons fire in populated areas."

He concluded with a stark warning: "No peacekeeping mission, however large, can substitute for sustained, high-level political engagement by all those with influence on the parties, to resolve the underlying causes of the conflict.... Ultimately, there can be no military solution to the crisis."

The problem, officials warn, is that in the Congo, as is all too often the case, UN peacekeeping is being asked to be all things to all people: both a robust military force, taking sides and engaging in active conflict, as well as a peace-making body, given the task of solving one of the world's most intractable conflicts, even as international attention lies elsewhere. It is a model under profound strain. ■

Pirates, Insurgents and More Strife in Somalia

Mark Turner

During her mid-January confirmation hearings, the new US secretary of state, Hillary Rodham Clinton, noted an unsettling parallel between the mounting crisis in Somalia in early 2009 and the situation 16 years ago, when her husband, Bill Clinton, assumed the American presidency.

In both cases, a Clinton inherited from a Bush a mounting sense of urgency surrounding the lawless Horn of Africa nation, the world's most failed of failed states. Only this time, the situation was preceded by 16 years of international failure and a marked lack of ideas as to how the situation might be resolved.

"At the beginning of the last Democratic administration, there was a humanitarian mission in Somalia that was handed off," Hillary Clinton told US senators. "And the beginning of this Democratic administration, here we are once again."

Back in 1993, a misconceived US operation to shift the balance of power in Somalia culminated in the notorious Black Hawk Down affair. Images of mutilated US troops dragged through the streets of Mogadishu were broadcast worldwide, horrifying the US public. The subsequent backlash is viewed as a major reason the US did so little to stop the Rwandan genocide in 1994.

More than a dozen years later, a long procession of international efforts to help stabilize Somalia—most recently through an Ethiopian occupation and an under-resourced African Union mission—has all come to naught.

Yet a dramatic rise in piracy, a resurgent Islamist insurgency, the effective collapse of the Western-backed "government" and a humanitarian crisis are muscling Somalia back onto the international priority list, creating a growing sense of urgency that something must be done. The problem is no one is sure what that something might be.

Pirates in the Gulf

The cost of doing nothing, by contrast, was becoming increasingly clear. Most celebrated has been a wave of piracy around the Gulf of Aden, where ships and their crew were being taken hostage until ransoms are paid.

In late 2008, the capture of a Saudi tanker carrying $100 million worth of oil made global headlines, but it was only one of some 140 foreign vessels attacked by Somali pirates in 2008. Western governments became seriously concerned at this mounting threat to world trade and dispatched several warships to the region.

The pirates remained undeterred, however, and continued their attacks. In late January 2009, nine countries from the region signed a pact to cooperate against the scourge.

But analysts warned that piracy was only a symptom of a much more fundamental problem. "The international community is preoccupied with a symptom the piracy phenomenon—instead of concentrating on the core of the crisis, the need for a political settlement," said a statement issued by the International Crisis Group.

"Several attempts to create a transitional set-up have failed, and the current one is on the brink of collapse, overtaken yet again by an Islamist insurgency.... Over the last two years the situation has deteriorated into one of the world's worst humanitarian and security crises."

In late January, Somalia's Parliament chose a new president after Abdullahi Yusuf, a former warlord, was forced to step down. Sheik Sharif Ahmed, who took Yusuf's place, was a leader of the Union of Islamic Courts, a group that controlled most of southern Somalia for six months in 2006 and has been described as moderate. There were hopes that Sheik Sharif could prove to be a more unifying figure than his predecessor, and he quickly pledged to curb piracy. Nonetheless, it remained unclear whether he could tame more radical Islamist elements, establish a positive relationship with neighboring Ethiopia and help bring much-needed stability to the troubled country.

Islamic Threats

Islamist insurgents, known as al-Shabab, had already taken over much of the south and center of the country and were threatening the capital, Mogadishu. UN reports have suggested that, over recent years, several other countries in the region have been involved in their training and supply. There was also some speculation as to what extent the spoils from piracy were helping fund their advance.

The potential cost to the west of another nasty civil war in a far-off Muslim country was hammered home in a January 2009 article in Newsweek, which revealed that around 20 young Somali-American men in Minneapolis had recently vanished, suggesting they had left to fight for al-Shabab in their homeland.

The article "Recruited for Jihad?" noted that the FBI and Department of Homeland Security had issued a bulletin warning that "for the first time, al-Shabab might try to carry out an attack in America—timed to disrupt the presidential inauguration."

Secretary of State Clinton sounded a similar note of caution before the Senate Foreign Relations Committee. "The idea that Somalia is just a failed state somewhere over there, where people are fighting with one another over heaven knows what, is a construct that we adopt at our peril," she said.

"I don't know the most effective way forward.... The Ethiopian troops are leaving. The African Union commitment is questionable.... The internal conflict is just as intense as it's ever been, only now we have the added ingredient of Al Qaeda and terrorists who are looking to take advantage of the chaos and the failure in Somalia."

It was perhaps inevitable, then, that the US and numerous other countries —including South Africa—started to put more pressure on the United Nations to send a new peacekeeping force.

For months, UN officials have been expressing deep resistance to the idea. They did not have the wherewithal, they argued, to intervene in a potentially hot conflict, with no clear political road map. They began a hunt for a country that might lead a multinational force instead. No one stepped forward.

A UN Mission?

In mid-January, with no progress in sight, the Security Council set the ball rolling for real, unanimously expressing its intent to establish a peacekeeping force. The final decision, however, has been delayed until June. Some analysts find it hard to believe they will follow through on such a dangerous course.

Alain Le Roy, the head of peacekeeping at the UN, has made his concern all too clear. "There remains no peace to keep in Somalia," he said in a stark summary in late January 2009.

Groups like the International Crisis Group were even more explicit. "It would be a bad idea to try to send a UN peacekeeping mission in now, as the US is urging the Security Council to do, when there is no viable peace process and sufficient troops cannot be found," it said in a statement.

"If hard-core elements reject negotiation and either press on to establish a more extreme regime or fall into conflict with each other, Somalia will become an even more chaotic and dangerous place. No conceivable peacekeeping force could reasonably be expected to bring order."

Privately, diplomats and officials have been warning for some months that what happens in Somalia—and the UN's role there—may be viewed as a defining moment for the future of the organization.

At present, it is clear that the UN does not have the resources to do the job. At the same time, however, the situation is fast becoming an international imperative—and no one else is stepping forward to do the work. Fears were already mounting that, once again, Somalia might prove to be a bridge too far: with too few people asked to do too much and with profound and long-lasting implications for the global security system. ■

Darfur's Ugly Conflicts, the Scourge of Africa
Mark Turner

For a new generation of international activists, the six-year conflict in Darfur has become the pre-eminent test of the world's capacity to stop genocide, human rights atrocities and war crimes—in many ways a test of the United Nations system itself. By that measure, it is a story of dismal failure, an indictment of the world's inability to put into practice the promise it made after the 1994 Rwandan genocide that such a thing would not occur again.

In 2003, even as a 20-year conflict between northern and southern Sudan appeared to be drawing to a close, a new war erupted in the western Sudanese region of Darfur, pitting the government and government-backed militia against two rebel groups seeking an end to years of oppression. The people of Darfur entered into a nightmare from which they have yet to awaken.

By 2004, it was clear that human rights atrocities and war crimes were taking place on a systematic basis—with the backing of the Sudanese government. Yet today, the situation continues to defy all efforts to end it. It is believed that up to 300,000 people have died since 2003 (many in the first two years), and at least two and a half million have been displaced from their homes. It is one of the most highly publicized wars in recent memory, arousing film stars, students, politicians, lawyers and humanitarians alike to cry out in horror. The International Criminal Court has made Darfur one of its highest priorities. Despite all these efforts to fix Darfur, widespread atrocities continue, from the murder of civilians to the rape of women and girls.

The Early Days and Responses
When alarm bells were first sounded in 2003 by the UN and humanitarian groups, few seemed to be listening. The Security Council was focused upon shoring up a north-south deal, and dreams of a new era of effective humanitarian intervention were crashing down. China, a permanent member of the council, was loath to jeopardize its burgeoning strategic partnership with Sudan. It found a willing audience among Muslim and developing world

countries that were outraged at the US invasion of Iraq in March. Russia was growing increasingly distant from the West and less willing to cooperate. On Sept. 9, 2004, Colin L. Powell, US Secretary of State at the time, said of the Darfur situation, "at this point, genocide is our judgment," adding that the international community had not made the same judgment.

Later that fall the council adopted two resolutions on Darfur, with the US as a co-sponsor of the first. The second was adopted unanimously at a two-day meeting in Nairobi, Kenya, with Ambassador John Danforth chairing the council, but the resolutions were weak.

As images from the war area became too painful to ignore, the world agreed to impose sanctions and to back an African Union mission to the region, even though it was clear that the fledgling organization had neither the capacity nor resources for such a task. A series of efforts was made to negotiate a peace deal without success. The killings continued. Finally, after long, painful negotiations and many months of resistance from Sudan and its allies, the council in mid-2007 authorized a hybrid UN-African Union peacekeeping operation, with a wide-ranging mission to protect civilians, provide security for humanitarian efforts and to promote peace. At full strength it is meant to have almost 20,000 troops and more than 6,000 police officers.

But the mission has been bedeviled by delays created by Sudanese obstruction and the failure of the outside world to provide the necessary personnel and equipment, most notably attack helicopters. For all the public concern in Europe and America, not one developed country proved willing to give the UN the air support it needed.

Now in Its Sixth Year

Late 2008 and early 2009 saw continued fighting and heightened security concerns ahead of the expected indictment of Omar al-Bashir, the Sudanese president, by the International Criminal Court. As rebel groups splintered and the government continued to fight, the political process had few results to show. As the conflict enters its sixth year, millions continue to live in refugee camps, dependent on the life-saving help of the humanitarian effort. The situation has not improved. Over the last six months alone, an additional 100,000 people have been displaced. In late December 2008, one year after the official handover of authority to the African Union-UN hybrid, Alain Le Roy, head of UN peacekeeping, issued the following warning: "It is of grave concern that year after year, the security situation remains volatile and unpredictable. Attacks on peacekeepers and humanitarian workers, as well as intertribal violence and clashes between the government and the armed movements, have intensified." In its first year, he said, 21 personnel of the joint force were killed. Despite a government declaration of cease-fire on Nov. 12, 2008, aerial bombardments and military clashes continued, with both government and rebel groups responsible for violence.

Le Roy issued yet another call for the necessary resources. "I reiterate my appeal to council members to urge troop- and police-contributing countries in a position to provide these capabilities to do so without further delay," he said. In early 2009, there were some glimmers of hope that the helicopters might be provided. On Jan. 5, 2009, two weeks before leaving office, President George W. Bush authorized the immediate use of US aircraft to transport supplies to the peacekeeping force. The size of the force by then was estimated at half of its authorized strength of 26,000 people. But peacekeeping officials insist that even in the best of circumstances, the joint force could not solve Darfur's problems on its own.

It was a message hammered home in late January 2009, as a new wave of fighting erupted between the government and the largest rebel faction, the Justice and Equality Movement. Aerial bombardments resumed. "Even when fully deployed and with its full capabilities," Le Roy said, the joint force could not by itself bring peace to Darfur. "Only a sustainable political settlement between the parties will end this conflict," he said. "The fundamental responsibility lies with the parties." ∎

In Haiti, Dire Conditions but Inklings of Success

Mark Turner

The United Nations mission to Haiti—the poorest country in the Western Hemisphere—rarely hits the headlines, but for four and a half years, the UN's 9,000 uniformed personnel and almost 2,000 civilians have faced some of the most extreme challenges on the peacekeeping agenda.

The latest in a series of outside interventions over two decades, the mission, known as Minustah, derived from the French version of its formal title, the UN Stabilization Mission in Haiti, was deployed in 2004, after a wave of violence that led to the overthrow of President Jean-Bertrand Aristide.

Since then, its thousands of Brazilian, Jordanian and other peacekeepers have faced a string of crises of sometimes biblical proportions and undergone more active conflict than perhaps any other mission except Congo.

The year 2006 was particularly dramatic, as peacekeepers battled criminal gangs street by street for control of Cité Soleil, a large slum in Port-au-Prince, the Haitian capital. The mission's relative success in reclaiming control may be remembered as one of the UN's recent successes.

A Run of Catastrophes

After a period of relative calm in 2007, Haiti's troubles returned with a vengeance in 2008. In April, huge food riots took place after the price of basic commodities rose worldwide, with the UN at one point facing down an angry mob as it tried to break into the presidential palace.

The government fell, and a new one was not installed until September.

Haitians were then battered by devastating hurricanes, even as they struggled to cope with the grinding daily challenges of surviving in a country with almost no functioning civic institutions.

Hédi Annabi, the UN special representative, characterized 2008 as a difficult year for Haiti. Speaking at a news conference in 2009, the text of which is translated here, he said: "The riots of April, the fall of the government, nearly five months of political impasse and, finally, four hurricanes in the space of less than four weeks have inflicted on the Haitian people a level of destruction and suffering almost without precedent."

As 2009 began, mission staff members were bracing themselves for what the year might bring. Large-scale security operations were over, for the most part, with Brazilians patrolling the streets of Cité Soleil. But many Haitians were coming to resent the presence of foreigners, and the country's own police force was in no position to maintain law and order itself.

Fundamental security challenges remained, including large operations by drug traffickers. The drawn-out process of rebuilding institutions and rehabilitating the economy were raising hard questions about when the UN might ever be able to leave. The international financial crisis was taking hold.

Gaining Positive Ground

Despite these challenges, Minustah probably counts among the UN's more successful peacekeeping missions. In an interview with UNA-USA, the mission spokesman, David Wimhurst, said: "We've clearly had a stabilizing effect on this country, ending the stranglehold of the gangs in places like Cité Soleil, which is all to the good." Since 2005 the mission has put 7,000 newly trained police officers on the streets, making a total of 9,000. (In 2005 there were only 3,500 police officers, and 1,500 were dismissed for corruption.) The goal is to have 14,000 by 2012.

Crime has been reduced, and new measures have been put in place to patrol the country's border and coastline. The judiciary is finding firmer footing—with its independence guaranteed by law—and there are efforts to reform the prisons. After last year's hiatus, there are also hopes the political transition is on track.

The problem, UN officials say, is that there is really only so much a peacekeeping mission can do to put a country back on its feet, especially one in such a dire economic state. Without economic development, peacekeeping is little more than a patch on a major wound.

While most Haitians probably still see the UN as an unwelcome but necessary presence, there is a clear danger that without marked economic progress, resentment will grow.

"Things are a lot better, but it's still very fragile," Wimhurst said. "Of most concern to us all is the very dilapidated state of socioeconomic infrastructure. There are no services provided by the state; massive unemployment; people survive on $2 a day. There is incredible poverty; real pockets of malnourishment."

"What this country needs is huge amounts of aid and development," he said. "If conditions are not improved there'll be trouble. We can't do development." ∎

The Peacebuilding Commission: Burundi and Sierra Leone

Jessica Hartl

Established in 2005, the Peacebuilding Commission coordinates efforts for reconstruction, creation of institutions and promotion of sustainable development in countries that are recovering from conflict. By developing "integrated peacebuilding strategies," the commission's Web site says that it aims to "help governments highlight key peacebuilding priorities" and "identify gaps in existing national strategies that could constitute a threat to peace and address peacebuilding challenges."

In tandem with the commission and at the request of the General Assembly, Secretary-General Kofi Annan established the Peacebuilding Fund in October 2006 to provide financing to post-conflict countries in the early stages of recovery. So far, in addition to the funds provided to the specific peacebuilding strategies for the four countries on the agenda of the commission—Sierra Leone, Burundi, Central African Republic and Guinea-Bissau—seven other countries will receive such funds, for a total of approximately $121 million allocated, of which $87 million in projects has already been approved.

In Burundi, for example, a project financed by the Peacebuilding Fund is training national defense forces in peacekeeping, a code of conduct, human rights, gender-related issues and HIV/AIDS prevention.

Here is what has happened in two countries that have received assistance from the Peacebuilding Commission.

Burundi

Burundi went through more than a decade of civil war between its Hutu and Tutsi populations, with the loss of 300,000 lives. The main part of the conflict ended with the Arusha Peace Accords in 2000 and was further solidified when a three-year transitional government was established in 2001. An African Union peacekeeping force was brought in during this period to stabilize what was still a volatile country.

In 2004, the Security Council passed a resolution creating a UN peacekeeping mission to Burundi, which brought the African Union troops under UN leadership. This mission aimed to continue stabilization efforts, in light of continued sporadic violence. With elections finally held in August 2005 to replace the transitional government, and a final comprehensive cease-fire agreement signed in 2006 to bring in the last rebel faction, Palipehutu-FNL, the peacekeeping mission ended in 2006 and was replaced with a UN integrated mission, or Binub, as it is known.

Over the last two years, tensions have remained in Burundi, and security still is a concern, because of differences between the parties over implementation of the 2006 cease-fire agreement. Of particular concern is the insistence by Palipehutu-FNL that it be recognized as a political party under its current name, which, given its status as a former rebel group and its affiliation with a particular ethnicity (the Hutu population), could cause political turmoil. Progress was made in November 2007, when a Government of National Unity was formed, incorporating members of the opposition.

Drafted largely in Burundi by the government and Binub, the Framework Document for the Burundi Integrated Peacebuilding Strategy was adopted in late June 2007, after a series of formal and informal consultations both in Burundi and at the UN under the auspices of the Peacebuilding Commission with donors, local and international nongovernmental organizations working in Burundi and the private sector. The strategy identified several areas as being essential to preventing a return of violence: promoting good governance, strengthening the rule of law (including access to justice), reforming the security sector and ensuring community recovery (with a particular focus on youth).

In August and September 2007, negotiations on the document continued, to develop a final strategy and a monitoring mechanism to track progress. In support of these efforts, the Peacebuilding Fund pledged $35 million. In December 2007, a monitoring mechanism was approved by the Peacebuilding Commission and was put into effect in 2008 in conjunction with the strategic framework.

In 2008, Burundi made several important advances. Most notable was the end of large-scale hostilities in May between the government and Palipehutu-FNL, resulting in the return of rebel leadership to the capital so that it could be involved in the political process. In addition, the government's establishment of a National Security Council in August 2008 was widely viewed as a major step toward security sector reform, since the council is to develop a comprehensive national plan that ensures accountability to Parliament. But by December 2008, the cease-fire agreement still had not been carried out fully.

The commission has discussed with the Burundi government a possible role in creating the right conditions for free, fair and peaceful elections in 2010. It is also discussing the possibility of assisting in garnering resources to support crucial immediate needs, like the disarmament and reintegration of former combatants.

Sierra Leone

Sierra Leone emerged from an 11-year civil war in 2002, after two failed attempts at peace in 1996 and 1999. The 1999 attempt involved UN peacekeepers, who helped stabilize the country enough to shepherd it to a final peace agreement signed in Abuju, Nigeria, in 2001. The Truth and Reconciliation Commission, established through the agreement, began work shortly after the agreement went into affect in early 2002. Its mandate was to create "an impartial, historical record of the conflict; address impunity; respond to the needs of victims; promote healing and reconciliation; and prevent a repetition of the violations and abuses suffered."

Nongovernmental organizations played a key role in the Truth and Reconciliation Commission's work, with more than 8,000 statements taken for the record and the Inter-Religious Council of Sierra Leone leading the reconciliation effort for the commission, which completed its work in 2004. The last peacekeepers withdrew in December 2005, with law and order maintained since by national troops and the police.

To bolster local efforts, Sierra Leone was placed on the agenda of the Peacebuilding Commission in June 2006, and in March 2007 the commission allotted Sierra Leone $35 million from the Peacebuilding Fund. The commission and the government have identified six critical areas to work on: youth unemployment and disempowerment, judicial and security sector reform, democracy consolidation and good governance, civil service reform, gender inequality, and improving the energy infrastructure.

By the end of 2008, multiple projects had been approved, totaling approximately $32 million. They include support for the electoral process and improving the judiciary; water and sanitation; health facilities; training and job programs for young people; and help for the police and the National Human Rights Commission, a body established to investigate allegations of human rights violations, to advise on legislation and compliance with international human rights treaties and to promote human rights.

Because the August 2007 elections and subsequent runoff were largely peaceful, fair and transparent, the Peacebuilding Commission and the government moved forward in adopting the Sierra Leone Peacebuilding Cooperation Framework in December 2007.

In 2008, the government made great strides in adhering to the framework and solidifying the transition to peace through such actions as local government elections. In his Agenda for Change, the president of Sierra Leone, Ernest Bia Koroma, has set clear priorities for the country's Poverty Reduction Strategy for 2009-2012. Among the issues it addresses are combating corruption (e.g. by encouraging government officials to declare their assets publicly) and investing in the country's energy, health, agriculture and education infrastructure.

Several daunting challenges remain. West Africa is becoming a path for narcotics trafficking, and while the problem is still in its early stages in Sierra Leone, it could ultimately pose a threat to peace there if is not addressed immediately. High unemployment among its young people and rapid economic development are also issues the country must continue to address. ■

Afghanistan: Regaining Ground

Eriks Berzins interviews Thomas R. Pickering

Nearly eight years into the US-led war in Afghanistan, the international community faces enormous challenges in bringing peace, security and viable economic structures to the country's fledgling democracy: how to deal with the resurgence of the Taliban, increasing opium production, widespread government corruption and public indifference, if not antipathy, to Hamid Karzai's administration, to name a few. Both the international community and the Afghan people are uncertain about what this conflict will ultimately cost, what can be done to end it and by whom.

In January 2009, Thomas R. Pickering, co-chairman of the board of the United Nations Association of the USA and a former US under secretary of state, gave an interview on the underlying causes of the Afghan problems, what has contributed to their persistence and how these lessons illustrate what the US, the UN and others can do together to develop a new, practical approach to success in Afghanistan. This interview was conducted in person a few weeks before the appointment of Richard C. Holbrooke as US special representative to Afghanistan and Pakistan.

Q: In the last couple of years, there has been a deterioration in the humanitarian, security and political situations in Afghanistan. Before this, Afghanistan was widely recognized as a war that the US and its allies were "winning." When did the tide start turning against the US in Afghanistan?

A: When we took forces out of Afghanistan prior to the March 2003 invasion of Iraq, in effect we took away a security element that was, in my view, to set the stage for the reconstruction and stabilization of the new Afghan government under President Karzai. So we did what we needed to do in military combat terms, but then immediately removed our potential for maintaining stability, and then took away our possibilities for rebuilding stability.

As a result, everything that happened after that was piecemeal, halfhearted in some cases, and certainly differentiated from a single overall plan to achieve success and putting the resources behind it necessary to do so. It was underplanned, undersecured and underfunded. I think the diversion of attention, resources and capacity toward Iraq meant that in Afghanistan, we lost the advantage we had created for ourselves with the very effective combat operation with very few forces. And probably did nothing as a result and for the post-combat operation in Afghanistan, nor have we even now decided on what our objectives are in Afghanistan. They sort of vary from ending Al Qaeda and its sanctuary to rebuilding Afghanistan into sort of a model Swiss democracy.

Q: You mentioned in the Afghanistan Study Group Report, produced in 2008 by the nonprofit Center for the Study of the Presidency, that its pro-

posals would be shared with relevant US policy makers and UN officials. What were the responses?

A: Almost nothing. We passed the report on to UN officials, though we didn't have a meeting with them to discuss it, nor did we actively seek out a response. I heard privately from some that they agreed with the report and the overall thrust, but that it would require US leadership to make a major change. In our public appearance at the Senate Foreign Relations Committee, the assistant secretary of state for Central and South Asian affairs took issue with a number of pieces in the report. But I have since then had a number of people from the Bush administration say to me that the report was very helpful, it refocused their attention on critical questions, and that it was taken seriously.

Q: Has the United Nations Assistance Mission in Afghanistan been an effective mission so far?

A: Until Kai Eide took over the mission as the UN special envoy to Afghanistan, it seemed to have been floundering. I think he has a very impressive grasp of the situation and a serious sense of purpose. I'm concerned that we haven't found a way to bring together the Afghan government, the UN, the US and other actors who are playing a significant role both in security and in stabilization and reconstruction in a coherent, single-minded and purposeful way.

My sense is that the failure to work out unity of command on the military side alone—which is something that Secretary of Defense Robert M. Gates has tried to remedy—was responsible for some of the failure of coordination. There also seems to be uncertainty about how to proceed with respect to civil-military coordination. Many people, at least in theory, support the idea that there ought to be unity of command—under circumstances where the issue is a mainly military question, the military should be in charge. If not, the civilians should be in charge. But that's a very hard bridge for the US to cross, and it has not done that successfully.

Q: What tangible steps can be taken to find a path to more effective coordination?

A: The Obama administration now has an opportunity, and apparently it's going to appoint a special envoy. That individual, who will not only have the question of being a senior diplomat, but potentially a senior leader in the region, certainly in Afghanistan, could undertake to put together the framework for that kind of coordination. I don't know whether that individual could conduct all the negotiations necessary to pull together the international aspects and at the same time operate, run and manage the domestic ones inside Afghanistan. But that individual could play an enormously important role in consulting with the Karzai government, with the US ambassador, with US military commanders, with our NATO friends and allies, with Kai Eide and the UN, and with others, to find a way to strengthen the framework.

If they will not all accept an individual, they might all accept a regular coordination mechanism that met frequently but at the same time stayed in very close touch through things like e-mail in order to put things together. Out of that coordination mechanism might come the capacity to prepare what I would call a "single overall operational plan," based on a common strategy, which is therefore something that could make sure that everybody pulls their own weight.

Q: Troop-contributing countries have been reluctant to commit sufficient numbers of troops and deploy them to where they are needed most. In what way could the Obama administration give greater incentive to these countries to provide the appropriate size military?

A: It will depend a lot on three factors. Firstly, on how much clarity can be achieved with respect to the strategy and plans. Secondly, on the extent to which Obama himself would want to jump into the fray. And thirdly, on how much these countries, who all have serious domestic political problems surrounding this question, can deal with their own public in a way that would permit them to take more risks than currently they seem prepared to take on, and at the same time put us in a stronger position to operate across the board with the military in a more effective way.

These have been very hard nuts to crack. In some cases, these countries have been deployed to areas where there is very little expectation of military activity, but having them there under a cloud, so to speak, merely invites the opposition to exploit that difference that exists on the allied side. I think the overall lesson is that for NATO, when it undertakes operations which involve the use of force or the threat of the use of force, ought to do so with a single commitment on rules of engagement. It ought not to accept commitments of a military character where the operational forces can't carry out the rules of engagement. If countries can't commit in that manner, then they ought to commit on the civilian side, making their contribution on that side equal in strength and capacity to what they've done militarily. This way, we could have a complete commitment to stabilization and reconstruction, while at the same time we have a complete commitment to rules of engagement that provide the security necessary to carry that out.

Q: Have Provincial Reconstruction Teams been useful in dealing with countries that do place troops in Afghanistan?

A: My sense is that they are a useful way of providing stabilization and reconstruction assistance in a situation of security uncertainty, with a complementary security presence. I think they have been badly understaffed with respect to the civilian side. In part that's a problem for the US State Department, USAID and other US government agencies, and in part it's been a funding problem from the US Congress in providing the resources necessary to do that. Also, third-party countries who are participating and running PRTs have some of the same problems.

Secondly, the PRTs have tended, according to our earlier Afghanistan Study Group Report, to report back to the leader's home country rather than to a central authority in Kabul and have not been part of a central plan. So what has worked well in one area is not necessarily transmitted to another, and as a result there have been areas of really differential performance. Some teams have worked a great deal better than others. So it is in fact an effort that could do with more reforming and beefing up and regularity if we expect it to achieve the kind of successes it's been charged to develop.

Q: Is there a UN role in PRTs as a coordinating body, or could UN officials be embedded in PRTs or other security forces?

A: It could come. The UN has hesitated to involve its civilian side in operations which are actively engaged in combat, but it would be a subject for discussion with UN Special Envoy Kai Eide. I think that there ought to be an overall civilian-directing element for the stabilization and reconstruction activities of the PRTs and for their active support, including for training personnel to go there. That might be multinational, and the UN might well play a serious and significant role in such efforts if the secretary-general felt comfortable with doing so or could get support from the Security Council to do so. The latter may be difficult if there are objections, particularly among the permanent members of the Security Council.

Q: Poppy cultivation for opium is increasing in Afghanistan, and there have been problems getting programs for alternative crops started. Why?

A: I think it's very hard. First, you have to decide what alternative crops have a chance to be successful. If the land is marginal, that further restricts the degree to which you can count on alternative crops to produce any income. We quoted one farmer in our last report who said if he could receive 50 percent of the income that he gets from the production of opium, he would go for it. I suspect that not everyone joins him in that, which means that selling the question of crops is very hard. Also, you need a marketing mechanism to make those crops profitable, which includes roads and all of the inputs, extension services, finances, technical advice and research that have been provided up until now by the drug dealers to those who raise opium.

Eradication efforts also have to be attuned with a successful introduction of alternative livelihoods. Otherwise you run the risk not only of impoverishing a lot of people that can no longer support themselves, but doing so when they might well gravitate back to opium production for failure to have any other significant alternative. So it's a very complex question that requires a significant amount of hard work and planning.

For example, if you go for orchard crops, which are preferred as a long-term alternative and continuing investment, then you have to wait years of maturation before taking advantage of produce. So it argues for careful choices. Another question is: Has that balance increased in the favor of drug production recently? It seems to me it might have, but I don't have the data.

Q: Has the increase in violence led to a decrease in governmental power beyond Kabul? Do you think that this will have an impact on the presidential elections, which are scheduled for later this year, or on the parliamentary elections in 2010?

A: Yes, which means that the Taliban has continuing capacity to exert use of force against the government and its allies, and it's likely that they have more control over territory. I suspect it will have an impact on elections, and it's hard to figure out where it will come from. Also, people have recently visited Afghanistan and come back with stories about Karzai's growing unpopularity.

Q: The disenchantment that people have with Karzai stems partly from government corruption, and people believe that he is unwilling to tackle it. Do you think it's an inability or unwillingness?

A: I think in all these cases it's a combination of both. "Inability" sometimes because collecting the data and bringing people to trial on corruption charges is a long, difficult and trying process, and people are often effective in hiding or masking it. Corruption is fairly widespread in Afghanistan, and in the second case, a number of the people who are engaged in it may be principal supporters of the government and its efforts, and therefore immunize themselves against being charged for corruption simply because they're supporting the government in a whole lot of other areas.

Q: In light of the coming presidential elections in August, what sort of leader does the country need?

A: Afghanistan needs a leader who can galvanize the country and therefore bring to bear resources of Afghanistan to dealing with the problem, mainly the human resources. That begins with finding ways to improve the training, the performance and indeed the regard for the Afghan National Police and Afghan National Army, which are the bedrock of security activities as allies and friends hope to exit.

I also think that Afghanistan will continue to be, for a long time to come, a federation where provincial leadership and provincial autonomy are still the prevalent form of government. So there needs to be a strong commitment of regional leaders to the same ideas and principles as the government and where indeed much of the corruption and poor performance takes place. All those are tremendous tasks for the next leader. There isn't anybody on the horizon who is an obvious choice, even potentially a more successful replacement for Karzai than Karzai.

Q: Has the Karzai government provided good transitional leadership for Afghanistan? What must be done to regain public faith in the government and national progress?

A: It started out with the potential to be a good transitional leadership. I think we have been seeing, over the years, the areas where it has been growing in its ineffectiveness, and as a result many serious questions now arise in my mind and in the minds of other people as to whether or not it can do the job.

Is there an alternative? If so, who is it? Can it promise to deliver better than the Karzai government? That's also a very big issue. To regain public trust, the Karzai government must work with others to formulate an approach which can deal with the problem realistically and set it out for his people and then actually deliver on it. It involves lots of regional cooperation as well. I think it can be done with lower levels of regional cooperation, but it's more difficult. If you get regional cooperation particularly from Iran and Pakistan and the northern bordering states, Turkmenistan, Uzbekistan and Tajikistan, this could help the solution.

Q: What is an effective way to deal with the cross-border attacks between Afghanistan and Pakistan, and what can the UN and US do to resolve the situation?

A: For improving security, we should look at some of the practices that have been followed in Iraq with the Sunni Awakening, as well as in other areas dealing with insurgencies. These have included finding new leadership—or the old leadership—of tribal groups in the area and finding ways to help them promote their leadership through direct financial assistance. Then the focus should be building local militias around that leadership, recognizing that over time those militias will have to be folded into a national force, either in Pakistan or Afghanistan. One should begin to build systems of support and assistance to the tribal areas: education is a main issue, and even more important is health care. Now we have the lesson from Pakistan, in which Americans were widely and positively received after the recent earthquakes because they brought relief: food, medicine, health care and support, fundamental things that the local people could benefit from.

I think that you then follow a gradual process of expanding these sorts of activities based on the notion that you begin by establishing a secure effort in a section which is close to the external borders or places already under control so that you can spread it outward; you don't get people beginning to change in isolated groups, completely surrounded by the Taliban. I think the UN could play a major role in stabilization and reconstruction support for benefits and assistance. I think that this kind of an approach has worked in other places.

However, the tribal structure in Afghanistan is quite different, and it would have to take that into account, as well as the notion that some of the strife that has been going on is intertribal. So it would have to work very hard to create mechanisms, maybe a smaller version of the Loya Jirga [Pashtun for "grand council"], to begin to resolve internal problems among tribes and others in Pakistan and Afghanistan and across the line. With some care, setting up such an operation, which would not be cheap or easy, would be a serious way to get at these important questions.

Q: Are there are other political or military lessons from Iraq that could be applied in Afghanistan to improve conditions there?

A: We ought to take a look at whether all of our many statements about a political settlement being very important to dealing with the problem shouldn't be implemented, and whether if we implemented those in Iraq, we shouldn't also implement them in Afghanistan. Over this past year, there has been an effort by the Saudis and others to bring some parts of the Taliban together with the government in Saudi Arabia, which might be worthwhile. One value of that is that it offers the Taliban an alternative—participation in the political system and some guarantee of safety and security—as part of an Afghan government structure rather than continuing to fight in the hilltops and trenches forever. Those kinds of activities have proved to be very difficult, but when successful they have been very important in finding ways out of insurgent situations.

Q: Would the UN be able to broker discussions with the Taliban? What is your take on the Obama administration's approach to such direct discussions with Taliban?

A: I think that right now the Saudis bring a great deal to the table, and we should continue to encourage them to pursue these efforts. They have credibility with both sides. They also have the financial wherewithal to helpfully encourage breakthroughs in negotiations. If both sides will accept the UN as neutral, in the way they accept the Saudis, it could play a similar role. But the UN is also fully committed to the established government of Afghanistan, as it should be. As a result, this may leave questions in the minds of the Taliban as to whether in fact they could expect fair and balanced treatment from the UN.

I don't know what the Obama administration is prepared to do with respect to discussions with the Taliban. Some have indicated reservations on the basis that the military situation is not sufficiently in our favor to talk with the Taliban. Of course, if that's the case, the Taliban are unlikely to talk to us. And so, you have to begin to set the stage, even if in fact you feel that all the cards on the table are not stacked in your favor. I think that having discussions on these kinds of issues is a way to build credibility.

Q: As a final thought, what are some ways the UN can engage more productively in Afghanistan?

A: The UN can reinforce consensus on many things and strengthen the willingness of the secretary-general and specialized agencies to work, particularly if it can offer an overview. I think that the Security Council could be very useful in supporting plans once they are put together with the Afghan government, for the process to go ahead and calling on other states to play a constructive role as well as endorsing those plans toward an outcome, and maybe reinforcing the role that the UN could play as an important arbiter of a solution to Afghanistan. At some point there may well need to be an international consensus, perhaps built around the Security Council, for a particular outcome, and if that outcome is achieved, maybe endorsing and supporting it. The Security Council could be useful in reinforcing the commitment of other countries to be of assistance. ■

Testing the UN's Indispensability in Iraq

James Cockayne

The United Nations struggle to deal with the challenges posed by Iraq has defined the organization in the eyes of a generation. For almost three decades, the UN has been dealing with Iraq as a threat to international peace and security. A succession of brutal images that have emerged from the country—chemical-weapons attacks, trench warfare, Scud missiles, mass refugee movements, humanitarian catastrophes, oil smuggling, weapons inspections, "shock and awe" bombing, looting, Abu Ghraib, terrorism, sectarian assassinations, sieges and war-crimes trials—have defined for a generation the security challenges confronted by the UN and its limited capacity to meet them. Iraq has repeatedly tested the authority and ability of the UN, and at times shown it wanting. But experiences in Iraq have also demonstrated the ultimate indispensability of the UN organization.

Hussein's Bloody Rule

Perhaps no single individual more often and more blatantly challenged the authority and capacity of the UN than Saddam Hussein. His reckless invasion of Iran in 1980 demonstrated the paralysis of the Security Council during the cold war. The UN stood by, essentially powerless to stop one of the bloodiest wars since World War II. Millions of Iraqi and Iranian conscripts were killed in trench warfare. And the council proved to be equally powerless when Hussein unleashed chemical weapons on Iranians and Iraqi Kurds during the Iran-Iraq war. It was not until the cold war began to thaw in January 1987 that UN Secretary-General Javier Pérez de Cuéllar could engineer a meeting of minds, end hostilities and send a UN peacekeeping force to the two countries.

The council's impotence in the 1980s no doubt factored into Hussein's second reckless invasion of another neighbor—Kuwait in August 1990. He did not appreciate how far things had changed in the UN, where an emerging détente between the US and Russia liberated the council and, especially, US power. Within a week of the Iraqi invasion, the US ordered 200,000 troops to the Persian Gulf. The council, rallying to support the US, then imposed only the third embargo in its history (after Rhodesia and South Africa). Western, Arab, Asian and nonaligned movement countries all offered diplomatic, military and even massive financial support.

Hussein dug in, even taking some Western diplomats hostage. But by the end of November 1990, the council had authorized a US-led war to remove Hussein's forces from Kuwait. That push began on Jan. 16, 1991, with six weeks of aerial bombing that massively degraded Iraqi military capacity. Iraq's efforts to escalate the conflict by firing Scud missiles at Israel failed. When the ground assault began on Feb. 24, 1991, Iraqi defenses crumbled.

Sensing an opportunity to break out from Hussein's repressive grip, both Kurdish militants in northern Iraq and Shiite Muslim groups in the south rose up in liberation struggles, encouraged by rhetoric from the West. But when the US decided not to march on Baghdad, these groups were quickly exposed to Hussein's wrath, which the UN once again proved powerless to stop. In the north, the Kurdish population fled into the wintry mountains, where the Security Council acquiesced in the establishment of Western-enforced safe havens, thus paving the way for later episodes of humanitarian intervention.

Security Council Resolution 687, which brought the Persian Gulf war (also known as the First Gulf War) to a close, effectively placed Hussein on probation. He was subjected to a novel system of supervision, containment and control through mandatory border demarcation, weapons inspections, judicial determination of reparations claims, imposition of new treaty obligations and the continuation of economic sanctions as an inducement to internal disarmament.

Oil-for-Food Program

Yet the council struggled to maintain this complex control through the 1990s. First, the terrible humanitarian toll it was wreaking on the Iraqi population became increasingly apparent, leading to calls for the relaxation of the council's grip on the country. Hussein used this leverage to drive a wedge among the five permanent members of the council. By 1996, he had engineered a major concession, with the council's adopting Resolution 986, allowing the creation of the $64 billion Oil-for-Food program, in which Hussein's regime controlled aspects of Iraqi oil sales and the distribution of humanitarian goods purchased with the proceeds of those sales.

Even then, many members in the council understood that the program, and their willful blindness to other illegal oil trading with Iraq, would allow Hussein to siphon off funds and open the door to corruption. The subsequent scandal around the Oil-for-Food program revealed that this had, in fact, occurred. But allowing the program to begin with was seen as a necessary evil, not only to ensure that the overall containment strategy set in place by the council could be maintained, but also to protect the lives of Iraqi civilians.

A UN report in March 1991 had described postwar conditions in Iraq as "near apocalyptic," and most observers thought that the situation had probably deteriorated further in the subsequent years. The Oil-for-Food program was meant to mitigate and perhaps reverse that decline, enabling the Iraqi government to import enough food to sustain all 27 million of its people, with the average daily caloric intake increasing 83 percent between 1996 and 2003. In addition, malnutrition rates in 2002 in central and southern Iraq were halved from rates in 1996 among children under age 5. In addition, chronic malnutrition decreased 56 percent. The program also helped reduce child mortality and eradicated polio.

It is paradoxical, then, that the Oil-for-Food program now stands as the symbol of UN incompetence, a symbol that the Bush administration used later to beat up the organization even further. Similarly, the administration later characterized UN weapons inspections as dithering and bureaucratic inefficiency, when the record suggests the exact opposite: despite Hussein's cat-and-mouse games, the inspectors were remarkably successful in depriving Iraq under Hussein of access to weapons of mass destruction, or WMD.

That was not, however, clear until after the US invasion of Iraq in 2003. During the 1990s, Hussein toyed with weapons inspectors, using them as a pawn to drive a wedge among the P5. He resisted their activities just enough to provoke the US, Britain and France into taking unilateral actions to "enforce" Security Council resolutions—like the creation and enforcement of no-fly zones and bombing raids. But he never resisted enough to induce Russia and China to support such unilateral action.

As a result, weapons inspections and sanctions became an increasing point of tension and disunity in the council. The first weapons inspection apparatus, the UN Special Commission, ultimately imploded at the end of 1997 under these pressures. A new apparatus, set up in 1999, called the UN Monitoring, Verification and Inspection Commission, had still not entered Iraq in 2001. By then, Russia and China were increasingly being joined by France and domestic lobbies in the US and Britain to question the carrot-and-stick approach of sanctions plus weapons inspections.

Hussein's tactics had created not only massive frustration and impatience but also chronic uncertainty within the permanent council members—and their intelligence communities, it turned out—over his exact intentions and weapons abilities. Hussein deliberately clouded the fact that Iraq's nuclear weapons program had essentially ended as early as 1993, as he sought to maximize his leverage and bargaining power and heighten the perceived risk of any attempt by the West to remove him.

Then came 9/11. Suddenly, the risk calculus in Washington changed.

The Iraq War

After 9/11, Hussein no longer appeared to be a minor irritant but a potentially major threat to US strategic interests. The primary concern was that he would develop WMD that he could pass to terrorists. Within days of 9/11, the White House set its sights on removing him as the leader of Iraq.

The efforts to engineer diplomatic support for such an effort were halfhearted. In a General Assembly speech in early October 2002, President George W. Bush made the choice for other UN member states clear: go along with the US invasion or be sidelined. European states called for more time for weapons inspections. US Secretary of Defense Donald Rumsfeld and others resisted, arguing that the "absence of evidence" of Iraqi weapons development was not the same as "evidence of absence."

The US would probably have ignored the UN altogether if Prime Minister Tony Blair of Britain had not insisted on a renewed push to get explicit Security Council authorization for the invasion. This effort culminated in the anticlimactic presentation by US Secretary of State Colin Powell to the council on Feb. 5, 2003, when he argued that Hussein was developing WMD and that Hussein represented such a grave threat to international peace and security that mere containment was no longer an option. Other council members were not convinced, and when it became obvious that a US-Britain resolution would not pass, the two countries decided to invade without a new resolution, arguing instead that their actions were authorized by earlier UN resolutions. Worldwide street protests against an invasion did not dissuade them.

The Iraq war (also called the Second Gulf War) began on March 19, 2003, with a massive aerial bombardment described by Rumsfeld as "shock and awe." It was nasty, brutal and short. By April 9, 2003, US forces had entered Baghdad and pulled down a statue of Hussein in Firdos Square. Hussein and the Baathist leadership vanished.

Bush's gambit appeared to have paid off. He "landed" a fighter jet on the runway of a US aircraft carrier on May 1, 2003, and spoke in front of a huge banner proclaiming "Mission Accomplished." On May 22, 2003, the Security Council passed Resolution 1483, recognizing the US and Britain as occupying powers and extending their authority, beyond that traditionally granted by international law, to allow them to undertake a massive democratic transfomation of Iraq.

The UN itself appeared to have sustained grave damage from the war in Iraq, having failed to prevent one member state from invading another, despite the clear opposition of most its membership. Secretary-General Kofi Annan, who for many embodied the UN, seemed physically crushed, and the day before the invasion called it "a sad day for the United Nations." The council appeared increasingly irrelevant, with no sure mandate or direction in Iraq, beyond the limited humanitarian assistance role the US and Britain would allow.

But then everything began to unravel. The US occupation faced increasing resistance inside Iraq. Widespread looting turned to widespread insurgency as Baathists, militant Islamists and laid-off Iraqi Army officers made common cause against the occupying forces. Coalition casualties mounted, and tales of sectarian assassinations and kidnappings emerged. The occupiers' inability to capture Hussein stood as a powerful symbol of their weakening grip over Iraq.

The UN Secretariat quietly set about positioning itself to assist the Iraqi population wherever it could. Annan took one of the UN's brightest rising stars, Sergio Vieira de Mello, away from his post as High Commissioner for Human Rights and sent him to Iraq in June 2003 to try to put the UN on the front foot. Vieira de Mello was largely ignored by the coalition authorities. Then, tragically, he was killed with 21 others in a terrorist bombing of UN headquarters in Iraq on Aug. 19, 2003. When a second attack followed soon after, Annan pulled UN staff out.

The attack on the UN signaled a significant escalation in violence in Iraq. The coalition occupation appeared to be losing its way. The capture of Hussein in December 2003 failed to stem the violence, only underlining the depths of the problems the occupiers faced. (Hussein was tried in a process widely condemned for its procedural failings and executed by Iraqi authorities in December 2006.) When pictures of torture and interrogation of Iraqis by American forces at the Abu Ghraib prison emerged in April 2004, the authority of the occupying forces suffered hugely not only outside Iraq but also inside.

More and more embattled, the US turned back to the UN to help it broker a political exit. Annan sent another much-respected senior UN envoy, Lakhdar Brahimi, who became a key intermediary between the coalition troops and local political and spiritual authorities, notably Grand Ayatollah Ali al-Sistani. And the UN played a crucial role in providing technical advice and support in planning and executing the elections through 2004 and 2005, which allowed the US to begin to hand control and sovereignty back to Iraq.

As this transfer of power continued through 2006 and 2007, the UN has stayed largely on the sidelines, quietly supporting the Iraqi population through technical assistance on matters as diverse as refugee movements, elections and health. The Security Council has repeatedly renewed the authorization of the ongoing international presence in the country, though more recently this has been based on a request by Iraqi authorities.

The UN's role in Iraq is currently not nearly as central as it once was. Still, as events in 2001 showed, that can change quickly.

Looking Ahead

At the end of 2008, with the close of the Bush administration nigh, the US and Iraq agreed to a timeline for the complete withdrawal of US forces from Iraq by 2011. Early this year, the Obama administration announced an end to combat mission by August 2010, leaving some troops in support-type roles. The path ahead for Iraq remains uncertain, with diverging sectarian aspirations, tensions over the distribution of Iraq's oil wealth and a rising cohort of young unemployed men who have been raised in an atmosphere of violence all threatening to steer Iraq back toward conflict.

It seems likely, therefore, that the international community will continue to play an important role in helping Iraq to avoid such violence. With the election of Barack Obama in the US and his stated policy of withdrawal from Iraq and decidedly more multilateral perspective than the Bush administration's approach, it seems likely that efforts to provide such assistance will be channeled through the UN.

At first, this will most likely take the form of technical assistance in areas like elections, development, health care and, perhaps, even security reform. But it also seems quite possible that the UN's Department of Political Affairs will be called on in 2009 and 2010 to help Iraq's communities engage in a peaceful dialogue to resolve the deep and challenging issues of resource distribution and intercommunal relations that will linger. The success of such efforts will probably depend as much on the attitudes of Iraq's neighbors as it will on attitudes in the US and the rest of the West. Should such political brokering fail, we cannot rule out that the UN will once again be called on to take a more hands-on military role in Iraq.

Either way, the long story of the UN and Iraq seems far from over. We can only hope that there will be more constructive engagement in the years ahead than there has been in the last three decades. Iraq has repeatedly tested the UN's authority and capacity and at times found it wanting—even as the UN has proven itself indispensable. ■

A Dual Role in the Middle East

Richard Gowan

The greatest recent challenges to the United Nations position in the Middle East have been the acute crises in Lebanon and Gaza. The UN Interim Force in Lebanon, the UN's third-largest peace operation with 12,500 troops, was not directly involved in the significant fighting that engulfed Beirut and the north of the country in the second quarter of 2008; its area of operations is limited to the Israeli border. But this violence resulted in a political victory for the political and military organization Hezbollah, which has gained a powerful position in the Lebanese government.

This leaves the UN Interim Force in an increasingly contradictory position, as its presence is intended to constrain Hezbollah's freedom of military action in south Lebanon. While it has built up a relatively good relationship with the Israeli army, it is unclear that the mission can retain credibility if Hezbollah further reinforces its political power in Beirut.

In early 2009, further questions over the force's future emerged as Poland, for budgetary reasons, withdrew its contribution of 500 personnel, and France also withdrew ships from monitoring the Lebanese coast. These moves raised fears that the world financial crisis will lead other Europeans to pull out, depriving the force of the skilled troops that are its backbone.

By early 2009, there was also attention focused on another part of the UN family in Lebanon: the Special Tribunal set up to investigate the 2005 murder of Rafik Hariri, the billionaire former Lebanese prime minister. This investigation is expected to submit its final report in 2009, and it may implicate senior Syrian figures. Such revelations might have an impact on Turkish-mediated talks between Israel and Syria, another diplomatic process that affects a UN mission—the Disengagement Observer Force on the Golan Heights—but one in which the UN does not play a political role.

While this UN observer force itself had a quiet year, the same was tragically untrue for the UN Works and Relief Agency and UN humanitarian officials working in Gaza. Through much of the year, Israeli restrictions on movement in and out of Gaza—imposed in mid-2007 in response to rocket attacks by Hamas—threatened to precipitate a humanitarian crisis. In June, a cease-fire between Hamas and Israel offered some respite, but Israel reimposed the blockade in early November. Secretary-General Ban Ki-moon warned Israel that it was depriving Palestinians of their basic human rights and endangering UN personnel.

The situation blew up on Dec. 27, 2008, when Israel invaded Gaza. In the violence, attacks affecting the UN became a focal point for international anger, especially after the deaths of Palestinians who had found shelter in a UN school compound. But in contrast to the resolution of the 2006 war, the UN had only a limited role in ending the violence. Although the Security Council adopted a resolution calling for an end to the fighting, with the US abstaining, and there was unfulfilled speculation about the deployment of UN and European Union monitors to Gaza, Egypt led the way in mediating a cease-fire.

Secretary-General Ban visited Gaza at the end of the fighting and expressed anger at the damage. When the new administration took office in Washington, one of its first actions was to appoint a new Middle East envoy, George J. Mitchell. Attention thus continues to focus on the US rather than on the UN as a mediator. Combined with the increasing role of regional mediators, this suggests continued limitation of the UN's political contribution, while the recent crises were another reminder of the UN's longtime operational relevance in the region. ■

Reining In Iran's Nuclear Ambitions

Eriks Berzins

The United Nations involvement with Iran has been markedly different from the stabilization and reconstruction roles it has assumed elsewhere in the Middle East. In Iraq and Afghanistan, UN agencies have operated amid complex intrastate conflicts to lead and coordinate humanitarian relief efforts, carry out infrastructure projects, promote civil-society organization, write constitutions and build electoral systems, to name a few. With Iran, the role of the UN as both forum and actor has focused on the country's nuclear program—an equally complex, though less conventional crisis, which has been addressed through the International Atomic Energy Agency (IAEA) and the Security Council.

The clandestine nature of Iran's nuclear facilities and a regional supply chain through which nuclear equipment was channeled, first discovered in 2003, prompted questions about how the UN should respond. Did Iran intend to apply such technology solely for generating power, as it has maintained, or was this nuclear program designed to build weapons, making the country an explicit threat to international peace and security? The IAEA and the Security Council share the responsibility for answering these questions.

For Weapons or for Power?

As the world's nuclear watchdog, the energy agency has tried to encourage greater transparency and cooperation from Iran regarding the country's nuclear activities and to ensure that it was complying with its obligations under the Non-Proliferation Treaty. To address any possible threats to peace and security after failing to get the full cooperation it sought from Iran, the IAEA referred the matter to the Security Council in March 2006. Invoking Chapter VII of the UN Charter, the council used sanctions resolutions to persuade or pressure Iran to cease its enrichment activities, which could later lead to developing nuclear-weapons ability. Iran vehemently denied any intentions of making bombs and pressed forward with its program, contending that it was in full compliance with the Non-Proliferation Treaty and that it was entitled to enrich uranium.

The UN Security Council passed Resolution 1737 in December 2006 and Resolution 1747 in March 2007, consecutive sanctions demanding that Iran stop its uranium enrichment. In fact, during this period Iran's centrifuge production increased rapidly, and by September 2007, according to the IAEA chief Mohamed ElBaradei, Iran had 3,800 fully operational centrifuges, crucial in making nuclear fuel.

Why, nearly six years after the discovery of Iran's nuclear program, are tensions continuing to mount? The energy agency and the Security Council view the Iranian nuclear issue from inherently different perspectives. The cumulative sanctions against Iran, while seeking its greater cooperation, have aroused its national pride and apparently only strengthened its determination to continue enrichment.

The tensions over this standoff have escalated in the last year for several reasons. First, the sanctions did not reflect full agreement among council members. The US, promoting a policy of no direct engagement with Iran, worked strenuously with the other permanent members of the council to reinforce the sanctions. The other permanent members were as concerned about Iran's nuclear program as the US, and many of the nonpermanent members shared American concerns. But Russia and China were not persuaded that sanctions would be effective. At the urging of some European companies, Russia and China initially delayed sanctions resolutions to determine if the IAEA could somehow reach an agreement with Iran on its activities. The reluctance of Russia, China and the European companies may also have come from superseding economic interests—Russia, for example, will have completed construction of an Iranian nuclear power plant at Bushehr by the end of 2009, and European firms have also continued doing business with Iran.

Under heavy US pressure, Russia and China voted to pass Resolution 1803 in March 2008, insisting that Iran halt its enrichment activities and extending sanctions. But the lengthy debate leading up to this third resolution raises doubts that a fourth resolution could be approved. And the inauguration of a new American president suggested that the US strategy in dealing with Iran might well shift toward direct discussions, which could mean taking a different approach to managing Iran's nuclear program and ambitions.

Anger but Hope

The rising discord is also a reflection of other factors. UN members disagree on how best to proceed, and anti-Western sentiments associated with the wars in Iraq and Afghanistan have increased. The growing international opposition to Iran's nuclear program has only strengthened support there, not just among the governing elite but among the Iranian people. As the sanctions tightened, the Iranian government felt free to issue louder and more aggressive denunciations of the "arrogant powers" on the Security Council and to use public speeches to showcase vials of enriched uranium and update the world on how many new centrifuges it had added to its supply.

In this way, Iran has clearly expressed its own assessment of the relative costs and benefits of subjecting its nuclear program to the unfettered oversight of outsiders. In squarely placing itself at odds with the Security Council, the Iranian government, with strong public support, curtailed its cooperation with the IAEA, which has continued to report the increases in Iran's centrifuges and stockpile of nuclear material and to issue periodic reports on the country's failure to comply with council resolutions. As a result, far from simply failing to engender a mutually acceptable resolution to the standoff, the perceived threat of a nuclear-armed Iran has grown in tandem with Iran's resolve to assert what it sees as its inalienable right to nuclear enrichment.

Recently, some positive signals have been noted. In February 2009, President Mahmoud Ahmadinejad's government pledged to revitalize Iran's cooperation with the IAEA. Bilaterally, the Obama administration has shown interest in direct talks with Iran about its nuclear program, and the IAEA has fully supported these pledges. In turn, the Ahmadinejad government has declared its willingness to begin discussions with the US, based on "mutual respect and dignity."

These positive signs should also highlight the need for an international effort to deal with Iran's nuclear program. It is unclear whether there will be an increasing role for the Security Council as the international community tries to seek greater Iranian cooperation with the IAEA and the Non-Proliferation Treaty. Member states of the energy agency understand that the most accurate and most helpful information about Iran's nuclear program comes from the IAEA inspections themselves and depends on continuing that access.

These differing approaches to Iran's nuclear program reinforce the multiple roles the UN will need to play in its efforts to encourage compliance with resolutions. Iran's case also reflects on the UN's ability to reconcile peace and security with member-state interests and international law. The major member states will need to work with Iran to find a way to open up the country's nuclear program, since continued UN sanctions alone are not getting the job done. Member states might be better off working directly with Iran and through the UN to seek greater cooperation from the country without isolating it further, thereby minimizing contradictory policies and competing interests among member states, all of whom need to act in close cooperation. ■

The Aftermath in Georgia

Richard Gowan

While the United Nations has maintained a monitoring mission in Georgia for 15 years, it played only a peripheral role in efforts to end the August 2008 Russian-Georgian war. It has since acted as convener of negotiations between the sides but is constrained by Russian resistance on the Security Council and a Continental preference for action through the European Union.

The UN Observer Mission in Georgia was created in 1993 to operate alongside a Russian-led peace operation authorized by the Commonwealth of Independent States—an association of states that were part of the Soviet Union. The two had a mandate to monitor a cease-fire between Georgia and the separatist region of Abkhazia. A similar arrangement had been established for the Georgian breakaway region of South Ossetia in 1992, but with the Organization for Security and Cooperation in Europe in the monitoring role. The 56-member intergovernmental organization deals with security and human rights issues in Europe, the Caucasus and Central Asia.

Although tensions were high in both regions throughout 2008, with the UN reporting cease-fire violations by both Georgia and Russia in the Abkhaz case, they finally spilled into war in South Ossetia on Aug. 7, 2008. Russia opened a second front in Abkhazia, and UN observer mission patrols were blocked, and sometimes physically threatened, by Abkhaz personnel as the conflict progressed. The UN resumed most of its patrols in September.

By then, the mission faced significant political obstacles. The Security Council had been paralyzed during the war, and the European Union, through the French president, Nicolas Sarkozy, took the lead in brokering an imperfect cease-fire. As the hostilities concluded, the Georgian government renounced the original agreement under which peacekeepers of the Commonwealth of Independent States had been deployed in Abkhazia, while Russia recognized Abkhazia and South Ossetia as independent states. As the original mandate for the UN monitoring mission recognized Abkhazia as part of Georgia, there were doubts over Russia's acceptance of its continued presence.

A 'Technical' Renewal

The Security Council sidestepped this problem in October 2008 when the mission's mandate came up for renewal. Secretary-General Ban Ki-moon reported that it was too early to define the role the mission might play in the future and won approval for a "technical renewal" until February 2009, which avoided reopening the mandate. In December, Russia demonstrated its readiness to dismantle the prewar peacekeeping system in Georgia by vetoing the continued presence in South Ossetia of monitors from the Organization for Security and Cooperation in Europe. But the European Union had hedged against such challenges by sending its own monitors to Georgia in September.

If the UN's future in Georgia was uncertain by early 2009, some factors worked in its favor. Both Russian and Abkhaz officials privately indicated a preference for the UN mission to continue operations. Members of the European Union wanted to keep UN legitimacy for their presence in Georgia. The EU, along with the UN and Organization for Security and Cooperation, jointly convened Russian-Georgian talks in Geneva in October, but these soon fell apart in acrimony.

When the UN mission's future returned to the Security's Council agenda in February 2009, a resolution extending its mission was agreed on, though it included deliberately ambiguous language on Abkhazia's status. The longer-term future of the mission will be affected by shifting American attitudes. The Bush administration was an extremely strong supporter of Georgia, and the new American leadership is unlikely to desert this position completely. But it may aim to take a measured approach to the conflict, favoring a continued role for UN mediation and monitoring. ■

Technical Maneuvering Helps Reduce Tensions in Kosovo

Richard Gowan

Kosovo turned out to be one of the most sensitive peacekeeping cases in 2008, dividing the Security Council and creating significant pressure on Secretary-General Ban Ki-moon to act. Yet by the end of the year, Ban had moved quickly enough to help create a technical compromise that reduced tensions—an important example of how the United Nations can moderate high-profile international disputes.

After nearly nine years under UN administration, Kosovo's government unilaterally declared independence from Serbia on Feb. 17, 2008. While Kosovo enjoyed the support of the US and most members of the European Union,

Russia and a majority of UN members refused to recognize it. The Serbian government reasserted its claim to sovereignty over Kosovo, and there were major clashes between Kosovar Serbs and peacekeepers from NATO and the UN in February and March 2008. One resulted in the death of a UN police officer.

The divide between Russia and the West precluded any agreement on Kosovo's status in the Security Council. This complicated plans, developed since 2006, for an EU police and justice mission, called Eulex, to take on rule of law duties from the UN transitional administration. While NATO maintained military security, it appeared unlikely that the Kosovo Albanian population would tolerate an indefinite UN presence.

With political agreement impossible, Secretary-General Ban attempted a technical maneuver. In June 2008, speaking in his capacity as the UN's chief administrative officer, he declared that UN transitional administration was no longer viable in its current form. As the year progressed, the mission was severely downsized, and it reduced its public profile, while the EU and the UN worked to persuade Serbia that Europe should take over international policing in Kosovo, with the condition that the new mission be "status neutral" rather than endorse independence.

These negotiations concluded successfully in November 2008 and were endorsed by the Security Council. While the EU police and justice mission rapidly increased its presence after a slow and somewhat disorganized start, the UN transitional administration also maintains a residual presence. This leaves all sides at least partly satisfied. Kosovo Albanians perceive the shift of responsibilities to the EU as de facto progress toward independence, while Serbia sees the UN transitional administration's survival and the EU mission's "status neutrality" as evidence of its claim to its former province.

This complex situation also assists the few EU members, like Spain, that have not recognized Kosovo for domestic political reasons—they can participate in the European operation without undermining their position. The compromise in Kosovo is imperfect and temporary, but the UN's technical maneuver helped stabilize a fragile situation. ∎

Kashmir, a Tinderbox?

Roger Nokes

The dispute over who should control Kashmir was one of the first issues addressed by the United Nations in 1948, and it lies at the heart of two major armed conflicts between India and Pakistan.

In 2000, President Bill Clinton referred to the Kashmir region as "the most dangerous place on earth," not only because at least 34,000 people have died in an insurgency that began in 1989 in the Indian-controlled part of the former princely state but also because India and Pakistan are now nuclear nations. And while turbulence over the region has calmed down in the recent past, no mutually accepted resolution has been developed. This remains so despite decades of effort by the UN and initial efforts by the Obama administration to have the issue addressed early in 2009 by Richard C. Holbrooke, the special US representative for Afghanistan and Pakistan.

How Tensions Began

The dispute over the territory started with the British partition of Pakistan and India at independence in 1947. Among other events, this resulted in the mass migration of 12.5 million people (primarily Hindus from Pakistan to India, and Muslims from India to Pakistan) and extensive violence. Pakistan was intended to be the homeland for South Asian Muslims, with the Radcliffe Commission, a British creation, charged with determining which areas would be designated into which country.

The area of Kashmir, however, was left out of the commission's evaluation, and instead the region was allowed to choose which country it wanted to join. The maharajah, or royal leader, of Kashmir, is a Hindu, and he preferred independent status. But when the state was attacked by Pakistani guerrillas, he could not protect it. He joined his state to India, therefore, to secure the aid of its army.

Pakistani tribesmen and local insurgents then began to rebel against Indian control and annexed the area that is now administered by Pakistan. In 1965, infiltration occurred from Pakistan into India, with India subsequently occupying positions across the previously determined cease-fire line. The conflict spiraled into a three-week war that ended through a UN-brokered cease-fire and Security Council resolutions. No concrete change occurred, however, until the civil war in East Pakistan brought India and Pakistan to arms once again in December 1971.

This conflict ended with the Simla agreement, which holds that no state will unilaterally attempt to resolve the Kashmir dispute.

A second insurgency broke out in 1989 in the Kashmir Valley, where Muslims are a majority. Pakistan has been accused of fueling this rebellion, which was widely supported by Kashmiri Muslims, while India has been accused by international human rights organizations of committing wide-spread abuses in efforts to quell the campaign. Allegations against Indian security forces include execution of suspected militants without trial and the killing of innocent civilians.

According to Human Rights Watch, the Indian security forces are protected in their actions by laws that in effect institute martial law and allow the use of lethal force against anyone suspected of violating the law. Further complicating the issue, the insurgency gained in strength and deadliness in the late 1990s, as combatants were joined by Islamic militants from Pakistan.

Cooled Relations Amid Decreased Violence

After the most recent standoff in 2002, when India blamed Pakistan for an attack at an Indian Army barracks, more than a million troops were placed in the border region. As a result, diplomatic relations cooled further because of regional and international fears that the situation would spiral into nuclear war. Then a dialogue between the Pakistani President, Pervez Musharraf, and the Indian Prime Minister, Manmohan Singh, began in 2004. Diplomatic engagement quickly snowballed when a bus route between the Pakistani and Indian sides was established.

Some degree of peace was apparent despite little resolution and continued dissent against Indian policies on both sides. In 2008, for instance, the number of militant attacks in Indian-controlled Kashmir decreased 40 percent from the level in these states in 2007. This represented the lowest level in the insurgency's history, according to an interview with the Indian Kashmir police director-general, Kuldeep Khuda, by Reuters in December 2008. Regional elections in Indian-controlled Kashmir also witnessed a high voter turnout (61.5 percent) despite a call for boycott by separatists, and while resistance to Indian control still exists, the rebellion has taken the form of less violent public demonstrations.

In addition, the UN Military Observer Group in India and Pakistan, which has been working in the region since 1949 to supervise cease-fires on both the Indian and Pakistani sides, has a correspondingly low staff count (about 120 people), and the Kashmir issue was not on the Security Council's Peace and Security Agenda at all in 2008.

Current conditions, however, do not translate into success or popular approval on the ground in the two Kashmirs. As The Wall Street Journal reported on Dec. 15, 2008, about the Indian-controlled side, "India now largely faces a different, and potentially more challenging, foe here: peaceful campaigners for self-determination, who borrow from Mahatma Gandhi's rule book of nonviolent resistance."

These protests are more challenging, according to the Muslim Kashmiris' spiritual leader, Mirwaiz Umar Farooq, because while India has the arms to defeat an insurgency, it has no way to quell the hopes of peaceful independence-seeking people.

According to The Journal, while attacks have dropped, popular dissent in the form of public protests has been the strongest in the history of the disputes and has a greater base of support, given the protests' nonviolent nature. Indian forces have at times answered protests with the same lethal responses they used against militant protests. Allegations have been made that voter turnout in the recent elections came about because India forces threatened citizens with violence.

Nuclear Threat

Despite some of these debatable improvements, the issue will continue to be of concern to UN members and could be addressed by the Security Council.

Considering that both countries in the argument are nuclear powers means that a flare-up could, in the worst-case scenario, result in major catastrophe, an aspect that makes the issue constantly relevant to nonproliferation efforts. The specter of nuclear warfare was also increasingly relevant when the US and India completed a treaty in late 2008 that allows the transfer of nuclear technology to India. This will require Indian nuclear facilities to be open to inspection by the International Atomic Energy Agency.

The concern by those who did not support the treaty is that it may result in an increase in India's nuclear arsenal, since only civilian nuclear plants will fall under the agency's oversight. In addition, India has spurned the nuclear Non-Proliferation Treaty, which states that parties cannot build bombs in exchange for access to civilian technology. Pakistan is also not a member of the Non-Proliferation Treaty.

The possibility of altered regional military strategy is also a related concern, as talks in India are focused on developing a "cold start" military doctrine, in which its traditional emphasis upon defense and a large number of troops will be abandoned for a leaner military force that could strike enemies soon after a crisis emerges. If such a "cold start" strategy were enacted, controlled incidents of violence could quickly spiral outward, given that a faster military reaction might bypass more careful analyses.

Considering the history of the Kashmir troubles, in which reactive measures have often characterized behavior in the region, member states of the UN may try to take action to deter such rapid-response ability.

Additionally important is the connection of Kashmir to terrorism in the region. In a Nov. 27, 2008, Backgrounder article on the Council on Foreign Relations Web site, William Milam, a former US ambassador to Pakistan, said that "the ISI probably would not define what they've done in the past as 'terrorism,'" referring to support of Islamic fighters in Kashmir by the Pakistani Inter-Services Intelligence. The agency has failed to contain these terrorist elements in Kashmir, according to Milam, and they are thought to be responsible for additional attacks in Pakistan along the Afghan border.

Furthermore, according to a Jan. 6, 2009, article in The New York Times, evidence suggests that the planners of the Mumbai attacks in 2008 had also sent operatives to Kashmir. While these reports do not necessarily mean that the operatives came from Kashmir, it illustrates the dispute's role as a possible trigger for regional militancy.

Additionally, if Pakistan moves its forces away from Afghanistan and redeploys them to the Indian border, less assistance is available for efforts against the Taliban in the tribal regions, Mark Sappenfield wrote in The Christian Science Monitor on Dec. 29, 2008.

As President Obama has said, "We can't solve Afghanistan without solving Pakistan," and because of its relation to terrorism, human rights and general peace and security, regional stability can also be affected more specifically by the continuing events in Kashmir. For this reason, the issue could end up on the agenda of the UN Counter-Terrorism Committee, as well as the Security Council's Peace and Security Agenda.

In an essay in 2005 in "A Global Agenda," Ishtaiq Ahmad, a Pakistani writer and scholar, called for an increase in the personnel and funds available to UN operations in Kashmir long before the Mumbai terrorist attacks and recent rise in tensions between India and Pakistan. (Right after the attacks, for example, Pakistan moved troops to its part of the Kashmir region, after intelligence suggested that India could launch an attack inside Pakistan, according to an article in The New York Times.) Given the heightened tensions between India and Pakistan, multiple branches of the UN could find themselves involved once again in the Kashmir quagmire of terrorism, human rights, nuclear proliferation and security.

For the topic to be taken up, it would have to be presented by a UN member. This is unlikely to be the US, which recently acquiesced to Indian demands that Kashmir be taken off the US special representative's agenda. Given Russian and Chinese concerns over their own internal independence movements, it is also improbable that they would encourage the UN to address another independence movement in another state. Kashmir therefore remains a classic example of being a case that is too politically sensitive for just the UN to handle. ■

Child soldiers from an anti-Tutsi militia, the Forces Démocratiques de Libération du Rwanda (FDLR), in eastern Congo, June 2008.

UN Photo/Marie Frechon

Child Soldiers:
Stealing Their Youth and Adulthood

Giselle Chang

More than 300,000 people under age 18 are believed to be currently involved in armed conflicts. They fight not only with weapons on front lines but also as messengers, spies and supply carriers. According to the nonprofit organization Human Rights Watch, since 1994 the recruitment and use of child soldiers have been reported in Angola, Burma, Burundi, Chad, Colombia, the Democratic Republic of the Congo, India, Lebanon, Liberia, Nepal, Sierra Leone, Sri Lanka, Sudan and Uganda, among others.

Sri Lanka and Sierra Leone

The Sri Lankan rebel group, the Tamil Tigers, has been notorious for abducting and recruiting young people as soldiers; at times in the past, the group was estimated to have recruited up to 4,000 children as young as 10 years old in its fight for independence in Sri Lanka.

Under the Sri Lankan government and international pressure, from Unicef as well as Radhika Coomaraswamy, a UN under-secretary-general, the Tamil Makkal Viduthalai Puligal, a breakaway faction of the Tamil Tigers, agreed to end child recruitment as of 2008, leading to the release of many children. But declarations on the part of armed groups to discontinue using child soldiers have proved disappointing. After a 2003 announcement that the group would stop conscripting child soldiers, Unicef and Human Rights Watch accused the Tigers of defaulting and conscripting Tamil children orphaned by the 2004 tsunami.

Sierra Leone's 10-year civil war is another infamous case of child soldier use on all sides. The Revolutionary United Front, the Armed Forces Revolutionary Council as well as the pro-government Civil Defense Forces all recruited children, first drugging them and then forcing them to commit atrocities. At Grafton Camp, a rehabilitation center managed by Unicef for recently demobilized child soldiers, the camp director said that many of the boys expressed great pride at having been effective killers. While boys were armed and pushed into the front of combat, girls were also abducted and sexually exploited. Hardship for many of the girls did not end when the conflict was over, as many of them, now young women, stigmatized and ostracized, are forced to survive alone for having lived among the rebel forces.

Superior Fighters?

Though children have been involved in many wars throughout history as combatants—as far back as the 1212 Children's Crusade and in the Spanish Civil War—the changing nature of war in the last few decades has greatly increased their role. Since the end of the cold war, conflicts have become mostly internal wars of rebellion with guerrilla groups fighting against colonial or totalitarian regimes. The advent of automatic weapons has greatly encouraged child recruitment as well, since even 8-year-olds can handle modern weapons like grenades and small arms.

Many guerrilla fighters argue that children are superior to adults as fighters because of their speed, agility and resilience. Furthermore, children can be tightly controlled and easily manipulated, making them vulnerable to military indoctrination and training techniques. Some armed groups force children to return to their own communities and kill someone they know as an initiation rite, which permanently severs a child from its home.

In response to the prevalence of child soldier recruitment and use, the Geneva Conventions, standards for international law on humanitarian concerns, added Protocol II in 1977. Under this and other parts of the conventions, parties involved in a conflict must take all feasible measures to protect children under 15 from being recruited and participating directly in hostilities.

Trial of Congolese Begins

In a monumental event, the International Criminal Court's very first trial, in January 2009, was against a militia leader from the Democratic Republic of the Congo, Thomas Lubanga. This is the first trial to focus solely on the use of child soldiers as a war crime; it is also the first time that victims, including former child soldiers, are to participate as witnesses. In fact, the first witness called to testify, a former child soldier, ended up retracting his testimony after the judge informed him he could face prosecution in Congo if he incriminated himself.

Humanitarian law and the International Criminal Court have taken only the first of many steps, however, in preventing the recruitment and use of child soldiers. The Geneva Conventions are vague, excluding from protection children age 15 to 17 as well as children carrying gear, acting as spies and guarding prisoners. Furthermore, the conventions are legally binding only if the warring parties have ratified them, and they apply only to certain violence.

Since 1994 the Human Rights Watch report recorded a decrease in the number of conflicts involving child soldiers from 27 conflicts to 17. But it attributed this drop to the ending of conflicts and not to the impact of efforts to protect children from use in war.

Peace Is the Solution

As conflicts break down societies, children are inadvertently separated from their families, removed from schools and forced to witness atrocities. Many take up arms to seek revenge for the murder of family members, while others desperately seek basic survival needs. To effectively protect children, international laws require order and structure in society, but civil wars take place outside this framework. Peace remains the main hope for permanently ending the use of child soldiers. ▪

This view of melting glaciers on King George Island, Antarctica, was taken in 2007 from the small plane in which Secretary-General Ban Ki-moon traveled to see the effects of climate change.

Protecting the Environment

Protecting the Environment

Roger A. Coate

Protecting the environment is more than a noble cause; it is the foundation of sustaining human life. Yet humans continue to use and abuse ecosystems with reckless abandon. The consequences may be devastating because potentially irreversible damage looms. As the international community moves into the 21st century, political momentum has been increasing to do something about it. A range of environmental issues—climate change, loss of biodiversity, deforestation, loss of cropland, diminishing water supplies and declining water quality, sanitation, toxic wastes, clean energy and sustainable consumption and production—vie for attention on the global agenda. For some, climate change appears the most devastating threat. For others, especially the poor and marginalized of the world who are mired in poverty, with squalor and death all around, the absence of safe drinking water, sanitation and adequate food represents the greatest obstacle to human security. The international community must respond effectively to both threats if the United Nations is to fulfill the promise of promoting the security of all.

Protecting the environment and ensuring the sustainability of life on Earth occupies center stage at the UN. In environmental affairs, the organization is committed to action. For well over three decades, the issues of environment and development have fused. Sustainable development means eradicating poverty and improving the quality of life for everyone in a way that ensures high quality for future generations. Protecting the environment is central to sustainable development, and some important progress has been made.

In regard to the critical threat of ozone depletion, for example, the international community, with institutional facilitation at the UN, has responded admirably. The production of ozone-depleting chemicals has been cut 96 percent. Looking ahead, Secretary-General Ban Ki-moon has called for a Global Green New Deal for the 21st century, and UN agencies are acting aggressively to make it a reality.

Climate Change

Carbon dioxide and other greenhouse gas emissions blanket the atmosphere and trap solar radiation, inhibiting its release into space. This results in a warming effect on the planet. Evidence of climate change is all around—severe weather, floods and droughts representing only the most obvious. As detailed in the United Nations Environment Program Year Book for 2009, climate change increases human vulnerability to weather and geological hazards. It intensifies soil erosion, water contamination and ice melt, which releases hazardous substances into rivers and ecosystems. These are a few of the problems related to climate change.

Many scientific experts and world leaders, including the secretary-general, consider climate change the defining challenge of our generation. It represents a potentially devastating threat to human security and the social and economic well-being of everyone round the world.

The international community is responding, but that response has been slow. The Montreal Protocol on phasing out ozone-depleting substances has been one of the premier success stories in global environmental politics: since 1986, over 96 percent of all ozone-depleting substances have been phased out. In September 2007 parties to the protocol agreed to speed up that process and make the target for complete phasing out of hydrochlorofluorocarbons within a decade.

These changes have had a positive impact on mitigating climate change, but direct action has been slower. In February 2007 the fourth report of the intergovernmental panel on climate change declared that there was unequivocal evidence of global warming and that most of the increase has very likely been caused by human activity, especially burning fossil fuels, which accounts for more than half of greenhouse gas emissions. These emissions, which increased by 30 percent from 1990 to 2005, continue to rise.

UN reports suggest that the small island states, the Arctic, large delta areas and Africa in general are especially vulnerable. Over the 21st century current trends are expected to intensify sharply. It is projected that developing countries, if unconstrained, will emit four to five times the amount of carbon dioxide emitted by the developed countries in the last century and a half. Even more devastating, countries of the Organization for Economic Cooperation and Development are expected to account for about 70 percent of the greenhouse gas emissions and other global-warming factors in the same time period.

The World Bank's Global Monitoring Report for 2008 concludes that it is a virtual certainty that air quality in urban areas will decline and that there will be decreased agricultural yields in warmer environments, although yields may increase in colder environments. It is very likely that demand for water will increase along with its contamination, while on the other hand water scarcity may decrease in some areas. Natural resources are a major source of income in poor rural areas, and dependency on natural resources makes them highly vulnerable to the effects of climate change.

The United Nations Framework Convention on Climate Change entered into force in March 1994. It was meant to achieve stabilization of greenhouse gas concentrations in the atmosphere at a low enough level to prevent dangerous interference with the climate system. An additional agreement, the Kyoto Protocol, concluded in 1997, entered into force in 2005. It set binding targets for reducing greenhouse gas emissions for 37 industrialized states and the European Union, which are parties to it. These targets amount to an average of 5 percent reductions from 1990 levels in a five-year period, from 2008 to 2012.

In 2007, participants at the UN Climate Change Conference in Bali initiated a new round of negotiations under the framework convention that is due to be concluded by the end of 2009. The so-called Bali Roadmap plots a course toward a legally binding international accord to replace the Kyoto Protocol when it expires in 2012, and to mitigate further climate change.

Meeting in Poznan, Poland, in December 2008, governments pledged to put negotiations on climate change in the forefront in hopes of reaching a satisfactory response by their scheduled meeting in Copenhagen at the end of 2009. Incremental steps were taken at Poznan, including movement toward creating the Kyoto Protocol's Adaptation Fund. There was also progress on adaptation, finance, technology, reducing emissions from deforestation and forest degradation, and disaster management. The final goal for Copenhagen is "an inclusive, comprehensive and ratifiable deal that will address the challenges and harness the opportunities that climate change presents."

Deforestation

Deforestation threatens biodiversity and is a leading factor in climate change. Forests act as sinks, absorbing carbon dioxide in the atmosphere, and also conserve soil and water resources. Between 1990 and 2005, global forest coverage was reduced by some 3 percent, largely in Latin America, which lost 7 percent of its forests, and sub-Saharan Africa, which lost 9 percent. Indonesia alone lost 18,700 square kilometers from 2000 to 2005. In 25 countries entire forests have disappeared, and in 29 more countries they have been reduced by 90 percent.

While deforestation continues more or less unabated, net forest loss has apparently slowed, largely because of increased planting and conservation. According to a 2008 Millennium Development Goals report, from 2000 to 2005 the net decline was 18 million acres a year, compared with 22 million acres a year in the previous decade. In 2008 over one-tenth of total global forest area was designated for biodiversity conservation, and 9 percent for soil and water conservation.

Loss of Biodiversity

Despite the creation of more than 114,000 protected sites—nearly 13 percent of the Earth's land mass—the planet's biodiversity is being increasingly reduced. Although attention to the issue has grown, by the end of 2007 only 0.7 percent of the world's oceans were under some form of protection and an even smaller percentage was being managed effectively. In 2002, the World Summit on Sustainable Development pledged to achieve a significant cut in biodiversity destruction by 2010. But biodiversity loss continues at an unprecedented rate, and over 10,000 species are threatened. The 2005 Millennium Ecosystem Assessment warned that the world was on the verge of a "massive wave of species extinctions" that threaten human well-being.

The UN Environment Program Year Book for 2009 reports that the total biomass (a traditional measure of organisms per area) of large commercially targeted fish species has declined by 90 percent since the 1960s. In terms of the marine environment, fully exploited, overexploited and depleted fisheries stocks have increased marginally in recent decades. At the same time, the proportion of underexploited and moderately exploited stocks has decreased.

Loss of Arable Land

Agricultural production is closely connected to environmental problems in complex ways. Because of the heavy dependence of people, especially rural people, in poor countries on natural resources and agriculture, it is estimated that unabated climate change will result in 40 million to 170 million more undernourished people by midcentury.

Agriculture is an environmental two-edged sword. On one hand, clearing dense rainforests for crops or grazing contributes to the release of carbon dioxide, presenting a classic dilemma. A 2008 World Bank-IMF Global Monitoring report estimates that from an individual perspective, the value of such cleared land has been estimated at $100 to $200 per hectare, representing a gain to those who clear the land. But in the process, 500 tons of carbon dioxide could be released into the atmosphere, compounding global warming problems for all.

On the other hand, acreage of available cropland per person is declining, and as a consequence, agricultural production is intensifying, leading to soil degradation. By 2008, soil degradation had affected 16 percent of the world's croplands.

Seven UN agencies recently undertook an international assessment of agricultural knowledge, science and technology for development and concluded that, if current trends continued, agricultural production would exhaust the world's agricultural resources and jeopardize future generations. The report warned that the way the world produces food will have to change dramatically to be sustainable.

Water Scarcity

Water is essential for survival. But more than 40 percent of the world's population—2.8 billion people—is experiencing some form of water shortage. About 1.2 billion live in areas subject to physical water shortage, and 1.6 billion others live under conditions of economic water shortage, meaning that economic conditions limit access to safe water. Clean drinking water is crucial to health, yet more than a billion people do not have safe water; 1.8 million people die of diarrhea each year (the second leading cause of child death after pneumonia), and many more become infected with water-borne diseases.

Lack of safe drinking water places an extreme burden on public health facilities. The World Health Organization estimates that more than half the hospital beds in the world are filled with people suffering from water-related diseases. Rural populations are far worse off than people living in urban areas. Less than 80 percent of rural inhabitants in the developing world have access to improved water sources, and only 30 percent of rural households have piped-in water. In these areas women bear an inordinate burden of collecting water and often must walk extremely long distances to do so.

But is the glass half empty or half full? Data indicates that 89 percent of the global population will have access to safe drinking water by 2015. In global terms, 87 percent of the population now has access to improved drinking water, a 10 percent improvement compared with 1990. But given the condition of the poor in the developing world, the challenge is clear and substantial. The Global Monitoring Report estimates that unsafe water and poor sanitation kill 4,100 children each day, nearly three children every minute.

Sanitation

Many of the world's people live in an environment polluted by human defecation. One out of four people in the developing world uses no form of sanitation, and 15 percent of the rest use facilities that put people in direct contact with human waste. This creates high risk for cholera, worms, hepatitis and other related diseases. According to the Millennium Development Goals report from 2008, defecation in the open is the only choice for 1.2 billion people worldwide. In Southern Asia nearly 50 percent of the population relies on it. Progress toward providing improved sanitation has been meager. Furthermore, it estimates that the number of people without improved sanitation declined by 8 percent from 1990 to 2006.

To focus the world's attention on the problems associated with lack of sanitation, the UN declared 2008 the International Year of Sanitation. The goals included increasing awareness of sanitation problems; strengthening institutional and human capacity for change; mobilizing governments; increasing financial commitments; creating sustainable solutions; and enhancing sustainability. Yet in 2009 sanitation problems continue to plague the world's poor and intensify other environmental problems like water contamination.

Toxic and Hazardous Waste

Human activities and industrial production yield an enormous amount of dangerous waste. This includes chemicals, pesticides, biomedical and health-care wastes, used batteries and motor oil and an almost endless list of others. Most toxic and hazardous waste remains inside national borders, but it is estimated that 8.5 million tons of hazardous waste move from country to country each year. The Basel Convention on hazardous waste, which has 170 parties, is one of the leading international efforts to protect human health and the environment. It was adopted in 1989 and came into force in 1992. In 2002, a conference of its members established an elaborate partnership program to provide more effective ways to manage waste. These partnerships bring together businesses, international institutions, environmental and other nongovernmental organizations, academia and government bodies. Of particular priority have been partnerships to deal with electrical and electronic waste, including used cellphones and computer equipment, and household waste containing hazardous materials like lead, cadmium, mercury and asbestos.

Air Pollution

Air pollution is a particularly bad problem in both urban and rural areas. People living in low-income countries are heavily dependent on biomass fuels, such as wood, manure, crops and the like. This dependence has decreased only marginally, from 55 percent of total energy use in 1990 to 48 percent in 2004. The use of such fuels generates significant indoor pollution and is especially a problem in sub-Saharan Africa.

Severe outdoor air pollution plagues many cities. Over 90 percent of urban air pollution results from vehicle emissions. More than a billion people are exposed to outdoor air pollution annually, and a million of those die from causes linked to air pollution. In addition, air pollution is responsible for a million prenatal deaths each year.

Urban Dwellers

By the end of 2008 for the first time over half the world's inhabitants lived in urban areas. It is projected that by 2050 the proportion will grow to 70 percent. At that point, 6.4 billion people—nearly the total world population in 2007—will be urban dwellers, and there will be 27 megacities with populations of 10 million or more. The stress on global as well as local ecosystems will be tremendous.

Currently, cities take up only 2 percent of the world's surface, but urban inhabitants account for 75 percent of global resource use and a significant portion of waste products and emissions. Urban dwellers are the main contributors to climate change. The UN Environment Program has developed a range of initiatives to mitigate the impact of cities on the environment. Among them are the Partnership for Clean Fuels and Vehicles; the campaign on cities and climate change; and the global partnership on cities and biodiversity. These initiatives represent partnerships with international, transnational and national participants. ■

Global Green New Deal

Roger A. Coate

In October 2008, Secretary-General Ban Ki-moon called for the Global Green New Deal, and the Green Economy Initiative was begun. The initiative represents a medium- to long-term strategy to blunt and turn around global environmental degradation. It incorporates three elements: the Green Economy Report, the Economics of Ecosystems and Biodiversity and the Green Jobs Report.

The Green Economy Report will provide an overview, analysis and synthesis of how public policy can accelerate the transition to a green economy. The Economics of Ecosystems is a partnership focusing on the economic value of biodiversity and ecosystem services, aiming to make a credible economic and development case for conservation and investment. It was initiated in March

2007 by the environmental ministers of the Group of 8 Plus 5—the eight major industrialized countries, Britain, Canada, France, Germany, Italy, Japan, Russia and the United States, plus Brazil, China, India, Mexico and South Africa. The first interim report, issued in May 2008, concluded that unless strong corrective action was taken, the decline in biodiversity and loss of ecosystem services might result in irreparable damage to certain ecosystems. The Green Jobs Report examines green-related employment trends.

Secretary-General Ban reiterated his call for a Green New Deal in Poznan, Poland, in December 2008 and called for "investment that fights climate change, creates millions of green jobs and spurs green growth."

Green investment is needed at all levels, including large-scale geothermal energy programs and eco-friendly mass transportation networks as well as local-level initiatives. Grameen Shakti, a company that pioneered a microfinance system in Bangladesh, is a good example. (The company is a project of Grameen Bank, which won the 2006 Nobel Peace Prize with its founder, Muhammad Yunus.) It finances photovoltaic panels for poor households, particularly those headed by women. They buy the panels and sell solar electricity to neighbors, thus becoming local suppliers of electricity. This new green energy source replaces kerosene at about the same cost.

Another element is the Green Jobs Initiative, a partnership of the UN Environment Program, the International Labor Organization, the International Trade Union Confederation and the International Organization of Employers. Its philosophy is that countries should formulate policies to deal with climate change that create green jobs; that is, jobs that reduce carbon emissions.

The objectives include promoting awareness and dialogue on the links between development, environmental challenges and employment; facilitating a "just transition" that reflects the environmental, economic and social aspects of sustainable development; and strengthening collaboration between the partners within the UN system and with the international business community.

In September 2008, the Green Jobs Initiative published a report, "Green Jobs: Towards Decent Work in a Sustainable, Low-Carbon World." It estimated the current global market for environmental products at $1.37 billion a year, a figure expected to grow to $2.74 billion by 2020. Globally, 2.3 million people are estimated to be employed in renewable-energy jobs: more than 600,000 in solar thermal; 300,000 in wind power; and 100,000 in solar photovoltaic. In just four countries—Brazil, China, Germany and the United States —1.2 million are employed in biomass-related jobs, like engineers, project managers and consultants in alternative energy industries. ∎

Clean Sustainable Energy Policies

Roger A. Coate

To stabilize climate change and mitigate all the associated environmental and social problems, greenhouse gas emissions must decrease. Accomplishing this will require a rapid shift to clean-energy technologies, which are in short supply in both developed and developing countries. Promoting renewable clean energy and improved energy efficiency and spurring development of a carbon market are two of the main approaches being used by the UN Environment Program to reduce emissions of greenhouse gases. Investment in sustainable energy has risen significantly in recent years and has broadened and diversified. The program's report, "Global Trends in Sustainable Energy Investment 2008," said that the total rose to $148 billion last year, a 60 percent increase over 2006.

Between 1998 and 2007, investment in renewables increased more than sixfold. Sustainable energy accounted for 23 percent of all new power-generation capacity worldwide, with wind leading the way. Large gains were also posted in biomass and waste conversion, cellulosic ethanol and thin-film solar technology.

Early-stage venture-capital investment rose 112 percent, to $2 billion. Investment in clean-energy companies more than doubled in the world's public markets in 2007. The report noted a shift in renewable capacity investment beyond Europe, to China and the United States. Chinese investment in non-hydro renewable technologies, especially wind, increased more than fourfold from 2006 to 2007. Other developing countries, such as Brazil and India, are attracting substantial new clean-energy investment.

The UN Environment Program has taken a lead in the bioenergy field. It supports the development of bioenergy planning and related policies with a special focus on fostering small agribusiness development. It is also engaged in the BioTop Project, designed to identify research needs and technical opportunities for Latin America, based on biofuel development in Europe. The agency serves as a clearinghouse for information on renewable energy, and in the area of energy governance, it undertakes analyses of the effectiveness of renewable energy policies.

Governance: Leading by Example

Although the UN Environment Program bears the sole responsibility within the UN system for keeping the world environmental situation under review to ensure that emerging problems get attention, there is little it can do alone. In this context, the UN Chief Executives Board, in October 2007, began the UN Climate Neutral Strategy, defined as "the entire set of policies that an institution uses when it estimates its known greenhouse gas emissions, takes measures to reduce them and purchases carbon offsets to 'neutralize' those emissions that remain."

The strategy aims to make all UN bodies and programs reduce greenhouse gas emissions by the time of the UN Climate Change Conference in December 2009. It requires agencies to commit to reducing greenhouse gas emissions as part of a comprehensive environmental management approach; to develop and implement measures to reduce greenhouse gas emissions; to make regular reports on the agency's emissions inventory, together with any targets or goals for reductions; to develop and implement a knowledge-management system serving the entire UN; and document initiatives, data, lessons learned and best practices.

The strategy identifies five focus areas and four crosscutting areas and the UN agencies in each that are to play convening roles. Following are the five focus areas and their respective agencies:

- Reducing emissions from deforestation and forest degradation; Food and Agriculture Organization, UN Development Program, UN Environment Program.

- Technology transfer: UN Industrial Development Organization, UN Department of Economic and Social Affairs.

- Finance (mitigation, adaptation): the World Bank, UN Development Program.

- Capacity building: UN Development Program, UN Environment Program.

- Adaptation: High Level Committee on Programs working group on climate change.

To integrate climate concerns more generally into UN activities, these four crosscutting areas were identified:

- Science, assessment, monitoring and early warning: World Meteorological Organization, UN Educational, Scientific and Cultural Organization.

- Supporting global, regional and national action: UN Development Program, UN Department of Economic and Social Affairs, UN Regional Commissions.

- Public awareness: UN Environment Program, UN Communications Group.

- Climate-neutral United Nations: UN Environment Program.

In support of the initiative, the Environment Program began the Climate Neutral Network. It strives to assist governments and others in achieving significant reductions in greenhouse gas emissions. Among other things, it acts as a forum and as a clearinghouse for sharing information.

The primary purpose of the UN strategy is to lead by example. It forces agencies and employees to think holistically about the environment. It includes renovation and construction; facilities management; procurement; field operations; management systems; networks; assessment methodologies; and, perhaps most important, organizational culture. One wonders if such an approach could possibly find its way into the UN's governing bodies as well as into other UN agencies, governments and individuals' daily lives. Of course everyone cares, but is anybody really listening, and are people individually and collectively willing to change? ▪

In Port-au-Prince, Haiti, members of the Jordanian battalion of a United Nations mission and others lead a rescue of children from an orphanage after Hurricane Ike lashed the region in September 2008.

Humanitarian Assistance, Economic Growth and the Millennium Development Goals

The Financial Chaos Challenges the UN's Humanitarian Role

Irwin Arieff

Soaring commodity prices and mayhem in world financial markets have presented the United Nations with extraordinary challenges in its traditional role as coordinator of global humanitarian assistance. These twin crises have forced the UN to rethink the fundamentals of its methods in combating world hunger and aiding victims of natural disasters as well as people caught in conflicts and other emergencies.

Rising fuel and food costs drove up the 2008 budgets of humanitarian agencies while also pushing millions more people into hunger and poverty around the world. By the end of 2008, a global economic crash deepened the problem, threatening both the needy and those seeking to help them.

While food and oil prices retreated to some extent by the year's end, they continue to have an effect on the cost of seed, fertilizer and the operation of farm machinery and trucks that transport agricultural goods to market. At the same time, these high prices encourage farmers to divert some food crops, already in limited supply, to the production of fuel.

The higher prices also increased global malnutrition and poverty along with the risk of economic and political instability, the UN Office for the Coordination of Humanitarian Affairs (OCHA) warned in its annual consolidated humanitarian appeal for 2009.

"This, combined with the deepening global financial crisis, which is straining government budgets, is likely to unravel traditional safety nets and increase humanitarian needs in the coming year," said the appeal, issued in November 2008.

Even before food prices began climbing in late 2007, 923 million people were considered to be undernourished by the Food and Agriculture Organization (FAO), a UN agency in Rome that coordinates efforts to feed the hungry.

Another 40 million people were pushed into hunger during 2008, primarily because the rising food costs priced them out of the market. In 2009, "the ongoing financial and economic crisis could tip even more people into hunger and poverty," the FAO warned in a Dec. 9, 2008, report. These increases were occurring after four decades of progress in international efforts to bring down levels of world hunger, the World Food Program (WFP), another UN agency in Rome, said.

Despite major price declines during the second half of 2008, the FAO food price index remained 28 percent higher in October 2008 than in October 2006, the agency reported in December 2008. ■

A 'Perfect Storm' Hits the World Food Program

Irwin Arieff

The pressure on food prices began building in 2007 in what Josette Sheeran, the World Food Program's executive director, described as "a perfect storm." The key factors include rising prices for fuel, fertilizer, seed and transportation; increasing demand for food, driven partly by the growing prosperity of population giants like China and India; and growing demand for corn and certain other crops that could be converted into ethanol for use as fuel.

The crisis has had a significant impact on the program, curtailing the amount of food that the agency can afford to buy while weakening donors' ability to continue contributing to its work, even as needs are growing.

While food-exporting nations stood to benefit from higher food prices, most developing nations were expected to be hurt because 55 percent are net food importers, according to the Food and Agriculture Organization. Nearly all the countries in Africa are currently net importers of cereals, the FAO said.

Buying More From Small Farms

The WFP, introduced by the UN in 1962, said it distributed food aid to an estimated 90 million people in 80 countries in 2008, after helping to feed 86 million in 80 countries the previous year. In 2009, it was planning to feed nearly 100 million people, it announced in December 2008.

To do so, WFP depends on both cash and equivalent contributions from its donors, which include governments, private relief organizations, businesses and individuals.

In recent years, seeking to make better use of its financing, the WFP has tried to obtain more and more of its food supplies from developing nations. In 2007, the latest year for which figures are available, $767 million of its $2.7 billion donations came in the form of cash. It spent 80 percent of that money to buy supplies in 69 developing nations. Topping the list were Uganda, where the WFP said it bought $55 million in goods; Ecuador ($51 million); and Turkey ($45 million).

In a five-year trial program begun in September 2008, the WFP is also trying to steer more of its business to small farms. The program, financed by $76 million in grants from the Bill & Melinda Gates Foundation, the Howard G. Buffett Foundation and the Belgian government, planned to reach out to 350,000 small-holder farmers in as many as 21 countries. Its first-year goal was to buy 40,000 metric tons of food (about 88 million pounds), enough to feed 250,000 people for one year.

Where the Hungriest Live

The FAO estimates that of the 923 million undernourished people worldwde, 907 million live in the developing world. In fact, 65 percent live in just seven countries: India, China, the Democratic Republic of the Congo, Bangladesh, Indonesia, Pakistan and Ethiopia, the FAO said in a December 2008 report, "The State of Food Insecurity in the World."

Nearly two-thirds of the world's hungry live in Asia, while about a third live in Africa. The ranks of the undernourished have been increasing in recent years in many parts of Asia and Africa, most notably in Congo. But some countries have gained ground by increasing agricultural production, the FAO said. Those achieving the biggest gains, it said, include Congo, Ghana, Malawi, Mozambique, Nigeria, Thailand and Vietnam.

Malawi, in southern Africa, has stood out for its success in one of the world's most enduringly hungry regions. The country went from being a major recipient of food assistance in 2003-06 to registering bumper harvests in 2006-08. The turnaround, while helped by good rainfall, came after the government started a subsidy program for seeds and fertilizer.

Providing small-scale farmers with the necessary tools for a successful planting season is a top priority for the FAO, which is seeking to increase food production in 106 countries. Working with the WFP, the World Bank and the International Fund for Agricultural Development, the FAO also sends assessment missions to help countries develop action plans for growing more food.

Seeking to improve the FAO's effectiveness, a panel of UN member states drafted a three-year reform plan in September 2007 that the agency has pledged to carry out beginning this year. The panel called for reforms after concluding that the FAO staff was top-heavy and averse to risk. The plan calls for staff cuts and streamlining the bureaucracy as well as additional funding for FAO programs.

Two-Track Approach

In the same vein, a report issued by a high-level task force on the global food crisis in July 2008 recommended major changes in the way the entire UN system looks at humanitarian needs.

The report called for a broader range of international agencies to participate in the effort to provide humanitarian aid, including the World Bank, the International Monetary Fund and the World Trade Organization. Ensuring food security required dealing with development, trade and financial questions as well as the more traditional challenges of getting more food and other vital aid to those most in need, it said.

The panel, led by Secretary-General Ban Ki-moon, set out two parallel tracks for action, one focusing on how to better meet the immediate needs of vulnerable populations and the other seeking to address the underlying factors driving the food crisis. Specific recommendations ranged from increasing food production by small farms and using the latest technology to holding down inflation, streamlining the international food market and developing international guidelines on the production of biofuels that give appropriate consideration to food needs.

"The financial implications related to this crisis will be considerable, will exceed the response thus far and will require substantial political and financial commitments from national governments first and foremost, but also from the private sector, civil society and the international system," the task force said, suggesting that an additional $25 billion to $40 billion a year would be required to ensure adequate food supplies globally.

Unfortunately, the report said, the huge demand for extra financing coincided with government cutbacks in their contributions to agricultural development aid.

While more countries have begun contributing to UN aid drives in recent years, only a handful of governments were meeting the longtime UN goal of donating 0.7 percent of their gross domestic product for official development assistance, according to the Organization for Economic Cooperation and Development (OECD), a policy group based in Paris. The 0.7 percent goal was officially adopted by the UN at a conference on financing for development in Monterrey, Mexico, in 2002.

Furthermore, just 3.4 percent of official development assistance was earmarked for agriculture in 2006, the latest year for which figures are available, compared with 18 percent in 1979, the task force said, basing its figures on OECD data.

Record Appeals

The primary UN vehicle for raising money for humanitarian help and distributing it is the annual appeal coordinated by the UN Office for the Coordination of Humanitarian Affairs. The 2009 consolidated appeal, which is typically supplemented throughout the year as additional emergencies occur, called for a record $7 billion in contributions from the international community for distribution among 31 countries. To ensure a coordinated and efficient global response, some 360 aid agencies helped formulate the needed programs and draft the appeal, which was issued by OCHA on Nov. 20, 2008.

Just five countries accounted for nearly three-quarters of the latest financing request, none a newcomer to the group: Sudan, Somalia, Congo, Zimbabwe and Iraq—all but Zimbabwe torn apart by war. They are listed in order of aid allotted, with the highest first.

Sudan: Nearly a third of the total 2009 humanitarian appeal, $2.19 billion, was reserved for this sprawling northeast African nation, which has been mired in conflict for decades. While a 2005 peace agreement officially ended the North-South war that raged since 1983, the situation between the two regions remains fragile, while a separate civil war has been under way in Darfur, in western Sudan, since 2003.

International experts estimate that up to 300,000 people have been killed and more than 2.5 million driven from their homes during the more than five years of fighting in Darfur.

OCHA said humanitarian assistance for 2009 would focus on aiding and protecting vulnerable populations and encouraging national recovery and self-reliance. In July 2008, the chief prosecutor of the International Criminal Court, Luis Moreno-Ocampo of Argentina, accused the president of Sudan, Omar Hassan al-Bashir, of genocide, crimes against humanity and war crimes, charging that he was orchestrating a massive campaign of ethnic violence in Darfur.

Somalia: A total of $919 million from the 2009 appeal would be channeled to this northeast African state, which has suffered from virtual anarchy since the collapse of its dictatorship in 1991.

In the latest shake-up, Ethiopia, which had sent troops into Somalia in December 2006 to help restore order and prop up an internationally recognized transitional government, withdrew its forces by early 2009 after falling short of its goal. Shortly afterward, the Somali Parliament elected Sheik Sharif Ahmed as the country's new president. Sheik Sharif ruled southern Somalia for six months in 2006 before being driven out by the Ethiopian forces. Before that, he served as chairman of the Islamic Courts Union, a religious alliance that had opposed the transitional government but more recently agreed to join its Parliament.

The chronic instability and on-and-off fighting among clans, warlords and rival governments have led to a surge in acts of piracy off the coast of Somalia and, according to OCHA, left more than three million people in dire need of humanitarian aid. The piracy has become a major obstacle to delivering humanitarian aid, and several ships carrying WFP supplies have been attacked by pirates off the coast. One food ship was seized and held by pirates for a few months in 2007. The incidents have obliged WFP to seek military escorts and alternative delivery routes.

Congo: Even before the start of 2009, relief officials acknowledged that the $831 million aid that they sought to raise for this long-troubled central African nation would fall far short of what was needed. "While the humanitarian community works hard to address the most urgent needs, it cannot address all of the needs related to extreme poverty and underdevelopment in this vast country," OCHA said. "Humanitarian aid allows vulnerable Congolese to survive emergencies, but it does not address the underlying causes."

Efforts in 2009 will therefore focus on helping communities resettle former residents displaced by war and curtailing aid dependence by encouraging self-reliance, OCHA said.

Relief workers have been seeking to stabilize and rebuild Congo since a 2003 peace agreement ended a five-year civil war that killed nearly four million people. But there is still fighting in the country's mineral-rich east, fed by tensions with neighboring nations, particularly Rwanda, and actions led by the warlord Laurent Nkunda, who was taken captive by Rwanda soldiers in early 2009. Aid workers and Congolese have criticized UN peacekeepers for failing to protect them from both rebel and out-of-control government soldiers active in eastern Congo. Rape, looting and shooting have been regularly reported in camps in the area housing displaced people.

Zimbabwe: Political turmoil and economic decline, including staggering inflation, have worsened in this East African nation after failed efforts to form a unity government occurred in the widely criticized March 2008 elections that left President Robert Mugabe in power. In February 2009, however, Morgan Tsvangirai, representing the country's main opposition party, Movement for Democratic Change, agreed to a power-sharing arrangement and role as prime minister.

OCHA estimated that 47 percent of Zimbabwe's 12.2 million people were undernourished while 56 percent were living in extreme poverty on a dollar a day or less. OCHA proposed $550 million in humanitarian aid for 2009, but aid workers have had a hard time carrying out their work because of disruption by the government and its deep mistrust of outsiders.

Iraq: While much of this troubled Middle Eastern nation was stabilized in 2008, many Iraqis who fled their homes after the US-led invasion in 2003 or in the subsequent violence have been unable to return, whether from other parts of Iraq or from neighboring nations.

OCHA called for $547 million in humanitarian aid in 2009, with a major focus on meeting the needs of Iraqis left homeless both inside and outside the country. The hope of aid officials was "to help Iraq create a better climate for safe, voluntary and dignified return," the UN appeal said. Another priority was to help the government restore public services and the rule of law while Iraq struggled to wean itself from foreign assistance, it said. ■ – *Irwin Arieff*

Dependence on Outside Help

In meeting global humanitarian needs, UN agencies work closely together and also rely heavily on thousands of public, nongovernmental and other private organizations to help get the job done. In many parts of the world, private aid personnel put their lives on the line alongside UN and other relief workers to carry out their mission, delivering food and other assistance amid conflicts and other trying and dangerous circumstances.

In 2007, the latest year for which figures are available, 2,816 nongovernmental organizations helped the World Food Program to deliver supplies and to campaign for global humanitarian aid. Money for the WFP and other UN aid programs also comes from private organizations, corporations and individuals as well as governments and other donors. Contributions to the WFP from corporate and private donors totaled $94.5 million in 2007, the organization said. And while the WFP runs the largest UN humanitarian relief program, it is just one of many UN aid agencies. The others, including Unicef, the UN refugee agency UNHCR and OCHA, also rely heavily on NGOs to carry out their work.

Aid Workers Under Attack

Free and unfettered access to the people who need help is a fundamental requirement of effective relief efforts. But aid workers have found themselves increasingly under attack in many parts of the world in recent years, making their work more dangerous and difficult.

Aid workers often find their way barred by weather conditions, floods, bad roads and other such unavoidable constraints. But human constraints, like a burst of military activity or a deliberate attack, have been a particular challenge in conflict-plagued areas like Darfur, Somalia and Congo.

Relief operations have also been disrupted in the Middle East by Israeli restrictions on access to Palestinian areas and in southern Asia by Sri Lankan restrictions on access to areas under the control of antigovernment rebels, John Holmes, the UN under-secretary-general for humanitarian affairs, told the Security Council in May 2008.

From July 1, 2007, to June 30, 2008, 25 UN staff members were killed as a result of malicious acts, a 36 percent increase over the same year-earlier period, Secretary-General Ban said in an August 2008 report to the General Assembly. In just one incident, on Dec. 11, 2007, 17 UN staff members were killed in a bomb attack on a UN office building in Algiers.

During the same period, other incidents involving the UN included 490 attacks, 546 harassment and intimidation cases, 578 robberies, 263 physical assaults, 119 hijackings and 199 arrests and cases of detention, Ban reported. There were also 84 forced entries and occupations of UN offices and 583 break-ins at UN staff residences.

Staff members of nongovernmental humanitarian organizations also paid a high price for their work during the period: 63 died from malicious acts, 236 were attacked and 173 were detained, according to Ban's report. Eighteen relief workers were killed in Somalia alone during the year.

"I am gravely concerned by the wide scale of threats, the rise in deliberate targeting of humanitarian and United Nations personnel and their vulnerability worldwide," Ban said. "In this disturbing trend, hostage incidents and targeted attacks against humanitarian and United Nations staff in areas of humanitarian emergencies continue unabated. Locally recruited personnel of the United Nations and humanitarian organizations are most vulnerable in conflict and postconflict areas." ■

HIV/AIDS, Tuberculosis and Malaria

Irwin Arieff

The UN plays a key role in the global battle against HIV/AIDS through UNAIDS, the UN umbrella agency, based in Geneva, that coordinates the efforts and resources of 10 UN organizations and works in more than 80 countries. It was set up in 1996 to help prevent new HIV infections, care for people living with HIV and mitigate the impact of the AIDS epidemic.

To help finance the fight against HIV/AIDS and other deadly infectious diseases around the world, the UN established the Global Fund to Fight AIDS, Tuberculosis and Malaria. The fund was set up in Geneva in January 2002 after Kofi Annan, the UN secretary-general at the time, called for its formation at a summit of African leaders in Abuja, Nigeria, in April 2001.

Since its establishment, the fund has become the main source of financing for international efforts to combat the three diseases, providing a quarter of all international financing for AIDS programs, two-thirds for tuberculosis and three-quarters for malaria. For AIDS alone, the fund funneled $15 billion into hundreds of programs in 140 countries by the end of 2008.

Up to two million people with AIDS were being treated with lifesaving antiretroviral drugs as of December 2008 through programs the fund supported, 43 percent more than were being treated in December 2007. Antimalaria programs that it supports had distributed 70 million insecticide-treated bed nets to families at risk of the disease, up from 46 million a year earlier, the fund reported. And more than 4.6 million people were being treated with tuberculosis drugs under fund-supported programs, it said. Tuberculosis accounts for as many as a third of AIDS deaths worldwide, according to the WHO.

AIDS nonetheless remains a major threat to world health, according to UNAIDS, which tracks the epidemic through regular monitoring and reports. An estimated 33 million people were infected with HIV worldwide as of December 2008, far more than the 20 million living with HIV when UNAIDS began in 1996. An estimated 2.7 million people are newly infected each year and two million people die, according to the most recent UNAIDS statistics. But more than three million people in developing nations are being treated with antiretroviral drugs, and the number of new HIV infections is dropping in many countries, UNAIDS said. About $10 billion is spent in developing countries on the disease.

"We are at a turning point in the epidemic," Michel Sidibé, who succeeded Dr. Peter Piot as the UNAIDS executive director at the start of 2009, said in late 2008. "We have shattered the silence and built a global movement. But an unprecedented collective effort is still required to prevent an estimated 7,000 new HIV infections each day" and an estimated 6,000 deaths each day. ∎

Are We There Yet? Midway Through The Millennium Development Goals

Roger A. Coate

The Millennium Development Goals, initiated in 2000 at the Millennium Summit, define eight aims, associated targets and measurable indicators to be achieved by 2015 to eradicate poverty and promote sustainable human development and security.

Since the summit, a strategy for the whole UN system has been designed to mobilize support and monitor progress toward these goals. The midway point was 2008, and UN members gathered in New York in September to assess progress. The picture was mixed.

Goal 1: Eradicate extreme poverty and hunger

In global terms, the world appears on track for meeting the target of halving extreme poverty by 2015. The number of people living in extreme poverty fell from 1.8 billion in 1990 to 1.4 billion in 2005. At the same time, the percentage of people living below the poverty line ($1.25 a day) fell from 41.7 percent to 25.7 percent. However, such aggregate statistics can be very misleading. Most of the reduction in extreme poverty occurred in eastern and southeastern Asia. Most of the other regions experienced a rise in the number of people living in extreme poverty. Sub-Saharan Africa still hovers around 50 percent. The target of achieving full and productive employment for all remains possible but not likely given current trends. Half of the world's labor force works in unstable, insecure jobs.

In global terms, the proportion of people suffering malnutrition and undernourishment has declined since 1990. Yet at the same time, the number of people lacking access to adequate food has increased. By late 2008, it was estimated that one billion people were going hungry and over half the population of the developing world was undernourished. Nearly half the children in southern Asia are underweight; in sub-Saharan Africa, progress on eliminating child malnutrition has been even poorer.

Goal 2: Achieve universal primary education

Education is crucial for development. Of the 10 regions covered within the MDGs, eight have primary-school enrollment rates of more than 90 percent. The number of children not attending primary school declined from 103 million in 1990 to 73 million in 2006. Although the most progress has been in education, persisting gender inequalities jeopardize worldwide attainment of the goal. Eighty-six countries have yet to attain universal primary education; of these 58 are not on track for reaching the target. Throughout the developing world, a large proportion of children do not attend primary school, and slightly more than half of the youth of appropriate age attend secondary school. In sub-Saharan Africa, the proportion of children attending primary school has increased to 71 percent; the figure for secondary school stands at 25 percent.

Goal 3: Promote gender equality and empower women

These goals are viewed as essential components of sustainable human development. Gender inequality is a major factor affecting all the goals. In 6 of the 10 regions within the MDGs, the gender-parity index in primary education is 95 percent or higher. Yet globally, progress toward meeting this goal remains off track. A hundred and thirteen countries failed to achieve parity in primary and secondary education by the target date of 2005, and it is projected that only 18 of these will reach the goal by 2015. On the positive side, from 2000 to 2006 enrollment of girls increased more than boys in all developing regions, and two-thirds of developing countries have already achieved parity at the primary level.

In the workplace, women in general are making progress slowly. From 1990 to 2006 the proportion of women in nonagricultural employment increased to 40 percent from 35 percent. Two-thirds of women still work in vulnerable jobs and lack employment security. In this regard, sub-Saharan Africa is at the bottom of the list.

The political advancement of women still lags, especially at the highest levels of government. In January 2008, only 7 of the world's 150 elected heads of government were women. And women constitute less than 10 percent of members in one-third of the world's parliaments.

Goal 4: Reduce child mortality

Progress in this arena has been very mixed. The target of reducing the mortality rate for children under age 5 by two-thirds between 1990 and 2015 is not on track. Overall, deaths of children under 5 has declined from 93 per 1,000 in 1990 to 72 per 1,000 in 2006; since 1960 there has been a 60 percent drop in general child mortality rates. Yet every hour, more than 1,200 children die. In 2006, the death toll stood at nearly 10 million. In 62 countries, conditions remain so bad that this goal will most likely not be achieved, and in 27 countries conditions are either getting worse or static. Sub-Saharan Africa has the dubious distinction of recording half of all child deaths in the developing world.

Goal 5: Improve maternal health

The primary gauge for maternal health care is maternal mortality. The aim is to reduce the number of women who die during childbirth by three-quarters between 1990 and 2015. The world is far off target on this goal. In fact, this goal demonstrates the least progress of the eight. From 1990 to 2005, maternal mortality decreased by less than 1 percent. Maternal and reproductive health problems are the leading cause of death of reproductive-age women worldwide. The situation is especially bad in sub-Saharan Africa and southern Asia. Although births to adolescents in developing countries as a whole have declined slowly since 1990, they have actually increased in sub-Saharan Africa. Crucial factors in averting deaths of women in childbirth are access to family planning and the presence of a skilled attendant at delivery. Yet in the developing world, skilled attendants are present in only 60 percent of deliveries. The greatest improvements in this regard have been made in Southeast Asia and North Africa, including Malaysia, Sri Lanka, Thailand and Tunisia, with the least improvement seen in sub-Saharan Africa and western Asia.

Goal 6: Combat HIV/AIDS, malaria and other diseases

In 2007 it is estimated that 33 million people were living with HIV/AIDS, up from 29.5 million in 2001. The number of people newly infected with HIV, however, fell to 2.7 million in 2007 from 3 million in 2001, and AIDS-related deaths declined to 2 million in 2007 from 2.2 million in 2005. The number of children under age 15 living with HIV has increased since 2001, but the rate of new infections has declined. Nearly 90 percent of children living with HIV live in sub-Saharan Africa. From 1998 to 2007 there was a tenfold increase in financing for anti-HIV/AIDS programs globally, but less than a third of those needing treatment had access.

Malaria is endemic in 109 countries and kills more than one million people annually. The vast majority of deaths (90 percent) are in sub-Saharan Africa, and 90 percent are children under 5. Progress toward eradication of tuberculosis has been mixed, and the target of halving the prevalence rate by 2015 is unlikely to be achieved. Nearly 15 million people actually have full-blown tuberculosis, and 90 percent of all cases are in the developing world. In 2006, TB accounted for 1.7 million deaths. Of the countries in the world with TB infection rates over 400 per 100,000, 12 of the 15 are in sub-Saharan Africa.

Goal 7: Ensure environmental sustainability

The main targets of this vast goal are integrating the principles of sustainable development into country policies and programs, reversing the loss of environmental resources, significantly reducing biodiversity loss, halving the proportion of people without access to safe drinking water and basic sanitation and improving the lives of 100 million urban slum dwellers.

The most visible and controversial global environmental issue is climate change. While major strides have been made since the 1987 Montreal Protocol in phasing out ozone-depleting substances, carbon dioxide and other greenhouse gas emissions continue to rise unabated, threatening the stability of the world's climate. Emissions increased on average by 30 percent from 1990 to 2005. While developed countries remain the world's leading generators of emissions, the greatest increases (82 percent) have occurred in southeastern Asia. Deforestation is also a large factor affecting world climate. Although it declined from 2000 to 2005, deforestation continues to pose serious challenges for meeting this goal.

In response to biodiversity loss, governments have acted to significantly increase the areas of land and marine environments under protection.

However, biodiversity loss continues to occur at an unprecedented rate. The number of threatened species is rising rapidly. More than 10,000 species, and perhaps more important, the world's fish stocks are under threat.

Inadequate access to safe water and sanitation plagues nearly one-half of all people in the world. Progress has been made in providing safe drinking water and basic sanitation in developing regions, and the world as a whole appears on target for halving the proportion of people who have no safe water supplies. Since 1990, nearly 1.6 billion people have gained access to safe drinking water with the largest gains being made in southern Asia. Yet one billion people remain without. Sub-Saharan Africa lags far behind, with 42 percent of the population still without access.

In developing regions nearly a quarter of the population uses no form of sanitation. More than half the people in the developing world, an estimated 2.5 billion people, lack basic sanitation facilities. Access has increased significantly since 1990, but the world is not on target for reaching this goal. There is a large gap between rural and urban populations, and 70 percent of people without basic sanitation live in rural areas. But this figure masks the situation in urban slums, where both safe water and basic sanitation remain extremely scarce. More than one-third of people in developing regions and more than 60 percent of those in sub-Saharan Africa live in slums. These conditions have not improved in any major way.

Goal 8: Develop a global partnership for development

This is by far the most complex and, in some ways, the most ambitious goal. It embodies the spirit underlying the Millennium Declaration, to eradicate poverty and make sustainable development work for everyone, requiring partnerships between developing and developed countries. This goal and its seven targets focus on steps that rich countries need to take to fulfill their side of the bargain. The targets have a broad range.

Trade. With regard to stimulating further development of an open, rule-based, predictable, nondiscriminatory trading and financial system, the situation has stagnated with the failure of the Doha round of negotiations in the World Trade Organization. Less than 80 percent of exports from less-developed countries are granted duty-free access to developed countries. Agricultural tariffs remain high, as do agricultural subsidies in developed countries.

Landlocked countries and small island states. These places confront special problems. The indicator of progress is the official development assistance received by landlocked countries or small island states as a proportion of their gross national incomes. Progress to date has not been good. In 2004, 72 percent of landlocked states and 80 percent of small island states received less aid as a proportion of their incomes than in 1994.

Jobs for youth. The developing world is home to nearly 90 percent of the world's youth. This age group is three times more likely to be unemployed than adults in developing countries as a whole, and young women are more likely to be unemployed than young men. The situation regarding youth employment has not improved much over the last decade, except in the countries of the former Soviet Union.

Access to affordable essential drugs. Progress has been made here, yet the situation is dire, especially for the poor. Only 35 percent of the drugs considered essential are available through the public sector. Unfortunately, on average these medicines cost 250 percent more than the international reference price. Two-thirds of essential drugs are available through the private sector, but at 650 percent the international reference price.

Overcoming the digital divide. The divide between developed and developing regions continues to widen in regard to technologies that drive information and communication development. Yet significant progress has been made in people's access to information and communications technologies, especially cellular telephones. More than 77 percent of people in the developing world have access to cellular telephone signals. This is a drastic change from 2001. Even in sub-Saharan Africa, the access rate is 54 percent. On the down side, more than 30 percent of people in the developing world and 74 percent in sub-Saharan Africa still do not have access to electricity.

Aid. Official development assistance is a cornerstone of the global development partnership. From its low point in 1997, development assistance rose steadily for eight years until it reached a peak of $106.8 billion in 2005. Then, 2006 witnessed a significant downturn, when the total fell by 4.7 percent; it dropped again in 2007, by 8.4 percent. The proportion of assistance allocated to agriculture and physical infrastructure, however, has declined a lot. In 2005, the Group of Eight industrialized countries committed to increase aid by $50 billion per year by 2010. However, to date little has actually occurred to fulfill this promise. Progress has been made in reducing the practice of tying aid to the purchase of specific commodities, services or products from the donor country.

Debt. Major progress has been made in reducing the unsustainable debt of poor heavily indebted countries. The Heavily Indebted Poor Countries initiative, begun in 1996 by the International Development Association of the World Bank Group and the International Monetary Fund, has served as the centerpiece for debt reduction. Debt relief has been or is being provided to 33 of the 41 eligible countries, canceling more than 90 percent of their external debt. At the same time, however, more than 50 developing countries were forced to spend more on debt service than on public health.

Looking Forward

In the words of Secretary-General Ban Ki-moon: "We have made important progress towards all eight goals, but we are not on track to fulfill our commitments. The challenge is clear, but in the context of the current global economic recession, ongoing widespread food shortages, increasing energy prices, climate change and other environmental problems and civil strife, the way will not be easy or fast. It will require strong leadership and follow-through." ■

Rescuing the World's Homeless and Persecuted

Tendai Musakwa interviews António Guterres

Last year was busy for the Office of the United Nations High Commissioner for Refugees. From evacuating refugees of postelection violence in Kenya to providing emergency aid to victims of a cyclone in southern Myanmar to establishing a temporary camp for displaced people in the Georgian city of Gori, the agency continued to respond to a wide range of extraordinary crises.

In 2009, it faces an increasingly complex set of challenges. Financing problems, attacks on refugees and personnel and an ever-increasing refugee population only add to the enormous tasks that the agency already deals with year after year.

The main concern is the sudden rise in the number of refugees. In 2006, the number worldwide fell to 10 million, the lowest level in almost 25 years. But by June 2008, the continuing war in Iraq and the conflict in Somalia pushed the total number of people seeking protection from the UN agency to almost 11.5 million.

To enhance its efficiency in the last two years, the agency has cut back on headquarters staff and devoted more money to field operations. Nevertheless, it still cannot fully meet the needs of the people under its care. For example, a December 2008 study by the Women's Commission for Refugees, a nonprofit group that works to provide long-term solutions, found little in the way of education or training available to displaced young people.

Finding money for the agency's programs is also a major undertaking. By Dec. 10, 2008, donors pledged $463 million toward its 2009 programs, but that is only a quarter of what the agency needs and 6 percent less than was pledged for 2008 by December 2007. The biggest donor is the US, which gave about a third of the agency's $1.5 billion budget for 2008. The top 10 donor countries are the US, Japan, Sweden, the Netherlands, Britain, Norway, Germany, Denmark, Canada and Italy. Together, they provided about $1.1 billion of the 2008 budget.

In 2007, the agency's top two private donors were the Bill and Melinda Gates Foundation, which gave $4 million, and the Dutch Postcode Lottery, which gave $3.5 million.

Paradoxically, it is mostly poor countries that house the largest number of refugees. In 2007, the latest year for which figures are available, the top five were Pakistan, Syria, Iran, Germany and Jordan, listed in order of the number of refugees admitted. Of these, Pakistan, Syria, Iran and Jordan were host to five million people, while Germany took in 600,000.

Like other UN affiliates, the refugee agency has limited capacity to provide physical security for its staff and beneficiaries. On Jan. 31, 2008, for example, it was forced to evacuate personnel from its eastern Chad office in Guereda after five hijackings at gunpoint.

António Guterres, who served as the prime minister of Portugal from 1996 to 2002 and succeeded Ruud Lubbers of the Netherlands as high commissioner for refugees on June 15, 2005, outlined the challenges the agency faces in 2009 in an interview conducted by e-mail in January 2009 with Tendai Musakwa, an intern at UNA-USA.

Q: What are the most urgent challenges for 2009? And how can the new US administration help?

A: It is clear that a series of adverse developments confronts us. We face more complex situations of forced displacement, higher numbers of internally displaced people, more emergencies and a worldwide financial and economic crisis—the worst effects of which are still to be felt.

First and foremost, our job is to provide protection and assistance to the world's refugees and other persons of concern. Currently, UNHCR counts nearly 32 million people of concern worldwide. Meeting the needs of millions of uprooted people is an enormous challenge, particularly given that we work in nearly 120 countries and in some of the most difficult places on earth. Support from governments, including the United States, is crucial to that work. We are almost totally dependent on government contributions, and the United States is our largest individual donor.

Q: How will the refugee agency fare in the financial crisis?

A: UNHCR is almost totally dependent on annual voluntary contributions from donor governments; only 3 percent comes from the regular UN budget. About 75 percent of our funding comes from just 10 donor countries, so we obviously need to broaden our donor base. Thus, we have placed increasing emphasis on individual and corporate giving.

In 2009, we are seeking a total of $1.86 billion for our worldwide work on behalf of refugees and others of concern. Raising such amounts every year is a major undertaking and a responsibility we take very seriously because every dollar we receive has an impact on the lives of some of the world's most vulnerable people. We are extremely concerned about the current global financial crisis and the potential impact this may have on support for humanitarian work in general and our own efforts for tens of millions of uprooted people in particular.

At a time when governments are spending tens of billions of dollars on financial rescue plans, we hope they will also continue to show similar concern for some of the world's most vulnerable people—refugees and the displaced—a majority of whom are hosted by poor countries whose own governments do not enjoy sufficient resources to care for them.

For our part, I can assure donors that UNHCR is doing its best to minimize its own costs by carrying out a sweeping reform program begun in 2006, aimed at making us a more effective, efficient and agile organization that is fully responsive to the needs of refugees. The changes include streamlining our Geneva headquarters to devote as many resources as possible to field operations. Our headquarters staff has fallen from 1,047 people at the begin-ning of 2006 to less than 750 today, with the number expected to drop below 700 by mid-2009. Globally, the proportion of staff costs has fallen from 42.5 percent in 2006 to a projected 33.3 percent in 2009.

Many of the headquarters posts were moved to a new UNHCR global serv-ice center in Budapest; others are being relocated to the field under an ongo-ing decentralization and regionalization program expected to conclude in mid-2009. More than $22 million in savings from the reforms, which also include an overhaul of our human-resources policies, have already made a real difference in the lives of refugees by addressing crucial gaps in the areas of malaria, malnutrition and reproductive health, as well as sexual and gender-based violence in situations as diverse as Algeria, Bangladesh, the Democratic Republic of the Congo, Ethiopia and Nepal.

Q: The refugee agency has corporate partnerships, like one with Nike, which developed the Més que un Club campaign involving the Nike-spon-sored soccer team FC Barcelona. The campaign raises money through the Més brand of merchandise and proceeds provide sports, education and other skills to young refugees. How are that and other partnerships faring?

A: UNHCR's partnerships with companies and teams such as these have brought significantly more support for sports programs for refugee youth. This has multiplied our reach to young boys and, of great importance, girls. UNHCR has had sport programs for refugee children in camps for the past decade, but most of that time we were severely limited in what we could do due to funding constraints.

Our new and expanding relationships with major companies and teams are instrumental to our efforts to use sport to help refugee children regain other-wise lost childhoods; to serve as a catalyst in teaching youngsters about coop-eration, rules and positive attitudes; to help guard against forced recruitment; and to bring young people together to discuss important issues such as health awareness and sexual and gender-based violence. More broadly, the wide reach of the major companies and professional teams that now carry the UNHCR message leads to greater public understanding of the plight of refugees around the world.

Q: What security challenges do agency personnel face in the field? What actions has the international community taken to make them more secure?

A: UNHCR works in some of the world's most difficult and dangerous places. More than 80 percent of our staff work in the field, and more than 60 percent are in so-called nonfamily duty stations, where the living conditions are diffi-cult and security is often a concern.

To help the world's uprooted people, we must be with them, on the ground. Our staff members understand and accept this. But at the same time, it is imperative that our people in the field work under the safest possible conditions so they can deliver the necessary protection and assistance to refugees. While we cannot eliminate risk, we can manage it.

For this reason, we have continued to pursue conformity with UN minimum operating security standards for all our offices and staff residences worldwide. Staff safety was one of the principal subjects in my recent mission to Baghdad, Ramadi and Najaf in Iraq, and in Kabul and Jalalabad in Afghanistan. All of this, of course, requires resources, and I am pleased that our donors understand the importance of funding these security measures.

Q: What steps has the agency taken to reduce violence in refugee camps — for example, the December 2008 murder of two children and the rape of a woman in camps in the eastern Democratic Republic of the Congo?

A: UNHCR is constantly striving to improve security for refugees in camps worldwide, particularly for women, children and the most vulnerable. In any refugee population, a majority of the uprooted people are women and children. Stripped of the protection of their homes, their government and often their family structure, women and girls are often particularly vulnerable. They face the rigors of long journeys into exile, official harassment or indifference and sexual abuse even after reaching an apparent place of safety.

Women must cope with these threats while being nurse, teacher, breadwinner and physical protector of their families. While overall security for refugees is the responsibility of the host government, UNHCR has developed a series of special programs to ensure women have equal access to protection, basic goods and services as they attempt to rebuild their lives. Details of these various programs can be found on the UNHCR Web site at www.unhcr.org/protect/3b83a48d4.html.

The specific incidents referred to in the Democratic Republic of the Congo are particularly tragic and underscore the immense difficulties UN humanitarian agencies face in trying to help internally displaced people in conflict situations. Under our mandate, most of our work over the past six decades has been with refugees who have reached relative safety in neighboring countries. Increasingly in recent years, however, we have been called on to work alongside other UN humanitarian agencies in providing help to internally displaced people—those who remain uprooted within their own countries and therefore are not covered by the 1951 Refugee Convention.

The United Nations has developed the so-called "cluster" approach in dealing with internal displacement situations, assigning specific roles to individual humanitarian agencies for various sectors. Providing adequate protection to the internally displaced can be extremely difficult and sometimes impossible in conflict situations. We see this in Congo, where all sides have been accused of horrific abuses that include widespread rape and murder. Recently, some 60,000 people who fled to a camp at Kibati, on the northern outskirts of Goma, in strife-torn North Kivu province, were caught between the front lines. Armed men roamed the camp at will, the displaced were sometimes caught in the crossfire, and aid workers were unable to reach them.

UNHCR is currently carrying out a difficult relocation program in which tens of thousands of people in the dangerous Kibati camp are being transferred to other sites to the west of Goma. But the situation remains precarious and will continue to be so until a long-term political solution is found to end the terrible violence in the eastern DRC. The recent approval of supplementary UN peacekeeping forces for DRC will help. In the meantime, we will continue to do everything we can to help the innocent victims of this prolonged and tragic conflict.

Q: What long-range plans does the agency have to reduce the numbers of refugees worldwide?

A: Displacement is first and foremost a political problem requiring political solutions. UNHCR is a field-based, nonpolitical humanitarian organization that deals with the human consequences of displacement caused by conflict and persecution. While the very near term remains unpredictable, longer-term trends are becoming increasingly clear. Climate change, extreme poverty and conflict are becoming more interrelated. Forced displacement is increasing as a result.

More natural disasters and the impact of the worldwide financial and economic crisis are prompting others to leave their homes in search of opportunities elsewhere, mostly in cities, accelerating both migration and urbanization. All this will inevitably have an impact on the delivery of the services for which we are responsible. More immediately, our job remains to find solutions for refugees, usually through three so-called "durable solutions"—repatriation, integration in countries of first asylum or resettlement to a third country. Over nearly six decades, UNHCR has helped find such solutions for more than 50 million people.

Unfortunately, too many refugees are caught in protracted situations in which they are left in exile for years and sometimes decades. Currently, there are some 6 million refugees in 30 different situations worldwide who have been in exile for at least 5 years. In December 2008, I convened an international dialogue in Geneva attended by more than 300 delegates from more than 50 nations as well as various agencies and nongovernmental organizations to focus on the specific challenge of finding solutions for these long-term refugees. That meeting brought renewed commitment from governments and UNHCR and led to a number of ongoing, follow-up initiatives, such as Core Groups, which will focus on resolving specific protracted situations in a coordinated, comprehensive manner. ■

Trying to Find Good Luck in America

Damiano Beltrami

Firas Taresh, 33, was one of 13,000 Iraqi refugees admitted to the United States in 2008 and one of two million Iraqi refugees worldwide, most of whom live mainly in Syria and Jordan, according to 2008 figures from the United Nations High Commissioner for Refugees.

Taresh, which is his grandfather's surname, used to work in Baghdad as an engineer for the Bechtel Corporation. According to Taresh, he was threatened by people identifying themselves as Al Qaeda members, demanding that he stop working for Bechtel because of its American affiliation. Here is his account:

"In September 2006 I received a death threat from Al Qaeda," Taresh said. "It was a printed piece of paper with the logo of Al Qaeda. We found it in our garage. It just said 'You are working with American people, you need to quit helping those atheist people or you will be considered a betrayer and you will be assassinated. To show us that you've quit your job you need to raise a white flag in your house within three days.'"

Taresh said that he put up the flag, but that he may not have quit Bechtel soon enough, and, he said, as a result one of his brothers was killed driving Taresh's car. Having escaped death—Taresh believes that his brother had been mistaken for himself—he fled to Syria and soon after, his father was kidnapped and murdered in Iraq.

In Syria, Taresh met an American filmmaker, Marie Maciak, who hired him as a translator because of his excellent English. Once Maciak returned to the US, she fought the bureaucratic maze to gain refugee status for Taresh, his brother Ali, 23, and their mother, Malkia, 57. The family arrived in the US in the summer of 2008 and stayed at Maciak's house on the eastern end of Long Island until they recently moved to a Sag Harbor cottage rent-free, through the generosity of a local resident. But they must leave the house before summer arrives and are looking for a permanent place they can afford.

Taresh works as a technician at the Ross School on Long Island and teaches evening Arabic classes to support his family. His brother and mother speak no English, and with few Arabic people in the area, they feel isolated and homesick. Ali spends most of his time chatting online with friends in Iraq. Malkia cries constantly and misses her grandchildren in Baghdad. Every week, Taresh catches a train to Brooklyn to go house-hunting in Bay Ridge, which has an Arabic community. As of February, he has had no luck. He is also studying to obtain a US engineering license so he can work his way up in his new country.

To do so, he said, he has to pass a fundamental engineering test. "The process of this application is complex for me," he added. "It requires a lot of patience. There are forms to send to a number of agencies, and I have to get my transcripts from the college where I graduated in Iraq. God only knows whether my former college will bother getting back to me. Inshallah, God willing."

Photo essay by Damiano Beltrami

Firas Taresh, 33, in front of the Sag Harbor, N.Y., cottage he is staying in with his mother and younger brother until the summer. A local resident is letting the family live temporarily in the house rent-free.

In a dark, quiet hour, Taresh's thoughts drift back to Baghdad, where his father and a brother were killed, he said, because Taresh was working as an engineer for Bechtel, an American company.

Taresh's mother, Malkia, is struggling to adjust to the American way of life since she arrived in the summer of 2008. She feels isolated on Long Island, where there is no Arabic community nearby, and she misses her grandchildren in Baghdad.

Every week, Taresh goes house-hunting in Bay Ridge, Brooklyn, hoping to find an affordable place for his mother and his brother Ali in an Arabic neighborhood.

Taresh checks ads online and in local papers in his quest to find a new home.

When Taresh finds an interesting apartment, he calls to set up a meeting with the landlord, but very often the apartments are too expensive or already taken.

Taresh hopes that better times are coming and that he can work his way up in in his adopted country.

From Bad to Worse? Afghans Journey Home

Dulcie Leimbach

Afghans have been returning to their country in droves through a longstanding United Nations voluntary repatriation program, with most of the refugees coming from the Northwest Frontier Province, just over the border in Pakistan. More than 270,000 refugees streamed back into Afghanistan in 2008, while a much smaller percentage came from Iran and elsewhere as well.

For many of those leaving, the main impetus was the closing of the Jalozai refugee camp in the Northwest Frontier Province, according to the United Nations High Commissioner for Refugees, which runs the repatriation program. The program, which has been in place since 2002, was suspended for the winter and will resume in the spring of 2009. Its 2008 budget was $115 million.

"What we have been doing since 2002 is to facilitate the return of those refugees who want to do so voluntarily," Vivian Tan, a public-information officer for the United Nations High Commissioner for Refugees in Islamabad, wrote in an e-mail message to UNA-USA. The agency is not, Tan added, "encouraging and has never encouraged Afghan refugees to return to Afghanistan," noting that under the Tripartite Agreement, signed in 2003 by Afghanistan, Pakistan and UNHCR, all parties agreed that repatriation must be voluntary and gradual, taking into consideration the turbulent situation in certain areas of Afghanistan.

Though the agency has 11 offices and field units in Afghanistan, with 450 staff members and 8 assistance centers operating in the county, its repatriation program is not equipped to take care of long-term survival issues. The agency and other development groups are beginning to address these problems with the Afghan government, which presented a five-year $509 million plan at a November 2008 conference in Kabul to strengthen reintegration projects focusing on issues like shelter, water, education, health care and jobs. At the conference, members of the international community (including representatives from Iran, Pakistan, the United States, Europe and Saudi Arabia) pledged to do more to support efforts to help those who are returning.

"Our main job these days is to advocate for returnees to be included in Afghanistan's national development strategy," Tan said.

Millions Have Returned

For decades, Afghans made up the world's largest refugee population; up to eight million people were living outside their country at the height of the exodus, with the majority ending up in Pakistan. In 2002, approximately 1.56 million Afghans returned home from Pakistan, having fled their country earlier because of the Soviet occupation, the ensuing civil war and the Taliban presence. The agency decided to get involved, Tan said, so that the returnees would receive assistance like food and relief supplies. Since that time, five million people have returned to Afghanistan, again, most of them from Pakistan, making the repatriation program the single largest such operation in the agency's 58-year history. The province of Kabul has received the most returnees, about 1.2 million as of December 2008.

In the fall of 2008, Ewen MacLeod, acting representative of the High Commissioner for Refugees, said at a press conference in Kabul that the large numbers for 2008 were attributed to not only the closing of the Jalozai camp but also from the rising prices of food and fuel, which have strongly affected Pakistan's economy.

The Jalozai camp, in one of the roughest areas of Pakistan, has long been considered a breeding ground for insurgencies plaguing this border region. Pakistan first announced the camp's closing, for security reasons, in 2006, but that did not end up happening immediately. In August 2007, the government took more concerted action to close Jalozai, with approximately 25,000 refugees repatriating in response. Meanwhile, the agency appealed to the Pakistan government to keep the camp in operation because of the onset of Ramadan and winter, so Jalozai did not shut down entirely until spring of 2008, resulting in an additional 54,000 Afghans moving back to their home country and others relocating in the Northwest Frontier Province or the Punjab Province in Pakistan.

The five million who have returned home represent a 20 percent increase in Afghanistan's population, overburdening an already collapsed infrastructure. About 4.3 million of the people were assisted through the UN program, with estimates that there are still 2.8 million registered Afghans living in Pakistan and Iran, a continuing source of tension there as well.

The refugees face severe hardships in their country, including such basics as lack of shelters, jobs, health care and education, not to mention violence from insurgents. Afghanistan's ability to absorb the stream of people poses yet another challenge to what is considered a seriously disabled government.

Stipends and Iris Scans

The refugee agency offers an average of $100 per person to those who return through its centers. The money helps cover transportation costs to get back into Afghanistan, as the returnees must hire their own trucks to take them home. To receive the assistance, the refugees must first go through the centers in Peshawar or near Quetta (in Baluchistan Province), where the staff check people's luggage and family history to make sure they are returnees and not people crossing for the cash.

At the centers, the Pakistan government deregisters the refugees from a database, and the agency performs an iris scan for all those over age 5 to ensure they have not returned through the agency before. Once the paperwork is done, the refugees leave on their hired trucks for the border, usually in groups of two to three families per truck. The centers stop processing the refugees by early afternoon to discourage them from traveling at night, Tan said. From Peshawar, the trucks drive on the main road to Jalalabad in eastern Afghanistan. It's a busy thoroughfare, full of vehicles carrying goods between the two countries, with the route going through the Khyber Pass to cross into Torkham in the Nangarhar Province of Afghanistan. Returnees from Baluchistan drive on the main road to the Chaman border before crossing into Kandahar Province in Afghanistan.

Once in Afghanistan, the refugees retrieve their cash payments and receive mine-awareness training and vaccinations for children from UN partners. The majority go back to their original homes and villages, primarily in the central, northern and eastern regions. Heart Province in the west and Kandahar Province in the south have received the fewest returnees.

More recently, returning Afghans have encountered serious difficulties in finding places to live. For example, Tan said, there are about 30,000 people this year who cannot resettle in their villages in eastern Afghanistan because of violence and lack of services, so they have set up makeshift settlements in Nangarhar and Laghman Provinces, sleeping in tents. ∎

Migration's Ebb and Flow

Georgianna Vaughan

From 1960 to 2005, the number of international migrants worldwide rose from 75 million to 191 million. The most distinctive feature of this increase was the high volume of temporary labor migrants emerging from a large number of developing nations. Comparatively, the developed countries are producing far fewer migrants, according to a United Nations report. In 2005, the 28 countries with the largest immigrant populations accounted for 75 percent of all migrants worldwide, the highest three being the United States, Russia and Germany.

The 2007 report, issued by the Population Division of the Department of Economic and Social Affairs of the United Nations Secretariat, also noted that these figures would only continue to grow because the population among the poorest countries was rising 18 times faster than that of the developed world.

In recent decades this uneven proportion represented benefits for both host and source countries. In the host countries, international migration enabled economic expansion by relieving labor shortages and encouraging market competition. For source nations, an outflow of large numbers of working-age people who sent remittances back to their families worked magic by both decreasing unemployment and putting money into the domestic economy.

Indeed, according to the UN's Economic and Social Commission for Asia and the Pacific, remittances made by migrants have a profound impact on the quality of life for millions of poor households in developing countries. In 2007, remittances sent to countries in the Asia-Pacific region by migrant workers exceeded $121 billion, a figure that accounts for officially recorded transfers only.

Migrants, Go Home

The current worldwide economic crisis has made traditional host countries far less welcoming to immigrants. With more developed, labor-importing economies facing rising unemployment, governments will face increasing pressure to cut the number of foreign-worker permits, offering incentives and disincentives to encourage unemployed foreigners to go home. For example, in February 2009 in Britain, nationwide strikes broke out in support of a mass walkout by energy workers in Lincolnshire, who were angry at the use of foreign laborers.

In Russia, the effects of the economic downturn are creating hostility toward the country's estimated population of 12 million foreign workers. The most recent report from the Moscow Bureau for Human Rights highlighted a dramatic rise in attacks on foreigners based on "aggressive xenophobia" since 2004. Such attitudes make migrants increasingly reluctant to settle permanently or pursue greater integration in Russian society. In 2007, a government program aimed at recruiting 250,000 immigrant workers to apply for fast-track citizenship attracted only 300 applicants.

In parts of the US, anti-immigrant sentiment has led to national legislative debates and fomented hostility and murder primarily against laborers from Latin America.

The tide of immigrants returning to their home bases is expected to be massive. Joseph Chamie, a former director of the UN Population Division, predicted in an article he wrote for YaleGlobal on Jan. 21, 2009, a "tsunami-like wave of migrants returning home, and falling remittances hitting the developing nations even harder."

The economic crisis is not the only event that will affect migration. A growing world population is sure to shift migration patterns. The UN Department of Economic and Social Affairs, for example, forecasts a rise of 2.5 billion people in the overall population in the next 43 years, an increase that will be absorbed mostly by less-developed regions. In fact, their populations are projected to rise to 7.9 billion in 2050 from 5.4 billion in 2007.

A growing worldwide population, widening demographic imbalances and the current global economy troubles will have two crucial influences on the movements of people. First, more people of an employable age will likely remain in their countries of origin, reducing remittances and swelling the ranks of job-seekers. To take a specific example, 10 percent of the population of the Philippines resides and works abroad. In 2008 these workers sent home $24 billion in remittances, representing 14 percent of the country's total gross domestic product. If even a fraction of these funds are lost, it will reduce living standards substantially, as well as damage markets throughout the developing world by reducing domestic consumption.

Second, it is highly likely that there will be a concomitant rise in the numbers of illegal immigrants. Although there have been several global initiatives aimed at tackling the problems of illegal immigration, most notably within Europe, the current challenges threaten increasing insecurity for all parties involved in international migration's web.

Higher levels of unemployment, combined with an uneven global demographic sprawl, in terms of absolute numbers and average age, will drastically change the look of migration soon if not in the immediate future. The economies of many developing countries will be caught in a pincerlike trap between expanding numbers of jobless workers and declining remittances, greatly expanding domestic poverty. Equally, more developed nations face a loss of cheap labor and a rise in social unrest if they fail to deal with the issue of illegal immigration. The natural instinct of many governments will be to curtail further influxes of unemployed workers. It remains to be seen how this matter, surely to loom larger in the years ahead, will be dealt with worldwide. ■

On Literacy: Reading Rates Rise But Regional Gaps Remain

Arnav Chakravarty

Global literacy rates have improved substantially since 2000, but marked regional disparities in education levels underscore the long road ahead for much of the developing world, according to a report released in 2008 by the United Nations Educational, Scientific and Cultural Organization, which also said that the world literacy rate would reach 87 percent by the year 2015.

The Education for All Global Monitoring report used six barometers to measure the effectiveness of literacy and other education programs: early childhood care and education, universal primary education, learning needs of young adults, adult literacy, gender equality in education, and educational quality. While major progress has been made in each area, large regional gaps remain.

Adults Still Lagging

The most striking area of concern is adult literacy. Although the global adult literacy rate rose to 83.6 percent in 2006 from 76 percent in 2000, 774 million adults still lack basic literacy skills. About three-quarters of illiterate adults live in 15 countries, including India, China, Bangladesh, Brazil and Nigeria. Of the 101 countries slow in the quest for universal literacy, 72 will not succeed in halving their adult illiteracy rates by 2015 at the current pace of improvement.

Gender inequality in education also remains prevalent. According to the report, sexual violence, insecure school environments and inadequate sanitation disproportionately reduce girls' self-esteem, participation and continuation in educational systems. In addition, the report states that "only 18 out of the 113 countries that missed the gender parity goal at the primary and secondary level in 2005 stand a chance of achieving" gender parity by 2015.

School-Enrollment Strides

The picture isn't all gloom and doom. As of 2008, compulsory education laws existed in 193 of 203 countries and territories, and the global net-enrollment ratio rose to 87 percent in 2005 from 83 percent in 1999, a significant improvement over the previous decade. During these six years, the number of children not in school dropped to 72 million from 96 million.

According to Nicholas Burnett, director of the report, "Good national policies and higher domestic spending supported by external aid are clearly making a difference to the lives of millions of children—for example, in Burkina Faso, Ethiopia, India, Mozambique, United Republic of Tanzania, Yemen and Zambia." Educational participation levels increased most rapidly in sub-Saharan Africa (23 percent) and South and West Asia (11 percent), the two regions with the highest illiteracy rates.

While Unesco's literacy initiatives are resulting in progress, more needs to be done. The agency estimates that at least $11 billion in annual external financing is needed if low-income countries are to reach the report's goals of halving illiteracy rates within their own countries by 2015.

However, outside contributions could become more unattainable than ever. Mark Richmond, the director of the division for the coordination of UN priorities in education at Unesco, said in an interview with UNA-USA, that "there is now a big question mark over the sustainability of existing commitments with the ongoing financial crisis." Richmond added that a vast majority of current external aid for education is "devoted to higher level education" and that not all the countries are committed to primary education.

The agency continues to work toward improving basic education for people at the margins. Its Literary Initiative for Empowerment focuses on countries that do not have the resources to reach a 50 percent increase in adult literacy rates without enhancing and accelerating related efforts. According to Richmond, adult literacy is a key precursor to achieving primary literacy, as a child is more likely to become literate if he or she has a parent who is literate. Moreover, Richmond said that the initiative is specifically targeted at 35 countries, including the 15 with the largest illiterate adult populations. It is a collaboration with partners from government institutions and ministries, NGOs, universities, the private sector, media and international donors. ■

Staying on Top of the Crises

Dulcie Leimbach

The following media resources provide information on news related to humanitarian crises:

ReliefWeb.int is an independent online source on humanitarian emergencies and disasters. The site, meant for the international humanitarian community, provides timely and relevant information as events unfold, while emphasizing "forgotten emergencies" as well. Introduced in 1996, it is administered by the UN Office for the Coordination of Humanitarian Affairs. In 2002, ReliefWeb received 1.5 million hits a week, and in 2004, the site received approximately 1 million hits a day. Shortly after the South Asia tsunami in December 2004, it received 3 million hits a day on average.

ReliefWeb maintains three offices: New York, Geneva and Kobe, Japan, all updating the Web site around the clock. The site's budget, about $2 million, is mainly supported by voluntary contributions. ReliefWeb reaches more than 70,000 subscribers through e-mail, allowing those with low-bandwidth Internet connections to receive information, too. The site posts some 150 maps and documents daily from more than 2,000 sources drawn from the UN system, governments, nongovernmental organizations, academia and the media. Its Map Center also creates original ReliefWeb maps. All documents posted on the site are classified and archived in a document database, which contains nearly 300,000 maps and documents dating to 1981.

IRINnews.org's principal role is to provide news and analysis about sub-Saharan Africa, the Middle East and parts of Asia for the humanitarian community. The network is geared toward relief agencies, governments, human-rights organizations, advocacy groups, academia and the media. IRIN (Integrated Regional Information Networks) is part of the UN's Office for the Coordination of Humanitarian Affairs, but its editorial service is independent. Based in Nairobi, Kenya, IRIN was founded in 1995 to improve the flow of information to people in relief efforts in the Great Lakes region of Africa after the 1994 Rwandan genocide. The service's coverage has increased since then, in terms of both geography and subject matter; regional desks are now in Johannesburg, Dakar and Dubai.

The core service is free to subscribers by e-mail and through the Web site. The services include PlusNews, specializing in news and analysis on HIV/AIDS; IRIN Radio, which is helping to develop programming in Africa (Ivory Coast, Somalia and Uganda) and Afghanistan; IRIN Film and TV, which makes documentaries on humanitarian matters and news events; and IRIN Photo, offering a public gallery of photos on humanitarian crises. The photos, which can be downloaded, are free.

Most of IRIN's services are in English, with some parts available in French. PlusNews produces material in English, French and Portuguese. IRIN Radio produces programs in more than a dozen languages.

AlertNet.org: is a Web publication sponsored by the Thomson Reuters Foundation. It aims to keep relief professionals and the public informed on humanitarian crises around the world. The site includes a network of 400 contributing humanitarian agencies and a weekly e-mail digest. Started in 1997 by the Reuters Foundation, an educational and humanitarian trust, it was set up during the Rwanda crisis of 1994, when the foundation became interested in media reports of poor coordination between emergency relief charities on the ground. It surveyed charities on what could be done to remedy this, and the service came into being.

In 2004, AlertNet conducted an analysis of humanitarian crisis reporting in collaboration with the Graduate School of Journalism at Columbia, resulting in the Fritz Report. With the support of the British Department for International Development, AlertNet is now acting on the report's recommendations in a project called MediaBridge. The project involves creating tools and services to help journalists cover difficult emergencies, such as:

- Crisis briefings: key background information on more than 70 emergencies.

- Country statistics: graphs comparing global humanitarian facts and figures.

- Who works where: directory of relief organizations and UN agencies that are willing to help journalists.

- Humanitarian heads-up: an e-newsletter for journalists that includes early warnings on looming crises.

- Hot-spot mapping: global emergencies on the map.

- Interactive training: online training modules.

- World press tracker: tabs on global trends in crisis coverage.

- MediaWatch: a daily selection of articles on humanitarian themes from the world's media.

- AlertNet Expresso: daily shot of humanitarian news delivered by e-mail. ■

Afghan girls attending
a Unicef literacy class
in 2008 in Bamyan.
The agency has set up
centers to teach girls
and women how to read
and write. In Bamyan
Province, the literacy rate
for women in 2007 was
6 percent and for men,
44 percent, according
to Unicef.

Protecting And Advancing Human Rights

Improving the Work of the Human Rights Council (2006-2008)

Jacques Fomerand

On March 15, 2006, an overwhelming majority of the General Assembly approved a resolution creating a new Human Rights Council to replace the Commission on Human Rights as the main UN body for promotion and protection of human rights. On June 19, 2006, the council opened its inaugural session in the presence of Secretary-General Kofi Annan; Jan Eliasson, president of the General Assembly; and Louise Arbour, high commissioner for human rights.

The goal was to strengthen the machinery to address human rights issues and respond to violations. The commission had come under increasingly fierce criticism for a membership that included nations with poor human rights records, for voting selective and politically driven condemnations and for general ineffectiveness in the face of blatant violations.

In inviting the assembly to establish the new council, Eliasson called it a "decisive moment, both for the promotion and protection of human rights and for effective multilateralism and the standing of the United Nations as a whole."

Has it proved to be a new beginning? On the whole, the first two years suggest that while there have been significant advances over the defunct commission, habit has prevailed over change. This may be no minor accomplishment, because the council's proceedings have been directed less by a concern to reform than by the need to preserve what progress was made by the commission in the face of efforts to turn the clock back.

One of the objectives of this essay is to show the causes of this pattern and its likely continuance. It must be understood, nevertheless, that it is far too early to judge the significance of the reform. Two years for a new institution is hardly enough time to assign a pass/fail grade to what continues as a work in progress.

From Commission to Council

Critiques of the old commission often overlook the truth that the concept of human rights has always been contested. Disputes over the scope, nature and universality of human rights and the UN's role in their "promotion" began in the drafting of the Universal Declaration of Human Rights in 1947 and flared again in the proceedings of the San Francisco Conference in September 1951. Cold war disputes and the clamors of newly independent nations simply built up the clash of contrasted visions, policies and practices.

In spite of these difficulties, the commission provided UN agencies, non-governmental organizations, national institutions and countries with an unmatched forum for defining and legitimizing human rights. It acted as the incubator of most major global instruments in the field and thus not only broadened the scope of internationally defined human rights but also laid down legal foundations and a framework for their protection. From the 1960s on, the commission considerably expanded its work by scrutinizing violations and complaints through the adoption of resolutions and the development of special procedures—investigations on a "thematic" or "country specific" basis. This change in paradigm was accompanied by increasingly intrusive activities by the commission that could hardly be labeled consistent or balanced. These set off political battles marked by accusations of politicization, double standards and ineffectiveness as well as general expressions of outrage.

Attacks on the commission reached greater intensity in the early 2000s. Civil-society organizations cried that the commission glossed over or appeared to tolerate blatant violations. Some countries complained that the commission aimed its "naming and shaming" resolutions primarily at poor Southern Hemisphere countries while ignoring the rich and powerful North. Still others—notably the United States, which led a posse of strange bedfellows—faulted the commission for allowing countries with dubious records to serve as members. Taking his cues from recommendations by the High Level Panel on Threats, Challenges and Change, Secretary-General Annan joined the critics in his 2005 Larger Freedom report, arguing that the commission's "declining credibility" required a creation of a new body.

Acting on more detailed recommendations of the secretary-general, the September 2005 World Summit outcome document included a commitment of support for a council and told the president of the General Assembly "to conduct open, transparent and inclusive negotiations" to establish a "mandate, modalities, functions, size, composition, membership, working methods and special procedures of the council." The new council came into existence after five months of intricate negotiations covering six drafts, more than 30 rounds of negotiations and countless backstage deals and compromises.

Votes Reveal Deep Problems

The General Assembly established the Human Rights Council, it said, to promote "universal respect for the protection of all human rights and fundamental freedoms for all without distinction of any kind and in a fair and equal manner" and to address and make recommendations on offenses, "including gross and systematic violations."

The council was also given the task of coordinating and promoting human rights in the UN system. Even this rested on a shaky and ambiguous consensus. At the request of the US, the resolution had been put to a vote, relatively rare in UN practice, an event that marks stubborn cleavages. Those voting for the resolution totaled 170; 4 were opposed (Israel, the Marshall Islands, Palau and the US); and 3 abstained (Belarus, Iran and Venezuela).

Throughout the negotiations, intense disputes—by and large along North-South lines—flared over the membership of the council, its role in the UN human rights architecture and its status in the UN system. Should the membership of the council be universal, as had been proposed by the High Level Panel and as was now pressed by developing countries and Russia, or should it be restricted to those with impeccable human rights credentials? How should these credentials be measured: by a positive record of cooperation with the commission's special procedures, the number of ratifications of human-rights treaties or voluntary contributions to UN funds? Alternatively, should countries that had been the target of sanctions by the Security Council be excluded, as the US argued?

Advocates of a council with a restricted membership generally embraced the idea of retaining the mechanisms of the commission's special procedures and country-specific resolutions. Conversely, those favoring an all-inclusive council, like China or countries that had been targets of special procedures, were inclined to do away with them. Some countries—Japan and those represented by the European Union—wishing to underline the importance of human rights, argued that the new council should be elevated to the status of a principal UN organ. Others were satisfied with the status quo or asked that the council be brought under the authority of the General Assembly.

The explanations of votes provide further evidence of the persistence of veiled but profound disagreements. Ambassador John Bolton of the US said he had insufficient confidence in the text and could not say that the new body would be better than its predecessor because US proposals had been sidelined. He also deplored the willingness of members to "settle for good enough, for a compromise, for merely the best we could do," rather than for an organization to ensure that governments were doing all they could to promote human rights.

The Cuban ambassador said the decision to create the new council had been driven by a need to end the "huge discredit" that had befallen the commission because of "political manipulation, hypocrisy and double standards imposed on its work by the United States and the European Union." In the Cuban view, nothing in the creation of the new council would bar a repetition of the maneuvering by the North to condemn third-world countries unjustly.

The representative of the Organization of the Islamic Conference said he was "far from being happy with the draft" because it did not contain unequivocal reference to acts of incitement, hatred and religious intolerance. The African group wished that the resolution had a stronger development agenda. China welcomed the resolution as reaffirming important principles, like the need to respect historical, cultural and religious backgrounds, but also criticized it as lacking effective guarantees against political confrontation caused by resolutions pointing to a particular country, which China described as a chronic disease of the commission. Sudan contended that the resolution contained "holdovers" from the commission that would make it easier for major powers to condemn small countries.

Less Than Harmony

Clearly, the resolution founding the council, identified as Assembly Resolution 60/251, can hardly be described as reflecting "common combined effort, intellect and aspirations." It was the best possible compromise at the time and no more than laid down the foundations of a new human rights architecture whose future hinged on the vagaries of the political process.

Under the resolution, the council came under the direct authority of the General Assembly. Its work was to be guided by principles of "universality," "impartiality," "objectivity and nonselectivity," "constructive international dialogue" and "cooperation."

It also aims to strengthen the capacity of UN members to comply with human rights obligations. In this regard, the resolution emphasizes the responsibilities of all countries to respect human rights and fundamental freedoms, without distinction to race, color, sex, language or religion, political or other opinion, national or social origin, property, birth or other status. At the same time, it acknowledges the important role that nongovernmental organizations can play at the national, regional and international levels in promoting and protecting human rights.

The new council is slightly smaller than the commission, with 47 members instead of 53, and its membership is based on a modified principle of geographic distribution. Seats are distributed among regional groups: 13 for the African group, 13 for the Asian, 6 for the Eastern European, 8 for the Latin American and Caribbean and 7 for the Western European and others group. Members serve three years. They are not eligible for immediate re-election after two consecutive terms.

The resolution thus establishes a principle of rotation and ends the Security Council permanent members' claim to perpetual membership. Membership in the council is open to all UN members, and to remedy problems of the former commission, the resolution specifies that each council member must be elected individually by a majority of the members of the General Assembly, meaning 97 votes of the 192 are required. Account is to be taken of the candidate's contribution to human rights. In addition, members of the council must uphold the highest standards in promoting and protecting human rights and may be suspended by a two-thirds vote of the assembly for gross and systematic violations.

An innovative and ambitious feature was put in place to meet criticisms that the commission had been selective in its review and assessment of national policies. The resolution envisions "a Universal Periodic Review," based on objective and reliable information, of each country's fulfillment of human rights obligations and commitments. This review is to be conducted to assure universality of coverage and equal treatment of all countries. Finally, the resolution requires the General Assembly itself to review the council's status five years after its establishment.

The Council Sets Up Shop

On May 9, 2006, the assembly elected the first 47 members of the council from the 65 countries that had campaigned for seats. They were elected to three-year terms, but to create staggered terms, the assembly randomly assigned expiration years, which means that some members will serve only one- or two-year terms. Further elections were accordingly held on May 17, 2007, and May 21, 2008. The members elected in 2008 will all serve full three-year terms.

The new mode of selection of council members and the mild requirements for membership given in the resolution brought about marginal improvements in the democratic nature of the council. The electoral bids of Belarus, Iran, Sri Lanka, Sudan and Zimbabwe were rolled back or defeated. At the same time, however, some countries with less-than-impressive human rights records—Russia, China, Cuba, Pakistan, Tunisia and Saudi Arabia—still got elected.

Although it sets only two criteria for membership—quotas for the regional groups and majority support in the General Assembly—the resolution does require that candidates uphold the highest standards of human rights and fully cooperate with the council. Note should be taken that all candidates have written pledges delineating their human rights agenda. But the quality of those pledges varies greatly, and the "standards" are nowhere defined in the resolution. In practice, they have been primarily equated with participation in major human rights treaties. In the same vein, members are instructed to take into account other contributions to protect and promote human rights. But assembly members are under no obligation to elect a candidate that can demonstrate commitments beyond ratification of international instruments.

Finally, the regional groups whose activities were held responsible for opening the old commission to countries more interested in averting criticism than in promoting human rights have not vanished from the process. Reciprocal favors in each region still prevail. Furthermore, slates of candidates submitted by regional groups, with the notable exception of the European group, have rarely exceeded the number of seats allotted to the region.

As a result, the degree of competitiveness for seats has been less than optimal, which might lead one to think that the results would have hardly been different if the US had prevailed with its proposal requiring a two-thirds assembly majority for council membership.

At Work: Special Sessions

The council met for the first time from June 19-30 in 2006. Since then, it has met three times a year. The ninth session took place Sept. 8-23, 2008. In addition, the council has held nine special sessions. The greater frequency of regular sessions (in contrast with the yearly meetings of the commission) and its special sessions (which may be called by one-third of the council's members, rather than a majority, as in the commission) has virtually made the council a standing body able to address emerging issues on short notice while monitoring and reviewing continuing ones.

The flip side, however, is that the convening of special sessions is not infrequently driven by political considerations. No fewer than three special sessions have been called about Israel at the request of Arab powers and/or the Organization of the Islamic Conference. The first, on July 5-6, 2006, dealt with "escalation" of the situation in the Palestinian Occupied Territories; the second on Aug. 11, 2006, concerned "gross human rights violations" in Lebanon; and the third, on Jan. 23-24, 2008, focused on human rights aspects of Israeli military incursions into Gaza.

The last special session, the ninth, was scheduled on Jan. 9, 2009, held at the request of Egypt, on behalf of the Arab group and the African group; Pakistan, on behalf of the Organization of the Islamic Conference; and Cuba, on behalf of the Nonaligned Movement. The stated purpose of the meeting was to address "the grave violations of human rights in the Occupied Palestinian Territory, including the recent aggression in the occupied Gaza Strip."

Other special sessions have received greater cross-regional support and have brought innovations. The request for a special session on Darfur, held Dec. 12, 2006, was sponsored by more than 30 nations; the meeting provided a forum for a large number of nongovernmental organizations. The fifth special session (Oct. 2, 2007) was called by Portugal in behalf of the European Union to discuss Myanmar. This resulted in a consensus resolution deploring the violent repression of peaceful demonstrations and asking the Special Rapporteur on Myanmar to monitor the response to the council's resolution. The presence of human rights defenders from Myanmar and a highly visible presence of the media were unusual.

Finally, the council's seventh special session, on May 22, 2008, was called at the request of Cuba to discuss "the negative impact of the worsening of the world food crisis on the realization of the right to food for all." Cuba's motion was supported by an unprecedented 41 states (out of 47) in the council. Perhaps more significant, this was the first session of the council devoted to a thematic issue of an economic or developmental nature.

It is too early to assess the long-term significance of the special sessions. The impact of council decisions has been minimal: they do not appear to have had brought about major change in the field. Overall, the new uneasily mixes with the old, and which one will prevail remains unclear. But some clues may be gleaned from an examination of the regular work of the council.

At Work: 'Institution Building'

One paradox of the "reform" of UN human rights work was that the commission was abolished before any agreement could be reached on the council's terms of reference and methods. The founding resolution in effect required the council to reform itself! In the language of the resolution, the council would have to review and rationalize the former commission system and within a year determine the modalities of the required Universal Periodic Review. While doing this, generally known as "institution building," the council was also to continue dealing with the work inherited from the commission.

In the first year, with the deadline looming, institution-building overshadowed substantive work in the council. After laborious negotiations conducted in three working groups, agreement was reached on June 18, 2007, on an "institution-building package." This package was endorsed by the assembly on Dec. 22 in a recorded vote: 150 in favor, 7 opposed (Australia, Canada, Micronesia, Israel, the Marshall Islands, Palau and the US) and 1 abstention (Nauru). The vote once again made evident areas of persistent discord and showed that the institution was by no means built yet.

The package revised some procedures of the commission, defined the modalities of the special procedures it used and established the broad guidelines of the periodic review. Other elements included the creation of an advisory committee to replace the Subcommission on the Promotion and Protection of Human Rights and a revised complaints procedure.

Some of the innovations are noteworthy. But by and large they do not add up to the significant advances that many reform advocates had hoped for. It was clear early on that institution-building was viewed by many members of the council not as an opportunity to strengthen the system but to weaken it. The political battles of the reform group thus focused primarily on containing attacks and preserving the protections developed by the defunct commission. The end product was modest improvements uneasily mixed with regressive steps.

Fruits of a Compromise

The package was a compromise between those who pressed for an agenda built around specific themes and rights and those seeking a more flexible thematic approach. The Canadian idea of having recourse to interactive dialogues with special procedures on specific issues, panel debates, seminars and roundtables was dropped in favor of language allowing the council to decide on such work formats on a case-by-case basis. Most important, the package preserves a right for nongovernmental organizations to participate, which had been won in the commission.

Close in importance is a procedure allowing individual complaints about "a consistent pattern of gross and reliably attested violations." The rules of admissibility for this, usually called the "1503 procedure," have remained essentially the same but whereas the old procedure permitting direct petitions by citizens was entirely confidential, petitioners may now get information on the progress of their complaint and its outcome.

Under the agreed modalities of the periodic review, all UN members will be scrutinized by the council in four-year cycles and on the basis of objective and "reliable" information. The European Union was able to secure some degree of involvement of NGOs and national human rights institutions in the process. The council rejected the demands of China, India and members of the Islamic group that the process be entirely state-driven and -controlled, subject to a consensus among all members of the council as well as the consent of the country under review. On this point, a compromise was reached that the report on a periodic review would include both recommendations adopted with consent of the country and those that were rejected.

Results of the Council's First Sessions

The continuation of the commission's "special procedures" was even more fraught with contention. Members of the Nonaligned Movement sought to eliminate all procedures for oversight of the record in an individual country by Special Rapporteurs, who are individuals assigned to examine and advise on human rights situations for country or thematic mandates. China proposed that such country-specific resolutions be adopted by a two-thirds majority. Eventually, Western states and NGOs were able to secure an ambiguous compromise making it possible to retain most mandates for examining the record of an individual country. The outcome, however, took a political toll: the mandates for Cuba and Belarus were abolished and all rapporteurs with mandates (country or thematic) would thereafter be subject to a code of conduct, an idea that originated in the African group and received support of all Asian states, Brazil and Ecuador.

The intention of the code is to define "the standards of ethical behavior and professional conduct that special procedures shall observe whilst discharging their duties." In that regard, the code reaffirms that rapporteurs must act in an independent capacity, free of any extraneous interference. But at the same time, the code requires them to exert their functions "in strict observance of their mandate." The information they gather must rely "on objective and dependable facts based on evidentiary standards that are appropriate to the nonjudicial character of the reports and conclusions."

Finally, their recommendations may not exceed the scope of their mandates. All these provisions, however watered down in comparison with initial proposals, still provide ample opportunity to opponents of special procedures to disrupt their operation.

Another backward step for Western states was the transformation of the Subcommission on the Promotion and Protection of Human Rights into a new Advisory Committee. The idea of an advisory think tank for the council was retained but at the price of major political concessions. In sharp contrast with the autonomous role that the old subcommision had, the Advisory Committee can provide expertise only "in the manner and form requested by the council and only in thematic issues." The advisers can make research proposals but may not adopt resolutions or decisions. They may not establish subsidiary bodies without council approval. In comparison with the powers and functions of the old subcommission, the new Advisory Committee has been made subservient to the political will of the council.

Political cleavages are equally evident in the regular work that the council pursued concurrently with institution-building. On June 29, 2006, at the end of its first session, the council created two major instruments. One was by acclamation, the International Convention for the Protection of All Persons From Enforced Disappearances. The other, a draft Declaration on the Rights of Indigenous Peoples, was adopted by a recorded vote of 30 in favor, 2 opposed, 12 abstentions and 3 absent.

The General Assembly endorsed the convention on Dec. 20, 2006. By December 2008, it had received 81 signatures and 7 ratifications. Twenty countries must ratify it before it becomes effective.

On the other hand, the Declaration on Indigenous Peoples, which had been in negotiation for more than 11 years, ran into the same difficulties—about language on self-determination and the definition of indigenous people—in the Third Committee of the General Assembly as in the council. It was not approved by the assembly until Sept. 13, 2007.

At the same first session, the council set up a group to draft a protocol on the Covenant on Economic, Social and Cultural Rights to allow for individual complaints. It completed its work in April 2008; its draft was endorsed by the council in June and by the assembly on Dec. 10, 2008.

The council has in its regular sessions continued the commission's custom of debating reports of special thematic and country-specific rapporteurs. A noteworthy development is a new practice of the council to cluster its reviews in the framework of "interactive debates" involving national delegations, national human rights institutions and nongovernmental organizations. The debates have thus gained in vitality, depth and substance, but most of the time, they have been politically divisive, providing opportunities to countries that wish to question the legitimacy of the special procedures or to criticize specific mandate-holders for exceeding their authority. They appear also to have led to a rise in shielding and lauding the countries under review.

Criticisms of Reports

Accusations have been made of "doubtful methodology," unwarranted "emotional statements" and "one-sided, selective and unreservedly biased" conclusions in reports by mandate-holders. This sort of language was apparent by the second session, when the Special Rapporteur on extrajudicial, summary or arbitrary executions was criticized by Nigeria for having addressed the continued imposition of the death penalty on lesbian, homosexual, bisexual or transgendered people. At that session, the US also attacked a report on detainees at Guantánamo Bay. Similar occurrences have been recorded at later sessions, bringing repeated calls for the dismissal of the Special Rapporteurs and termination of their mandates, or reassertions by the countries under review that they will not cooperate with the mandate-holders.

The renewal of the mandates of the Special Rapporteurs is an increasingly contentious issue, as was the case of Burundi and the Sudan at the ninth session of the council. The number of countries placed under the scrutiny of the council is pitifully small: Burundi, Haiti, North Korea, Liberia, Myanmar, Somalia and the Sudan, in addition to the Palestinian Territories.

Accusations of "selectivity" and "double standard" have predictably been made, most of the time by Northern Hemisphere countries and organizations that excoriate the council for ignoring "serial human rights abusers" such as China, Cuba, Russia and Saudi Arabia. But in turn, some of the values underpinning the positions of the North have also come under attack, underlining the growing polarization of the council along North-South lines.

When the mandate of the Special Rapporteur on the right to freedom of opinion and expression was renewed by the council at its seventh session, its terms of reference were broadened at the behest of Egypt and Pakistan and other members of the Organization of the Islamic Conference. The broadening included a review of "instances of abuse of the right of freedom of expression that constitutes an act of racial or religious discrimination."

Western countries resisted the move, arguing that it was a threat to freedom of expression, a view widely shared by such NGOs as Reporters Without Borders and Human Rights Watch. Similar North-South divisions in the development field came up at the eighth session, when the council extended the mandate of the special representative of the secretary-general on human rights and transnational corporations and business enterprises. The tame and ambiguous language of the consensus resolution to do this merely papered over the clash of North and South visions of the scope of the representative's mandate. The South pressed for strong international legal instruments to address transnational business practices, including establishment of a complaint mechanism. The North argued that these proposals were at best premature.

Universal Periodic Review

The Universal Periodic Review was probably the most innovative aspect of the resolution creating the council: for the first time in UN history and in contrast to bodies that monitor the policies only of those subscribing to human rights treaties, the human rights of all countries would come under scrutiny of the UN membership under a common system. Not surprisingly, discussions of details provoked inconclusive debates throughout the institution-building process.

The underlying issue, unstated, was how expansive, thorough and intrusive of national sovereignty should the review be. What constituted "objective and reliable information," the basis on which the review would be carried out? Who would be allowed to provide such information? What did the assembly mean when it stated that the review should be a "cooperative mechanism"? Who would be involved in "interactive dialogues" the assembly called for? What was the desirable outcome of the review: naming and shaming, prodding for improvement or business as usual?

The council's resolution of June 18, 2007, setting up the review system was a compromise among widely differing views. The review would take the form of a three-hour debate on each country, leading to adoption of recommendations by the council. The "peer review" would be sustained by three documents: one report presented by the country concerned and two prepared by the Office of the High Commissioner for Human Rights summarizing information gathered by the UN and presenting the positions of nongovernmental organizations. Each review would be facilitated by a group of delegates from three other countries drawn by lot. They would draft a report on the record of the country under review.

First to Be Examined

The calendar adopted by the council in September 2007 stipulates that the entire membership of the UN would be reviewed in the first cycle, from 2008 to 2011. In each session, the council would examine 16 countries. In the first review, held April 7-18, 2008, Bahrain, Ecuador, Tunisia, Morocco, Indonesia, Finland, Britain, India, Brazil, the Philippines, Algeria, Poland, the Netherlands, South Africa, the Czech Republic and Argentina were discussed, in this order. At the second, May 5-16, 2008, it was the turn of Gabon, Ghana, Peru, Guatemala, Benin, Korea, Switzerland, Pakistan, Zambia, Japan, Ukraine, Sri Lanka, France, Tonga, Romania and Mali. In the next session, Dec. 1-15, 2008, the countries were Botswana, the Bahamas, Burundi, Luxembourg, Barbados, Montenegro, the United Arab Emirates, Israel, Liechtenstein, Serbia, Turkmenistan, Burkina Faso, Cape Verde, Colombia, Uzbekistan and Tuvalu. In 2009 three more review sessions are to be held: one in February, one in May and another late in the year.

Results Are Mixed

It is probably premature to assess this project—because it can be described as having only yielded mixed results. Being driven by its members, the process has been tame. On the whole, countries commenting on those under review have been overwhelmingly positive and most frequently timid. Such sycophantic statements sometimes strain credibility, and they are always in sharp contrast to the pointed critiques of speakers for NGOs who take the floor. Members of regional groupings profusely commend their allies but with equal eagerness strongly rebuke members of another group or subject them to intense questioning. The overall impression is that countries appear unwilling to be fully engaged in the review process.

It is telling, in this respect, that disputes over the scope of the general debate on the reviews flared at the last session of the council and are likely to resurface. At issue is whether the debate should be used to consider updates on the impact of recommendations. The institution-building text does stipulate that the council should have (as a standing agenda item) discussions of the review system. Nevertheless, a group of delegates led by China, Egypt in behalf of the African group, and Pakistan in behalf of the Islamic group are insisting that no attempt should be made to create "new layers of review or follow-up."

Concluding Thoughts

The founding resolution said the council should be guided by principles of "universality, impartiality, objectivity and nonselectivity, constructive international dialogue and cooperation with a view to enhance the promotion and protection of all human rights." Clearly, such a culture of dialogue and cooperation has failed to take root. This should hardly be surprising even to countries like the US, which have taken the view that it is better to stay out of a council dominated by what detractors call "repressive regimes"—and unable to improve upon the "discredited practices," as Kofi Annan said, of its predecessor body.

But should anyone be perplexed by the council's behaving in a politicized and selective way, perhaps even more so than the commission did, in spite of procedural improvements? Should there be perplexity that the council tries to muzzle nongovernmental criticisms of members?

A useful clue can be found in the comments of a former UN deputy-secretary-general, Louise Fréchette. In an interview in January 2007, she said: "To a certain extent we have sought institutional responses, institutional fixes, through reform to problems that are more fundamental and more political."

"The Human Rights Commission was deemed to be ineffective by a lot of countries," she said. "The answer was to transform it into a new institution called the Human Rights Council. But it's not performing all that much better than the Human Rights Commission because the world is composed of countries that have very different views on human rights. And unless there's real political action to really strengthen the solidarity of all the countries that do believe in human rights across the North-South divide, you shouldn't be surprised that you have the exact same results. I think there's not enough attention paid to building this political consensus among countries that share the same views, and too much on the machinery."

Secretary-General Ban Ki-moon, in a statement in December 2008 marking the 60th anniversary of the Universal Declaration of Human Rights, went to the heart of it in exhorting the council to rise "above partisan posturing." One should not entertain high hopes that it will. ■

Strengthening the Office of
The High Commissioner for Human Rights
Jacques Fomerand

Judging from her latest reports to the General Assembly, strengthening the Office of the High Commissioner for Human Rights appears to be a priority for Judge Navanethem Pillay, who took over as high commissioner in September 2008, becoming the fifth person to hold the office.

In addition to her routine commitments to the Human Rights Council and assisting it in its institution-building, Judge Pillay has continued to expand its presence in the field. As of August 2008, her office had 53 "field presences" (offices and advisers worldwide), broken down by 9 regional offices and 9 country offices (not counting those in Kosovo and the occupied Palestinian Territories, which are not recognized as countries by the UN), 17 human rights departments in UN peace missions and 16 human rights advisers. Additionally, the office of the high commissioner plans to open regional sites in southwest Asia and North Africa and deploy human rights advisers to Moldova, the Philippines and Vietnam during the 2008-09 biennium.

At headquarters in Geneva, the office's rapid-response capacity and advisory functions for national human rights institutions have been reinforced; 100 of these institutions currently receive technical advice from the office, which opened in 1955. A key goal has been to build support for national systems that protect human rights and to help eliminate mechanisms that allow violations with impunity. This work involves advice on legislation, training, public reporting and fact-finding or investigative missions. Further efforts include counsel on eliminating poverty, reducing global inequalities, help with development, integration of the right to development in policies of key institutions involved in human rights, gender issues and women's rights. Priority is given to the issue of women's access to justice and safeguarding their economic, social and cultural rights.

A Difficult Post at Best

In seeking to enhance the effectiveness of human rights machinery and endeavoring to expand human rights monitoring and reporting, Louise Arbour, Judge Pillay's immediate predecessor as high commissioner, hardly broke new ground. She built and expanded on the work of her predecessors. That alone was enough to incur the wrath of a strange coalition. She was accused of turning a blind eye to violations in many countries, most particularly Russia and China, while focusing her public criticisms on US counterterrorism policies and Israeli actions in the Occupied Palestinian Territories. For some, her statements were considered tantamount to perpetuating the "selectivity" and "politicization" that tarnished the reputation of the Commission of Human Rights, which the Human Rights Council replaced.

In working on the council, she clashed with several Arab and Asian countries, which wanted more control over her authority to open field offices. At the same time, she was faulted as contributing to the demise of the Special Rapporteurs on Cuba and Belarus. Caught in this crossfire and no longer displaying the influence she had under Secretary-General Kofi Annan, Judge Arbour announced on March 7, 2008, that she would not seek another term.

The search for a replacement began immediately with nongovernmental organizations, notably Amnesty International and Human Rights Watch, calling for a "transparent, consultative process" in the selection. They exhorted the secretary-general to be aware that "appointing an extremely capable and highly qualified high commissioner is crucial at this time when fundamental principles of human rights are challenged and the independence of the high commissioner's office is under attack."

From a short list of candidates that included Francis Deng of Sudan, José Ramos Horta of East Timor and Luis Alfonso de Alba of Mexico, Secretary-General Ban Ki-moon chose Judge Pillay, who is from South Africa. In late July, the General Assembly endorsed her appointment.

Landmarks in Rwanda Trial

Judge Pillay brings a distinguished record in law and human rights to the office. In South Africa, she had been a prominent opponent of apartheid and an advocate of women's rights. From 1995 to 2003, as a judge on the International Criminal Tribunal for Rwanda, she lead the way in landmark decisions defining rape as a weapon of war. Since 2003, she had been a judge on the International Criminal Court. Nongovernmental organizations called her résumé admirable.

A spokesman for the secretary-general said that Ban was "committed to ensure that human rights remain high on the agenda," and the secretary-general himself said that he expected the new high commissioner to preserve the independence of her office and to maintain effective working relations with the General Assembly and the Human Rights Council.

In many ways, Judge Pillay inherits a political situation that is financially tenuous and politically perhaps even more treacherous than that of her predecessor. At the 2005 World Summit, UN members called for a doubling of her office's regular budget over the next five years. Accordingly, during the 2004-05 biennium, the office received $67.6 million; in the 2008-09 biennium, it received $119.2 million.

The budget of the office, which was $265 million for 2006-2007, remains puny in comparison with the scope of its assignments. In addition, two-thirds of the budget comes from the UN regular budget, the remainder from voluntary contributions of a small number of donors that often link their gifts to knotty conditions.

More disquieting, the Human Rights Council is deeply divided. The majority of its members have conceptions of human rights that diverge from those of Western countries. Their prickly concern for the norms of sovereignty and the primacy of national cultures often takes precedence over consideration of individual rights. The volatile mixture provides fertile ground for accusations and singularly narrows the scope for transformational leadership by the high commissioner.

Some of the writing is already on the wall. One of the unenviable tasks of the high commissioner is to prepare for Durban II, scheduled for April in Geneva, a follow-up to review the progress since the 2001 conference against racism held in Durban, South Africa. Addressing the Human Rights Council in the fall, Judge Pillay made an impassioned statement condemning racial and sexual discrimination as "totally incompatible with the Universal Declaration of Human Rights and the UN Charter" and urged all members to participate in the April conference. Her plea was praised by Islamic states, the African bloc, Cuba, the Nonaligned Movement and Russia and triggered angry accusations from Northern Hemisphere countries that said she was implicitly criticizing the world's most tolerant democracies instead of violators of human rights like Sudan and Iran. ■

Promoting and Protecting the Rights of Children

Jacques Fomerand

At its beginning in 1946, when it was called the United Nations International Children's Emergency Fund, Unicef was given the task of providing for the needs of children in war-torn Europe. Since then, Unicef has grown to deal with children's health, development, education and rights worldwide. The expansion can perhaps best be measured by perusing the 60-odd subjects covered by the agency's press releases. Topics range from abducted children to breastfeeding, child labor to girls' education, HIV/AIDS, landmines, poverty, sexual exploitation and on to water, environment and sanitation.

Issues concerning children are discussed not only in the Executive Board, the fund's governing body, but also in the Security Council; the Third Committee of the General Assembly, which is concerned with social, humanitarian and cultural issues; the Economic and Social Council and its subsidiary bodies; the Human Rights Council; and the Committee on the Rights of the Child. For this brief overview, the focus is on the survival, protection and development aspects of Unicef's work and that of the UN in support of children.

In 1996, a leading advocate for women and children, Graça Machel of Mozambique and South Africa, published a report, "Impact of Armed Conflict on Children," which drew global attention to the problem. After creation of the Office of the Special Representative of the Secretary-General for Children and Armed Conflicts, putting an end to such violence against children and guaranteeing their rights have become important concerns of the UN.

The children's special representative has so far submitted 11 reports to the General Assembly. The latest, which was also submitted to the Human Rights Council, highlighted progress made in the struggle to end people's ability to violate children's rights with impunity and in the incorporation of concerns for the child into the mandates and activities of UN. Against this backdrop, the representative proposed that her office continue to strengthen efforts to breach walls of impunity that protect violators, to stress child-protection issues in peacekeeping, peacemaking and peacebuilding and to advocate strategies for reintegration, psychological healing, funding and sustainability. These recommendations were endorsed by the General Assembly on Dec. 18, 2008.

Impact of Rome Statute

Concurrently, legal standards have been established. The Rome Statute of the International Criminal Court classifies the recruitment of children into fighting forces as a war crime and a crime against humanity. Several cases investigated and/or prosecuted by the court involve atrocities against children. The Optional Protocol to the Convention on the Rights of the Child, which entered into force in 2002, enjoins governments not to compel children under 18 years old to serve in their armed forces. By the end of 2008, the protocol had been ratified by 126 states. The Executive Board of Unicef, at its first regular session of 2008, reviewed the agency's role and concluded that children in armed conflict should stay under its protection.

Since 1999, the Security Council has held several debates on such grave violations as abduction, sexual violence, child soldiers, killing and maiming, attacks on schools and hospitals and denial of humanitarian access. Under a resolution of the council, the secretary-general established a monitoring and reporting mechanism that now operates in 18 areas of concern. A working group on children and armed conflicts, created in 2005, makes recommendations to the council on possible additional measures.

On Feb. 12 and July 17, 2008, the council held two debates involving a large number of participants. These resulted in presidential statements reiterating the council's commitment to issues of children and armed conflict and reaffirming the need for countries and forces at other levels to comply with their obligations under the Convention on the Rights of the Child and its Optional Protocols. The council had received reports from the secretary-general about children and armed conflict in Uganda, Somalia, the Philippines, Nepal, Burundi, Myanmar and Sri Lanka. Vietnam also circulated a paper about the development problems that lead to the involvement of children in armed conflicts.

Caring for the Children

The development aspects of child survival are examined in Unicef's latest annual "State of the World Children," which focuses on primary health care for mothers, newborns and children. The report documents gains in improving the quality and reach of primary health care, reducing deaths among children under 5 and improving their health and nutrition.

In 1960, some 20 million newborns did not live beyond the age of 5, but by 2006, the annual number of such child deaths had fallen below 10 million. Since 1990, China's under-5 mortality rate has declined 47 percent, India's 34 percent and in countries like Bangladesh, Bhutan, Bolivia, Laos and Nepal, the reduction has been 50 percent or more. But, as the report shows, achieving a two thirds reduction of under-5 mortality worldwide by 2015, as called for by a Millennium Development Goal, would require lowering child deaths from 9.7 million to 4 million.

In turn, to achieve this target would entail greater efforts in regard to other millennium goals, notably reducing poverty and hunger; improving maternal health; combating HIV and AIDS, malaria and other major diseases; improving water quality and sanitation; and providing affordable essential drugs on a sustainable basis.

The challenges are daunting. Only half of the world's regions are on track to meet the goal for reduced child mortality, and 62 countries, two-thirds of them in Africa, have made no progress or insufficient progress toward this goal. In fact, in some countries of Southern Africa, the spread of HIV and AIDS has reversed previously recorded declines in child mortality.

More extensive health interventions are advocated by the report. Among these are early breastfeeding, immunizations, vitamin A supplements and the use of mosquito nets as well as greater access to treatment and means of prevention at the community level. As the report puts it in stark terms, investing in the health of children is not only sound economic policy, but it is also a human rights imperative. The secretary-general made similar observations in a report to the General Assembly on actions taken to follow up to the assembly's 2002 special session on children. The secretary-general noted that failure to achieve the goals of the special session would significantly undermine efforts toward the realization of the goals of the Millennium Declaration.

Changes in the Legal Area

The growth of children's rights law is one of the striking transformations of the postwar international legal system. The Convention on the Rights of the Child is the keystone in the sense that it is the first instrument to enumerate the rights whose fulfillment is necessary for a child to survive: adequate food, shelter, clean water, formal education, primary health care, leisure and recreation, cultural activities and information about their rights. The convention also spells out the participatory rights children are entitled to.

On the basis of country reports, a committee monitors the carrying out of the convention and two protocols prohibiting the involvement of children in armed conflict, the sale of children, child prostitution and child pornography. The committee examines each report and describes its concerns and recommendations to the member. At the prodding of the committee, many governments have passed laws, created mechanisms and put into place other measures to ensure the protection of and realization of these rights to those under the age of 18.

Since 2006, the committee has considered reports in two parallel panels of nine members each, "as an exceptional and temporary measure" to clear the backlog. The committee also publishes its interpretation of the human rights provisions in the form of general comments. Previous comments of the committee focused on the aims of education, the rights of children with disabilities, HIV/AIDS and the child's rights, the treatment of unaccompanied and separated children outside the country of origin, the right of the child to protection from corporal punishment and other cruel or degrading forms of punishment. The latest comment in 2009 was to provide states with guidance on implementing their obligations under the Convention on the Rights of the Child with respect to indigenous children. ■

Progress for Women: A Long Way to Go

Jacques Fomerand

For almost a decade and a half, the Beijing Platform of Action has guided efforts to promote women's rights, gender equality and the empowerment of women. The platform, intended to create a transformation, identified 12 critical areas of concern: poverty, education and training, health, violence against women, women in armed conflict, women and the economy, women in power and decision-making, mechanisms for career promotions and advancement, human rights, the media, the environment and the girl child.

The platform also called upon the international community to take policy steps on each issue. Since 1995, the UN has mobilized on all of them, but it is difficult to quarrel with the feminist and Finnish UN leader Hilkka Pietila, who contends that UN work on gender issues has yet to match expectations. "Unfinished work" is the phrase that could be applied to all the areas dealt with in the Beijing Platform. This is particularly striking in regard to women and poverty and women in armed conflicts, two issues that were high on the UN agenda in 2008.

Role in Prevention Emphasized

In many respects, the resolution of the Security Council on women and peace and security, adopted on Oct. 31, 2000, was a landmark step. For the first time, the council not only called upon all parties in armed conflicts to take special measures to protect women and girls from gender-based violence, but it also stressed the vital role of women in preventing and resolving conflicts; in negotiations, peacebuilding, peacekeeping and humanitarian responses; and in postconflict reconstruction.

In the years since the resolution's adoption, increasing emphasis has been placed on the need to ensure women's equal participation in maintaining and promoting peace and security. In brief, the debate has moved so as to give equal weight to the need to protect a vulnerable group and incorporate gender perspectives into all UN peace and security efforts. This shift can be detected by comparing the initial study that the secretary-general submitted to the council in 2002 with reports produced yearly by the Secretariat since then.

The council's two open debates on women in armed conflicts, on June 19 and Oct. 29, 2008, vividly illustrated the trend. The first debate was devoted to sexual violence, the second to women's equal participation in peace and security. The June debate, held at the ministerial level at the initiative of the US, resulted in Resolution 1820, recognizing sexual violence as a security problem requiring a systematic response while affirming the council's intention to consider targeted sanctions against perpetrators.

The resolution also asked the secretary-general to develop guidelines and strategies to improve the ability of peacekeeping operations to protect civilians from sexual violence. The secretary-general was asked to report by June 30, 2009, with proposals incorporating ways to measure progress in reducing the prevalence of such acts.

The October debate brought 50 speakers and closed with a strong condemnation of violations of international law committed against women and girls during and after armed conflicts. The council reaffirmed its commitment to full implementation of earlier resolutions and urged members as well as international, regional and subregional organizations to take steps to raise the participation of women in conflict prevention, conflict resolution and peacebuilding, and to strengthen the role of women as decision makers in those areas.

Finally, the council asked the secretary-general to appoint more women to pursue good offices on his behalf, particularly as special representatives and special envoys. The secretary-general is expected to report to the Council in October 2009.

There is a steady momentum in the council to continue the agenda created in 2000 in a more integrated manner. Awareness is growing among council members that sexual violence against women and women's political empowerment are two facets of the same issue. The council has increasingly addressed women's participation under other agenda items, notably the prevention of armed conflict, peacebuilding, the protection of civilians in armed conflicts, the role of the UN in justice and the rule of law and peaceful settlement of disputes.

But the elimination of gender-based violence in armed conflicts raises daunting challenges, including institutional fragmentation, inadequate financing for gender-related projects and lack of capacity for oversight and accountability, as well as acts of sexual abuse and exploitation by UN peacekeepers themselves. Women remain sorely under-represented in all aspects of peacekeeping and peacebuilding.

The Millennium Development Goals endorsed in September 2000 by the General Assembly are targets for combating poverty, hunger, disease and environmental degradation. They have also evolved into a framework and benchmarks for measuring, assessing and correcting the development work of governments, intergovernmental agencies and nongovernmental organizations. Most goals do not focus explicit on women (a notable exception is Goal 3, which calls for an end to disparities between boys and girls in education), but the Millennium Declaration acknowledges that beliefs about the roles of men and women in society can promote or hinder development. In that sense, attainment of all the goals has a direct bearing on the advancement of women.

At the Halfway Mark

An event convened by the secretary-general and the president of the General Assembly to review progress on Sept. 25, 2008—the halfway point to 2015—provided a timely opportunity to assess achievements for women. A report by the Department of Economic and Social Affairs provided hard evidence of what had been done in each of the world's major geographic regions. Its main finding was that despite impressive gains, "the limited progress in empowering women and achieving gender equality is a pervasive shortcoming." Further, the report said, the "relative neglect of, and de facto bias against, women and girls continues to prevail in most countries." This assertion buttressed assessments by other UN agencies.

The facts speak for themselves. Two out of three countries have achieved gender parity at the primary level, according to the above report, but girls account for 55 percent of the out-of-school population, and the gender gap widens in secondary and higher education. Women have more income-earning opportunities than ever before, but almost two-thirds of women in the developing world work in vulnerable jobs, which can be unpaid domestic work or self-employment, subject to instability. Maternal mortality remains unacceptably high across much of the developing world, and mortality rates in sub-Saharan Africa and parts of Asia have barely changed over two decades.

Globally, the percentage of women and girls living with HIV and AIDS has risen from 41 percent of the people with HIV/AIDS in 1997 to just under half today.

Other indicators are no less comforting. If change continues at its current glacial pace, it will take women approximately 40 years to reach 40 percent parliamentary representation in developing countries. Only one-sixth of bilateral aid (money that is transferred directly from one country to another) in 2005-06 was earmarked for projects contributing either to gender equality or women's empowerment.

To reverse these trends would require new efforts to achieve gender parity in primary and secondary school enrollments, according to the report, improved support for women's self-employment, rights to land and other assets and "above all, an equal role with men in decision-making at all levels, from the home to the pinnacles of economic and political power."

French students demonstrating in Paris in 1968 may have had a point when they invited their compatriots to be "realistic" by asking for the impossible! ▪

Convention on the Rights of Persons With Disabilities

Jacques Fomerand

On Dec. 13, 2006, the General Assembly adopted by consensus the Convention on the Rights of Persons With Disabilities and its Optional Protocol. Both entered into force on May 3, 2008. To date, 137 countries have signed the convention and 47 ratified it. The Optional Protocol has received 81 signatures and 27 ratifications.

Widely heralded as a milestone in efforts to promote, protect and ensure full and equal lives for the disabled, the convention was negotiated in an ad-hoc committee of the assembly from 2002 to 2006. That process continued an effort started in the 1980s when the UN proclaimed 1981 as the International Year of Disabled Persons and then began a World Program of Action for Persons With Disabilities. The goals were to improve prevention, rehabilitation and equal opportunity for the disabled. The strategy was to build a framework for policy efforts over a United Nations Decade of Disabled Persons, 1983 to 1992.

Mexico Gets It Moving

Further progress was made in 1993 when the assembly adopted the Standard Rules on the Equalization of Opportunities for Persons With Disabilities, a set of guidelines, legally nonbinding, to improve the rights of the disabled.

Another step was taken in 1993 with the Vienna Declaration and Program of Action, which was the first human rights instrument to enfold the rights of the disabled. But efforts in 1987 and 1989 by Italy, Sweden and nongovernmental organizations to move toward a convention failed, and it was not until 2001 that Mexico finally put on track negotiations that led to the convention.

Why did it take more than two decades? To a large extent, the answer is, as its advocates say, that the convention encapsulates a "paradigm shift" in defining solutions for problems of the disabled, and for a long time, political support was found lacking for this shift.

The convention, as a human rights instrument, was the latest among the "core" treaties originated through the UN and designed, like its companions, to address the special needs and vulnerabilities of a sizable population group. The purpose of the convention is to promote, protect and ensure enjoyment by the disabled of all human rights, including self-determination, physical access, personal mobility, health, education, employment, habilitation and rehabilitation, participation in political life, and equality and nondiscrimination.

Equally important in the convention is the concept that disabled people are not merely vulnerable subjects entitled to special protection but should be able to become active members of society. Considering that 80 percent of the 650 million disabled people in the world live in developing countries and that roots of their difficulties are poverty-related, the convention turns a human right into a social development goal.

Looking at a Price Tag

The aspiration to social inclusiveness obligates governments to develop and carry out policies, laws and administrative measures to secure the rights recognized in the convention. More specifically, signers are expected to organize, strengthen and extend comprehensive habilitation and rehabilitation services and programs in health, employment, education and social services.

These broad obligations have a price tag, of course. For a long time, nongovernmental organizations representing disabled people and developing countries pushing for the convention had pressed for a document acknowledging that such improvements required aid and international cooperation. Countries in the Northern Hemisphere feared that developing countries could use the argument of inclusiveness to justify claims for more money for development.

The stalemate was resolved with adoption of a mildly worded (and elusive) article simply saying that the signers "recognize the importance of international cooperation and its promotion, in support of national efforts for the realization of the purpose and objectives of the present convention, and will undertake appropriate and effective measures."

How the convention will be carried out remains to be seen. A Committee on the Rights of Persons With Disabilities, a group of 12 independent experts that will oversee the carrying out of the convention, is being constituted. An interagency support group has been formed at the UN. The US was involved in drafting the convention but made it known that it would not sign. The

Obama administration may reverse this position, and there have been moves in Congress toward this as well. The Commission for Social Development, at its session in February 2008, began examining the subject of disability in the development agenda. The elaboration of the convention involved an usually strong participation of civil society, and there is no doubt that there remains a constituency ready to carry out the convention. ■

The Durban Declaration: A Follow-Up Overview

Karen Freeman

"We recognize that racism, racial discrimination, xenophobia and related intolerance occur on the grounds of race, color, descent or national or ethnic origin and that victims can suffer multiple or aggravated forms of discrimination based on other related grounds such as sex, language, religion, political or other opinion, social origin, property, birth or other status. . . ."

—From the Declaration of the 2001 World Conference Against Racism, Racial Discrimination, Xenophobia and Related Intolerance, held in Durban, South Africa.

When the United Nations convened the Durban conference in 2001, the aim was to create a blueprint for fighting racism in the 21st century. Mary Robinson, then the UN High Commissioner for Human Rights, the conference organizer, expressed high hopes, saying: "This World Conference has the potential to be among the most significant gatherings at the start of this century. It can be more: it can shape and embody the spirit of the new century, based on the shared conviction that we are all members of one human family."

Instead, the conference, which became known simply as the World Conference Against Racism, showed just how hard it can be to get representatives of all the members of the human family just to sit down together. And it was the disagreements, not the shared convictions, that took center stage. As delegates prepare to gather for the follow-up conference in Geneva in April, it's not just the agenda that seems familiar. It's the same disagreements—especially over Israel's handling of its conflicts with the Palestinians—that stand in the way.

In 2001, a Palestinian intifada aroused anger against Israel at the conference, especially during a parallel meeting of nongovernmental organizations. The language coming out of those sessions included denunciations of Israel as a racist nation engaging in ethnic cleansing. Robinson criticized the "hateful, even racist" atmosphere at the NGO meeting, and personally rejected the declaration it drafted. Israel and the United States left the conference.

A Legacy Is Neglected

The positive outcome of the Durban conference is often overlooked. The declaration from the conference itself actually refers to the Middle East conflict in balanced terms. The Israeli Foreign Ministry said, "Israel is satisfied that the clauses full of hate and incitement against it and the Jewish nation were removed from the conference's final document." Whether the meeting in Geneva, often called Durban II, will achieve success will probably depend on how closely it sticks to following up on that 2001 declaration and on how much rein is given to the NGOs, and on how many nations decide to join Israel in boycotting the conference.

Durban II, scheduled for April 20-24, is a turbulent time in Israeli-Palestinian relations, as it was in 2001. But one difference is that the US now has a president who has said he wants the nation to resume its active role in international diplomacy and whose ethnic background could be thought to give him more of a personal investment in human rights in the developing world. That could be viewed as a good sign for Durban II, but similar hopes were voiced in 2001 when Colin Powell became the first African-American to serve as a secretary of state, and the United States wound up abandoning the conference.

Secretary of State Hillary Rodham Clinton addressed the Durban II issue in 2008 when she campaigned for the presidency. Speaking to the American Israel Public Affairs Committee's annual policy conference, she said: "Our vigilance against anti-Semitism must go beyond the Middle East. It must receive no quarter anywhere in the world. The next president will face a test of resolve on this issue at the 2009 Durban conference. ... I will never forget how the world's first conference against racism became a mockery of itself when it descended into anti-Semitism and hatred. The debacle at Durban must never be repeated. We should take very strong action to ensure anti-Semitism is kept off the agenda at Durban II. And if those efforts fail, I believe the United States should boycott that conference." As of publication date, the US decided not to participate in the Durban conference unless the final document is changed to drop all references to Israel and its criticism of religion. ∎

Durban Review Conference

Jacques Fomerand

Preparations for the meeting to review the 2001 World Conference Against Racism, Racial Discrimination, Xenophobia and Related Intolerance are being made by the Human Rights Council. They started in the summer of 2007 with an organizational meeting of the council but began in earnest in 2008 when the council met in late April and in October. Regional preparatory meetings were held in Brasília in June for the Latin American region, and in Abuja,

Nigeria, in August for the African region. The Asian region, the European Union and the Organization of the Islamic Conference have limited their preparations to joint written contributions. Negotiations on a draft outcome document were in full swing by the winter.

Overall, the process has been bumpy. Many of the controversies that rocked the original conference have resurfaced, and new ones have crept up. The first conference—one of the main vehicles for creating the Third United Nations Decade to Combat Racism and Racial Discrimination—was supposed to identify policies to protect vulnerable groups such as Africans and people of African descent, indigenous peoples, migrants and refugees against discrimination. Instead, it evolved primarily into a forum resonating with demands for reparations for wrongs of colonialism and slavery.

Hostility in Two Forums

Taking place as the Palestinian intifada was raging, the conference was over-shadowed by attacks on Israel by Iran and a number of Arab states. Meanwhile, the parallel NGO forum produced an even more strident declaration calling for a virtually universal principle of self-determination, labeling Israeli counterterrorism measures as "war crimes" and endorsing an international strategy to isolate Israel patterned after the anti-apartheid campaigns.

In her speech on Oct. 6, 2008, the high commissioner for human rights, Navanethem Pillay, sought to unlink the two events. She reminded her listeners: "Seven years ago at the 2001 World Conference Against Racism, the virulent anti-Semitic behavior of a few nongovernmental organizations on the sidelines of the Durban conference overshadowed the critically important work of the conference."

Measures were taken to address this betrayal of the core principles of the Durban conference, and the NGO document was not forwarded to the conference. But the high commissioner's admonitions may have fallen on deaf ears of those who have conflated the NGO declaration with the one the conference itself formulated.

Suspicions that Durban II could be a copy of Durban I have been heightened by the selection of Libya as chair of the bureau for the Preparatory Committee and of Cuba, Iran, Pakistan, Russia and South Africa to serve among the 19 vice chairs. The draft outcome document at one stage portrayed the West's counterterrorism policies as racially motivated. The Asian group has proposed language that accuses Israel of engaging in "a new kind of apartheid, a crime against humanity, a form of genocide and a serious threat to international peace and security."

Equally thorny is the insistence of the Organization of the Islamic Conference that the document include "internationally binding normative standards" to guarantee against defamation of religions. From the perspective of this group, the proposal is designed to combat Islamophobia. Western countries view this proposal as thinly concealed threats to freedom of speech. These countries have repeatedly warned that their participation hinges on the conference's remaining focused on an evaluation of progress since 2001 in combating racism as well as an examination of further steps to be taken. Numerous nongovernmental organizations have joined the fray, saying that discussion of questions related to the incitement of racial or religious hatred must protect freedom of expression, belief and religion and must balance the rights of free expression with the right to be free from discrimination.

As the outcome document from the Preparatory Committee went to press, the question of who would participate and who not was far from settled, and there may be no clarity until the conference convenes. Or perhaps not even then. ■

Fact sheet
The United Nations Role in Advancing Human Rights

NO.1: UN HUMAN RIGHTS COUNCIL
February 2009 *Prepared by Simon Minching*

The United Nations plays a notable role in advancing human rights by elevating international human rights standards to the status of international law, promoting them through education and dissemination of information and carrying them out by responding to violations through mediation, mobilization of shame or enforcement when the Security Council identifies a link between violations and threats to international peace and security. To enforce those roles, the UN sets up appropriate UN bodies and mechanisms, creating new ones as needed. Among the most important means by which the UN fosters human rights are the Human Rights Council and the Office of the High Commissioner for Human Rights

This fact sheet is meant to clarify frequently asked questions about the Human Rights Council.

What is the Human Rights Council?
The Human Rights Council (HRC) is a Geneva-based intergovernmental body composed of 47 of the UN member states. The council was created by the General Assembly on March 15, 2006, replacing the UN Commission on Human Rights, which had lost credibility partly because of the presence of member states with poor human rights records, which used their positions to block scrutiny of themselves and other violators. The purpose of the council is to promote respect for human rights, recommend new treaties and norms,

periodically review human rights compliance by all member states and directly address serious human rights violations.

What are the criteria for membership on the council?

Members of the council are expected to "uphold the highest standards" of human rights and "fully cooperate" with the council itself. The General Assembly is advised to take into account the contribution of candidate countries to the promotion and protection of human rights and their voluntary pledges and commitments when choosing council members. A country sitting on the council can be suspended for gross and systematic violations of human rights (with two-thirds majority vote by those present and voting).

How does the General Assembly choose council members?

The council allocates a defined number of seats to each of these regional groups: 13 for Africa, 13 for Asia, 6 for Eastern Europe, 8 for Latin America and the Caribbean and 7 for Western Europe and other countries. Members are elected for staggered terms of three years by a secret ballot, with an absolute majority of the General Assembly required to win election. If any of the candidates fails to receive the required 97 votes in favor, the member must compete in further rounds until an absolute majority is obtained. There have generally been competitive elections for council seats, although the African group and sometimes the Latin American and Asian groups have nominated slates equal to the number of seats open, thereby avoiding competitive elections. Yet these groups have been praised at times by nongovernmental organizations (NGOs) for attempting to nominate countries with generally responsible human rights records.

How is the council an improvement over the discredited commission it replaced?

The council has a smaller and more selective membership than the former commission. It has six fewer members, and countries need 97 votes (as opposed to 28 required in the commission) to gain a seat in the council. The council meets at least three times a year and can more readily call special sessions, requiring approval by one-third of the council's members, instead of a majority as with the former commission, which met regularly only once a year. The council's new Universal Periodic Review process provides an opportunity for advocates to hold all UN members up to international human rights standards. The council is an intergovernmental body like the commission, however, and suffers when politics prevent its members from fairly and forthrightly addressing human rights situations.

What is the Universal Periodic Review (UPR)?

The review is a new mechanism that the council created in 2006 to assess all 192 member states' human rights records with each state looked at once over a four-year period. The state under review is required to submit a report on its fulfillment of human rights commitments. The Office of the UN High Commissioner for Human Rights compiles information submitted by non-governmental organizations and official UN human rights reports on the country under review. A dialogue with the state under review then takes place in the UPR working group, made up of the 47 members of the Human Rights Council, and is headed by its president. An outcome document for each state is produced and includes assessments of positive developments and challenges faced by the state under review, identification of best practices, accepted and rejected recommendations for improvement in its promotion and protection of human rights, provision of technical assistance and voluntary commitments by the state. The state under review is expected to respond to all recommendations made by other states. The mechanism is designed to allow an objective review of human rights records of all UN member states, addressing charges of "selective reviews" undertaken by the former commission, although so far results have been mixed.

What are the arguments for and against the United States' running for a seat on the council?

Those who oppose the United States' running for a seat argue that the US should not lend the council any credibility, and since any member state can speak to issues before the council, a seat would not necessarily give the US a greater voice over human rights deliberations. Furthermore, because membership is geographically based, if the US won a seat, it would replace one of the seven countries already representing the Western Europe and Other States group, which tend to vote in a similar fashion to that of the United States. The fundamental belief among those arguing that the US should run for a seat on the council is that it can influence the body by example and its moral authority and can best do so by seeking a seat, as opposed to acting as an outside critic. According to such advocates, by coming front and center on the council, a tool for cooperation, the US can inspire and impart its broader vision on human rights for the world. Expecting the European Union to substitute for an American voice on human rights is simplistic, they contend, because the US benefits in some parts of the world from its lack of a long colonial history; it also has a different story to tell on human rights and a distinct diplomatic style, while Europe acts through consensus and joint statements on human rights policy, where strong pro human rights voices are consistently drowned out in favor of the "lowest common denominator" approach.

Are there proposals to improve the effectiveness of the council?

Many human rights activists believe an effective US leadership in the council can improve the council's agenda. The council needs to directly and forcefully address many egregious human rights situations around the world that it has previously ignored and approach the Israel-Palestinian conflict in a fair-minded manner. Various proposals are under discussion for the 2011 review of the council in the General Assembly, including having council elections by open rather than secret ballots, or having a universal membership of all UN member states rather than a selective membership. NGOs would like to see a greater role for independent experts and for NGOs in the council's Universal Periodic Review procedure. The council can make those changes in Geneva without waiting for the review conference. ■

This fact sheet was first published by UNA-USA in December 2008 and was updated in February 2009. It was prepared by Simon Minching, a former intern in the Global Policy Programs of UNA and now a publications researcher for UNA-USA.

Fact sheet
The United Nations Role in Advancing Human Rights

NO.2: OFFICE OF THE HIGH COMMISSIONER FOR HUMAN RIGHTS
February 2009 *Prepared by Nikolina Saso*

The United Nations plays a notable role in advancing human rights by elevating international human rights standards to the status of international law, promoting them through education and dissemination of information and implementing them by responding to violations through mediation, mobilization of shame or enforcement when the Security Council identifies a link between violations and threats to international peace and security. To carry out those roles, the UN sets up appropriate UN bodies and mechanisms, creating new ones as needed. Among the most important means by which the UN works to foster human rights are the Human Rights Council [view fact sheet No.1] and the Office of the High Commissioner for Human Rights. This fact sheet is meant to clarify frequently asked questions about the Office of the High Commissioner for Human Rights.

What is the Office of the High Commissioner for Human Rights?
The Office of the United Nations High Commissioner for Human Rights (OHCHR) was created by the General Assembly in 1993 after years of pressure from states and many NGOs. The US government was an active supporter, and several US-based organizations, like the Carter Presidential Center, worked to create the post. As of April 2007, the office employed more than 850 people, is based in Geneva and New York and has 11 country offices and 7 regional offices around the world, including a work force of some 240 inter-

national human rights officers serving in UN peacekeeping missions. It also provides assistance to states with their human rights law and human rights education. The appointment of Navanethem Pillay as the fifth UN High Commissioner for Human Rights was approved by the General Assembly; she took up the post on Sept. 1, 2008.

Who funds the office?

The office receives financing from the UN's regular budget and voluntary contributions from member states, intergovernmental organizations, foundations and individuals. In the regular budget funding for the 2008-2009 biennium, $119.2 million (2.89 percent) of the UN's global budget was appropriated to the office. This represents an increase of $35.8 million over the previous biennium. Voluntary contributions amounted to $95.7 million in 2007—an increase of $10.4 million compared with 2006. Since 2002, the level of contributions has risen more than 130 percent. The $10.5 million that the US donated in 2007 made it the largest voluntary contributor to the office's budget. Member states provided some 91 percent of all voluntary funding in 2007. International organizations, including the European Commission, contributed about 8 percent. Private donors, including foundations, companies and individuals, accounted for just over 1 percent of voluntary funding. The number of institutional donors (governments, foundations and companies) increased from 65 in 2006 to 74 in 2007.

What is the relationship between the high commissioner and the Human Rights Council?

The council is a UN body that can assign tasks to the high commissioner, like conducting studies or providing technical assistance to member states. The high commissioner's office acts as the secretariat of the Human Rights Council, supporting and servicing council meetings and the Universal Periodic Review. The high commissioner can also make recommendations for actions. Yet, it is very a delicate relationship, as the high commissioner seeks to maintain independence, while some members of the council try to exert influence over the high commissioner's office through resolutions. The council cannot make budgetary decisions regarding the high commissioner's office and has no jurisdiction over it.

What is the relationship between the high commissioner and the Security Council?

Many conflicts on the agenda of the Security Council involve severe human rights violations. In the last decade and a half, the Security Council approved operations that often included a human rights component, and the high commissioner's office has been asked to provide staff and expertise. The Security Council has also a set of unique tools to use against violators, like sanctions and the use of force in the most extreme cases. The high commissioner seeks opportunities to address the Security Council when there is a clear link between serious human rights violations and threats to international peace and security. Human rights violators often attempt to prevent the high commissioner from having direct contacts with the Security Council. In recent years, some member countries have argued that human rights violations should be addressed only in the Human Rights Council.

What are some criticisms of the high commissioner's office?

Some countries criticize the office for being "donor-driven" and opaque and have thus proposed that the allocation of voluntary contributions should be decided or approved by member states. The office has taken steps to inform all member states of its planned activities, use of resources and contributions received. It has also encouraged donors to reduce earmarks, and so nonearmarked contributions have grown from 10 to 50 percent in five years. The high commissioner and human rights NGOs argue that requiring member state approval of use of extrabudgetary funds would be inappropriate as it would lead to a decline in contributions, impair the office's ability to act and politicize the office's work.

What are some challenges facing the high commissioner's office?

According to human rights observers, the office remains short of staff and funds. At the 2005 World Summit, the member states committed to doubling the office's regular budget within five years. Accordingly, during the 2004-05 biennium, the office received $67.6 million; in the 2008-09 biennium, it received $119.2 million. Additionally, Kofi Annan, the secretary-general at the time, had suggested that the office could play an enhanced role through greater interaction with relevant UN bodies, a matter that is possible if the high commissioner had a high-level representative in New York. Currently, the office has a director-level representative, who is prevented from attending meetings that are reserved only for assistant- or under-secretaries-general. Appointing an assistant-secretary-general in New York would help put human rights on equal footing with the other Secretariat departments and provide access to meetings with the UN secretary-general. Such a move would cost an estimated $20,000 yearly in administrative expenses.

What is an immediate issue facing the high commissioner's office?

The office has been given the tough task of administering the follow-up conference on racism, which is set to take place in Geneva on April 20-24, 2009, and encouraging all member states to participate, including those who have said in 2008 they would not attend (like Canada, the US and Israel). ■

This fact sheet was prepared by Nikolina Saso, an intern in the Global Policy Programs of UNA-USA and was updated by Simon Minching.

Thomas Lubanga, a former Congolese warlord, is the first suspect to be tried by the International Criminal Court in The Hague. Lubanga is charged with war crimes, including recruiting children as soldiers to kill in eastern Congo.

Promotion of International Justice And the Rule of Law

Issues Before the Courts

Irwin Arieff

The United Nations plays a central and sweeping role in international justice, ranging from making laws and interpreting them to administering its own court and assisting in the creation and administration of a number of special-purpose tribunals.

The General Assembly, for example, helps establish international law by serving as the forum for writing treaties and conventions that take effect after their ratification by UN member states. The Security Council can adopt resolutions that are binding on the international community.

A UN court, the International Court of Justice, was established as part of the UN system after World War II to resolve legal disputes among governments and to advise UN bodies and agencies on legal questions.

The International Criminal Court, while independent from the UN system, was created by an ad hoc group of nations working under UN auspices. The court, which began operation in 2003, was created to try people accused of the most serious international crimes: genocide, crimes against humanity and war crimes.

Before the ICC's creation, the Security Council established two special-purpose criminal tribunals to pursue allegations of genocide, war crimes and crimes against humanity in Rwanda and the former Yugoslavia. These two courts report directly to the council. Later, the council asked the UN Secretariat to help set up additional international tribunals in Sierra Leone, Cambodia and Lebanon. While these three courts are not considered part of the UN system, they were established with the organization's help and operate with UN administrative and financial support.

The UN also plays a multifaceted role, through the Convention on the Law of the Sea, in regulating the world's oceans, navigation, fishing rights and exploitation of offshore oil and other undersea mineral resources.

Weighing Disputes Among Nations

The International Court of Justice, often referred to as the World Court, is the only judicial entity created by the UN Charter as a "principal organ." (The other principal organs are the General Assembly, the Security Council, the Economic and Social Council, the Trusteeship Council and the Secretariat.) That said, the World Court rarely finds itself in the international spotlight, because its cases frequently unroll over long periods of time and focus on obscure international disputes.

The court, located in The Hague, is the sole UN principal organ housed outside New York. Its 15 judges, who serve nine-year terms, are elected by separate but simultaneous votes of the 15-nation Security Council and the 192-nation General Assembly. The court has jurisdiction only over disputes among nations, and it can take up a dispute only when asked to do so by one or more countries. Since it is not a criminal court, it lacks the authority to prosecute individuals accused of war crimes or crimes against humanity.

Its judgments cannot be appealed, although parties to a particular case can seek clarification by requesting a further interpretation of a ruling. Under the UN Charter, the court's decisions are binding on all 192 member states. However, there is no real enforcement mechanism other than governments' commitment and diplomatic pressure, and governments occasionally resist judgments or even reject them outright.

World Court Cases

It took Nigeria six years, for example, to give up the resource-rich Bakassi Peninsula after the World Court resolved a border dispute in October 2002, awarding the area to Cameroon, its West African neighbor. Similarly, Israel flatly refused to honor a court advisory opinion issued in July 2004, which concluded that a barrier Israel was building on Palestinian land in the West Bank was illegal and should be dismantled. The General Assembly had requested the ruling at the Palestinians' request. Israel argued that the barrier was justified on security grounds, but the Palestinians called it a land grab ahead of the eventual demarcation of a border between Israel and a future Palestinian state.

The United States, the biggest contributor to the UN budget, has also wrestled with the question of the court's reach. President Ronald Reagan announced in 1984 that Washington would no longer recognize the World Court's authority after the court ruled that US support for the Contra rebels fighting Nicaragua's Sandinista government was illegal and ordered the US to pay reparations.

Then, in 2004, the court ruled that the US had violated the 1963 Vienna Convention by failing to allow 51 Mexicans facing the death penalty in US prisons to have access to Mexican consular officials before their trials. The court said the Mexicans should be given court hearings to determine whether the violation had affected the outcome of their cases. President George W. Bush announced that while he opposed the judgment, states would have to follow it because World Court rulings were binding on the US.

But when Texas appealed Bush's decision to the federal courts, the US Supreme Court ruled, in a 6-3 opinion issued in March 2008, that Bush had exceeded his authority. Neither the International Court of Justice nor the president could impose their will on a US state, the Supreme Court concluded. Mexico then returned to The Hague, asking the World Court in June 2008 for an interpretation of its earlier ruling and seeking to have the court declare that despite the Supreme Court ruling, the US was obliged to ensure that the convicted Mexicans' cases were reviewed and that none of them be executed before the reviews were carried out. The ICJ is still weighing Mexico's request.

A Powerful Tool Against Genocide

The International Criminal Court opened its first trials in 2009, nearly 11 years after the international community laid the groundwork for creating this first permanent global criminal court.

The idea for the court grew from the ashes of World War II and the Nuremberg trials, which helped expose the horrors of the Holocaust. But it took more than half a century for the General Assembly to set the process in motion: it voted in 1998 to convene a diplomatic conference to draft the court's governing statute. After five weeks of negotiations in Rome, representatives of 120 nations agreed in July 1998 on a text creating the court.

The ICC aims to bring to justice those accused of the world's worst offenses: war crimes, crimes against humanity and genocide. It took until 2002 for the court to open offices in The Hague, and a year later it swore in its first judges and a chief prosecutor, Luis Moreno-Ocampo of Argentina. It took at least five more years before the first defendants could be brought to trial.

"The court has grown into a full-fledged independent judicial institution," backed so far by 108 nations that have agreed to become parties to its governing statute, Judge Philippe Kirsch, the court president, told the General Assembly in late 2008. But because many governments—including the US, Russia, China, India and Indonesia—have declined to join the court so far, its reach and its success will be limited, Kirsch cautioned. "For it to exercise jurisdiction truly globally, universal ratification will be necessary," he said.

Trials are expected to open in 2009 in as many as three cases, each linked to central Africa. The court's first trial got under way on Jan. 26, in the case of Thomas Lubanga, leader of the Union of Congolese Patriots, an ethnic militia. Lubanga faces three charges of recruitment of child soldiers in the Ituri Province in eastern Congo in 2002 and 2003.

Trial for 2003 Crimes

In a second case, Mathieu Ngudjolo Chui and Germain Katanga each face seven charges of war crimes and three charges of crimes against humanity for their actions in 2003 as leaders of other ethnic militias in Ituri. Ngudjolo is the former chief of staff of the Front for National Integration, while Katanga is the former chief of staff of the Patriotic Force of Resistance in Ituri, a Front for National Integration ally.

In the third case, which could be heard by the ICC beginning in late 2009, Jean-Pierre Bemba, an unsuccessful candidate for the Congo presidency and the leader of the Movement for the Liberation of Congo, is charged with five counts of war crimes and three counts of crimes against humanity. The charges center on allegations of rape, torture, looting and killing committed by his men during their intervention in a conflict in neighboring Central African Republic in 2002 and 2003. Bemba had fled Congo to live in exile in Portugal, but he was arrested by Belgian police during a May 2008 visit to Brussels.

The highest-profile case pending before the ICC is aimed at President Omar Hassan al-Bashir, who remains in power in Sudan at this time. The court voted in March 2009 on a request by Moreno-Ocampo to issue a warrant for Bashir's arrest on charges of genocide, crimes against humanity and war crimes in Darfur, in western Sudan. Moreno-Ocampo told the Security Council in late 2008 that he has compiled evidence that Bashir ordered brutal attacks against villages and camps for displaced persons in Darfur in 2003, which killed at least 35,000 people and led to the rape of thousands of women and girls. Bashir has repeatedly denied the charges.

Some governments have urged the Security Council to delay ICC action against Bashir on grounds that his arrest could slow diplomatic efforts to bring peace to Darfur, which has been devastated by a brutal civil war since 2003. Moreno-Ocampo said that aides to Bashir had threatened further violence in Darfur if the arrest warrant was approved. After the warrant was actually issued in early March and Bashir defied the indictment, many humanitarian aid agencies were suspended from working in the region, leaving millions of refugees in worse straits.

There are several other ICC cases in which allegations of serious crimes have been investigated and charges issued but trial cannot begin because the defendants remain at large. These defendants include Joseph Kony, Vincent Otti, Okot Odhiambo and Dominic Ongwen, leaders of the rebel Lord's Resistance Army in northern Uganda; Bosco Ntaganda, a leader of a rebel eastern Congolese movement known as the National Council for the Defense of the People ; and Ahmad Harun and Ali Kushayb of Sudan. Harun is Sudan's current minister of state for humanitarian affairs, and Kushayb is a former commander of Sudan's government-allied Janjaweed militia.

While the ICC is not formally a part of the UN system, it was created under a UN umbrella, and its work overlaps with many UN agencies, including the Security Council and peacekeeping operations, in particular. This aspect of its work has troubled the US, which under the George W. Bush administration flatly rejected joining or working with the court and pressured other governments to do the same. The Bush administration, which said it feared politically motivated ICC prosecutions of US military or government officials, worked within the UN system to prevent the tribunal from benefiting from any UN financing or other resources, including even the use of UN meeting rooms.

Grappling with a seemingly intractable crisis in Darfur, however, the US administration later softened its hard-line opposition to overt UN cooperation with the ICC, leaving court-watchers wondering whether the new Barack Obama administration might seek closer ties with the court or even call for the US to join the ICC by ratifying its governing statute.

The first sign of a softening came in March 2005. The US, by abstaining, allowed the Security Council to formally ask the ICC to investigate the situation in Darfur. (The council's referral resolution at the same time prohibited the ICC from investigating or prosecuting US nationals and barred the UN from bearing any of the costs of the referral.) Then, in June 2006, John B. Bellinger III, a State Department legal adviser, acknowledged in a newspaper interview that the ICC "has a role to play in the system of international justice." ■

Special Tribunals Fill In Gaps

Irwin Arieff

The UN has created or helped establish several temporary international courts to deal with particularly serious crimes in places where it determined that national courts were not up to the job.

The International Criminal Tribunal for the Former Yugoslavia, the oldest, was created by the Security Council in 1993 on evidence of mass atrocities and other war crimes in the Balkans after Yugoslavia's breakup. The court, the first war-crimes court since the trials in Nuremberg and Tokyo after World War II, has indicted 161 individuals accused of acts committed during conflicts in Croatia (1991-1995), Bosnia (1992-1995), Kosovo (1998-1999) and the former Yugoslav republic of Macedonia (2001).

By the start of 2009, the tribunal had completed action on 116 of the accused, including former Yugoslav President Slobodan Milosevic, who died in detention in March 2006 while on trial for 66 counts of genocide, crimes against humanity and war crimes. Five of those indicted are still awaiting trial in the tribunal's courtrooms in The Hague, while 13 have been transferred to national courts in Bosnia, Croatia or Serbia. Just 2 of the 161 remain at large after the arrest in July 2008 of Radovan Karadzic, the former Bosnian Serb political leader who faces 11 charges of war crimes, genocide and crimes against humanity. His trial is scheduled to begin in 2009. The two remaining fugitives are Ratko Mladic, Karadzic's military chief during the Bosnia conflict, and former Croatian Serb leader Goran Hadzic.

Under pressure from the Security Council, the tribunal is trying to wrap up its trials by 2010 and all appeals by the end of 2011, but "it is likely that a small number of appeals will spill over into 2012," the Yugoslavian tribunal president, Patrick Robinson, acknowledged in December 2008. The council, in a formal statement, said that a temporary mechanism might have to be set up to carry out any unfinished business once the tribunal is shut down.

"Few would have imagined, only 20 years ago, that it would have been possible to bring before an international tribunal high-level individuals, including heads of state, accused of the most heinous crimes," Robinson told a council briefing in late 2008. "I represent a court that has tried more persons for breaches of international humanitarian law than any other judicial body."

The International Criminal Tribunal for Rwanda was created by the Security Council in November 1994 to prosecute serious violations of humanitarian law in the slaughter of 800,000 people over 100 days in 1994. Tribunal courtrooms and offices were set up in Arusha, Tanzania. At the end of 2008, the court had issued judgments against 37 accused, while 8 were awaiting judgments. Trials were going on for 20 accused, another 6 were awaiting trial or retrial, and 13 defendants remained at large. Rwanda tribunal judges have blocked attempts to transfer the cases of 4 detainees and 1 fugitive to

Rwandan courts, for fear that potential witnesses might be unwilling to travel to the country to testify.

Like the tribunal for the former Yugloslavia, the Rwanda court is also under council pressure to complete its work and shut down. Dennis Byron, the court president, told the council in December 2008 that officials were hoping to complete all initial trials by the end of 2009 but that it might be prevented from doing so if current fugitives were arrested.

The Special Court for Sierra Leone was set up jointly by the UN and the government of Sierra Leone to try those who bear the greatest responsibility for atrocities during a brutal civil war in that West African nation from 1996 to 2002. Thirteen people have been indicted by the court, and proceedings against eight of these have been concluded. Two indictments were withdrawn in December 2003 after the accused died.

The court's best known defendant is Charles Taylor, the former president of Liberia and the first African head of state to appear before an international tribunal. Accused of supporting Sierra Leone's Revolutionary United Front rebels in the civil war, Taylor faces 11 charges of war crimes and crimes against humanity growing out of killings, mutilation and sexual violence involving thousands of victims, as well as the recruitment and use of child soldiers. Although the special court is based in Freetown, Sierra Leone, Taylor is being tried in The Hague for security reasons. Court officials say that the Taylor trial will be concluded in 2009 and that the rest of the court's business will be concluded in 2010.

A special Cambodian court was approved in principle by the Cambodian government and the UN in 2001 to try the leaders of the Khmer Rouge regime, which ruled Cambodia from 1975 to 1979. The Khmer Rouge is blamed for the deaths of some 1.7 million people in its notorious "killing fields." But three decades after the movement was driven from power, the court has been snarled in corruption charges, just five individuals have been indicted, and only one trial has begun.

In mid-February 2009, the court began hearing the case against Kaing Guek Eav, better known as Duch, the commandant of the Tuol Sleng prison, where thousands of people were tortured and died. Under a 2003 agreement between the UN and Cambodia, the court was set up as part of the Cambodian judicial system, but it has some international judges, a Cambodian and a foreigner as co-prosecutors and some outside administrative and financial support.

But the court's establishment and investigations have proceeded slowly, and allegations of corrupt employment and procurement practices have further delayed proceedings by impeding international funding commitments. Meanwhile, several top Khmer Rouge leaders have died, including Pol Pot, the movement's leader, who passed away in 1998.

A Special Tribunal for Lebanon is on track to begin working in The Hague in March 2009, taking up cases expected to grow out of a yearslong UN investigation of the assassination of former Lebanese Prime Minister Rafik al-Hariri, UN Secretary-General Ban Ki-moon announced in November 2008. Daniel Bellemare, the chief UN official investigating the February 2005 bomb attack in Beirut, told the Security Council in December 2008 that he believed the case could be solved but required more time.

The International Independent Investigation Commission, headed by Bellemare, is looking into the death of Hariri and 20 other bombings and assassinations that have taken place in Lebanon since October 2004 and are suspected of being linked to the Hariri case. In a March 2008 report, the commission said it had established, "on the basis of available evidence, that a network of individuals acted in concert" to assassinate Hariri and that this network was also linked to other bombings and assassinations.

Hariri's assassination brought a global outcry, which forced the withdrawal of Syrian troops from Lebanon after decades of Beirut's domination by Damascus. Hariri had been a critic of Syria's presence in Lebanon, and some anti-Syrian Lebanese politicians have said that Syrian officials were behind his murder. Because the commission's conclusions could have an explosive political impact in both Lebanon and Syria, the commission has maintained silence on many aspects of its work and has not publicly identified any suspects. ■

An International Pledge to Help: R2P

Irwin Arieff

While the UN has helped develop a range of mechanisms to punish the world's most heinous atrocities after they have been committed, governments have historically been slower to try to prevent such crimes before they take place or to end them while they are still going on. With that in mind, leaders attending a UN world summit in New York in 2005 formally approved a long-debated principle known as the Responsibility to Protect, known colloquially as R2P.

The principle, set out in the world summit outcome document adopted on the UN's 60th anniversary, states that governments have the obligation to protect their people from mass atrocities—including genocide, ethnic cleansing, war crimes and crimes against humanity. Furthermore, it says, the international community "should, as appropriate, encourage and help states to exercise this responsibility and support the United Nations in establishing an early warning capability."

The summit document also sets out a framework for international action, should a government fail to meet its obligations. It is the responsibility of the international community, acting through the UN, "to use appropriate diplomatic, humanitarian and other peaceful means . . . to help to protect populations from genocide, war crimes, ethnic cleansing and crimes against humanity," it says. The international community is "prepared to take collective action, in a timely and decisive manner, through the Security Council," in accordance with the UN Charter, including the use of force in the event that peaceful means fail "and national authorities are manifestly failing to protect their populations," the document states.

R2P had evolved informally over the years since World War II. It was formally adopted by the international community, by a vote of the General Assembly, after a series of international failures to protect vulnerable populations in the Balkans, Rwanda, Cambodia and elsewhere. But it has become clear even in the few years since 2005 that the international community has yet to fully grasp and put into practice the concept of the Responsibility to Protect.

Despite UN efforts to prevent genocide and grave abuses of human rights, to promote democracy and to peacefully resolve international disputes, "the world has continued to witness appalling acts that violate human dignity," Secretary-General Ban Ki-moon said in December 2008. "Too often, the international response has been inadequate. Far from being consigned to history, genocide and its ilk remain a serious threat. Not just vigilance but a willingness to act are as important today as ever."

On the plus side, diplomats say with pride, the UN stepped in to help resolve a disputed election in Kenya and a long-simmering civil war in Burundi, after ethnic clashes in these countries raised the specter of more widespread atrocities.

There has also been extensive international involvement in Darfur. But outside intervention there has fallen short of its goals as mass atrocities by the government and allied militias continue despite the presence of international peacekeepers, many international aid groups and investigators from the International Criminal Court.

Similarly, rebel groups in eastern Congo still kill, rape and plunder despite UN pledges to protect innocent civilians. Fighters from the Lord's Resistance Army continue to sow terror in Congo, Uganda and Sudan despite international pledges to shut them down and despite ICC war-crimes charges against four of its leaders, who remain at large. And in Zimbabwe, cracks in an international campaign to install a unity government have enabled President Robert Mugabe to retain power despite his disputed re-election.

To help guide the international community's commitment to R2P, in 2008 Ban named Edward C. Luck, senior vice president and director of studies at the International Peace Institute in New York, as his special adviser on the Responsibility to Protect. Ban is also preparing a report on the principle's implementation for submission to the General Assembly in early 2009.

One problem with carrying out the principle has been skeptical governments' questioning whether the Responsibility to Protect was being abused by the major powers to justify intervention, for their own ends, in smaller countries' internal affairs. During debate on whether the principle should be included in the world summit outcome document, developing nations, in particular, questioned whether it could have been used by the United States to justify the invasion of Iraq, Jean Ping of Gabon, the president of the General Assembly in 2005, said recently.

"It would be true to say that they were frightened by the proposal, and with the Iraqi syndrome—what happened in Iraq—at the back of their minds, they saw it as an instrument that could be used by the powerful countries against the weaker ones. Some talked of their fear of abuse and double standards," Ping said in an address in Ethiopia in October 2008.

To win over developing nations, the principle was modified to link the Responsibility to Protect solely to the crimes of genocide, war crimes, ethnic cleansing and crimes against humanity, Ping said.

But in August 2008, Russia invoked the Responsibility to Protect in justifying military intervention in the former Soviet republic of Georgia, a military action that Georgia rejected as an unjustified invasion.

"Just before the land invasion began in the early hours of August 7th—after days of heavy shelling had killed civilians and Georgian peacekeepers—we urgently sought to refute claims that 2,100 South Ossetian civilians had been killed by Georgians," Georgia President Mikheil Saakashvili told the General Assembly in September 2008. "This was the excuse used by the invader for what is called a 'humanitarian intervention'—a profound perversion of the Responsibility to Protect." Sergei Lavrov, the Russian foreign minister, insisted its intervention was necessary to protect civilians from a Georgian offensive.

The Responsibility to Protect has also sparked controversy in the international response to natural disasters. When a cyclone struck Myanmar in May 2008, leaving nearly 140,000 people dead and 800,000 homeless, the reclusive Southeast Asian nation's military rulers initially refused to allow in foreign aid workers and relief flights. Vital help was delayed, and humanitarian organizations and Western nations accused the government of callousness. But over time, the junta eased its opposition to outside assistance and gradually assembled a broad and generous relief program, with significant UN participation. ■

Policing the High Seas

Irwin Arieff

Before 1982, the world's oceans were considered beyond the reach of normal laws, leaving governments regulating only narrow strips of water along their coastlines and the rest of the waters left to a doctrine of "freedom of the seas." But with many governments unilaterally carving out fisheries, underwater mineral resources and zones of military influence in the mid-20th century, UN members began lobbying for an international convention to regulate the oceans. A series of conferences culminated in the adoption in 1982 of an international treaty, the UN Convention on the Law of the Sea, governing matters ranging from navigational rights and territorial limits to the exploitation of seabed resources and the conservation and management of marine life.

The convention also set up a binding procedure for the settlement of ocean-related disputes among nations and created three international bodies to help carry out the treaty: the International Seabed Authority, the Commission on the Limits of the Continental Shelf and the International Tribunal for the Law of the Sea. Because the convention left gaps in its regulatory scheme relating to some of the most contentious ocean-related disputes, parties to the convention meet regularly under UN auspices to monitor outstanding issues and debate the need for new regulatory steps, whether through new international agreements or self-regulation.

Despite the rapid depletion of many fish species in recent years, strong demand for seafood and intense economic rivalry among national fishing fleets have made the conservation of marine life one of the most challenging issues facing the convention. UN member states have left much of the policing to the major fishing nations and regional self-regulatory fisheries management organizations. But environmental and conservation groups, including Greenpeace and the Deep Sea Conservation Coalition, argue that international steps have failed so far to control overfishing and destructive fishing practices like bottom trawling.

On another matter, after a surge in piracy off the coast of Somalia, the Security Council voted in 2008 to shore up the Law of the Sea convention by authorizing ships from other nations, for a period of six months, to use "all necessary means" to crack down on pirates operating in Somalia's territorial waters. The council acted unanimously after numerous ships were seized or threatened and Somalia said it could not secure its coastline on its own.

"Over the last 25 years, considerable progress towards the goals of the convention has been made," Asha-Rose Migiro, the UN deputy-secretary-general, told the General Assembly in 2007. "Potential conflicts over maritime space and resources have been avoided. Pollution is being addressed through various instruments, and many sources of pollution are the subject of strict regulation. Our knowledge of the oceans and their ecosystems, albeit still expanding, has considerably improved through marine scientific research."

"At the same time," Dr. Migiro said, "it is necessary to recognize that the implementation of some of the provisions of the convention has lagged behind. The world's fisheries continue to be depleted. The marine environment continues to be degraded by pollution from various sources, including pressure from growing coastal populations and climate change. Transnational organized crime, such as illicit traffic in narcotic drugs, the smuggling and trafficking of persons, acts of piracy and terrorist acts also present major threats."

To date, 157 nations have ratified the Law of the Sea convention. One major power missing from the list, again, is the US. While Washington has promised to respect the treaty's provisions, the pact has never been put to a vote in the US Senate, mainly because of criticisms that it could compromise US sovereignty and threaten US economic interests. In May 2007, however, President Bush called on the Senate to ratify the pact, and Barack Obama has pledged to seek a Senate vote. ■

Perspective:
The Challenges and Promises
Of the International Criminal Court
Matthew Heaphy

This is a defining moment for the International Criminal Court. After years of preparation, its very first trial began on Jan. 26, 2009: Thomas Lubanga, leader of the Union of Congolese Patriots militia, faces three charges of recruitment of child soldiers in eastern Congo in 2002 and 2003. In another development, in March 2009, President Omar Hassan al-Bashir of Sudan was issued an arrest warrant by the court on charges of war crimes and crimes against humanity.

It is also an important time for the court, as it has successfully investigated other individuals, including past and present senior government leaders who are allegedly responsible for atrocities. The court continues to develop as an institution: its governing body, the Assembly of States Parties, is preparing for the 2010 Review Conference of the Court's Rome Statute.

As the court matures, it is showing that it can fulfill its early promise and cope with the challenges that it faces. It is functioning as designed—a true criminal court that holds individuals accountable for the most serious atrocity crimes. Its main challenges remain the universal ratification and domestic implementation of the court's governing treaty, known as the Rome Statute, including approval by the United States; enforcement of arrest warrants and sentences; and its institutional maturity.

The court investigates and tries individuals for genocide, war crimes and crimes against humanity and seeks to end impunity through its own cases and by encouraging national investigations and prosecutions. The court's supporters hope that by ensuring that the worst perpetrators do not go unpunished, the court's existence and the cases it prosecutes will deter future crimes.

The ICC also provides justice for victims of affected communities and a sense of redress by allowing them to participate in the proceedings and affording them financial and other reparations. The Rome Statute also established the independent Trust Fund for Victims, which helps victims of ICC crimes.

A Close Look

In the international community's establishment of a permanent criminal court, there are many demands on it, including universality of the court's law, enforcement of its actions and its institutional maturity.

Universality: The ICC is the world's first treaty-based criminal court. It can try only crimes that were committed in the territory of the states parties—that is, nations that have ratified the treaty—or by nationals of states parties. Without universal ratification of the Rome Statute, it cannot investigate certain persons or places or prosecute certain cases. To date, 108 nations have ratified the Rome Statute, though the world's largest—including the US, Russia, China and India—have not joined the ICC. In the long term, the court will not be effective if there are two tiers of international justice, including one in which individuals from some nations are beyond the reach of the law.

A related challenge is the evolving US policy toward the court after the hostile policies of the Bush administration. The US and the ICC now need to learn how to coexist and work together as effectively as possible so that in time the US will become comfortable enough to join the court. Until then, the US will most likely break with past policy by attending meetings of the Assembly of States Parties and cooperating with the ICC on cases in America's national interest beyond Sudan, especially Darfur. The court can succeed without the US, but both the US and the ICC would be well served by constructive American participation.

A third aspect of universality is reducing impunity. In many situations, the ICC takes cases when national court systems are broken or ineffective. It is intended to investigate and try those individuals bearing the greatest responsibility for the most serious crimes; it does not have the capacity to try any and all cases. The ICC and the international community must therefore work with national court systems to ensure that there are concurrent judicial mechanisms so that all perpetrators of atrocities face justice.

Enforcement: The ICC has no police force to arrest suspects, no permanent mechanism for relocating witnesses and no prison of its own where convicts serve their sentences. (It does, however, have a detention center in The Hague, where the accused are held during trial.) Instead, it must ask ICC states parties to fulfill their obligations by carrying out arrest requests and agreeing to witness relocation programs and to imprison sentenced persons. Without the active cooperation of states, the ICC will not be able to collect evidence, protect witnesses or bring suspects to trial, let alone jail those it convicts. States must do more to ensure that the warrants, orders and the goals of the ICC are fulfilled by cooperating and by asking how they can cooperate.

Institutional Maturity: The court is a relatively young institution. The Rome Statute was adopted in 1998 and entered into force on July 1, 2002. It took several years for the court to get up and running, opening its first formal investigations in the summer of 2004 and achieving its first arrest in 2005. Parallel to its judicial work is the development of its own governing body, the Assembly of States Parties. Now that the ICC has been working for five years, its institutional maturity will be tested.

First, the court is beginning to experience a turnover of leadership. Can it continue its important judicial work without interruption, and can it maintain its institutional memory? Within a six-month period in 2008-2009, the ICC will have a new Assembly of States Parties president, six new judges and a new president of the court. In 2012, the assembly will elect a new chief prosecutor and, at most, only 5 of the original 18 judges will remain. As the court evolves, these changes will show whether it is a sophisticated international institution or whether its success relies on people who champion its cause.

Second, in its legislative work, the assembly must ensure that it functions effectively to support and oversee the expanded judicial work of the ICC. So far, the assembly has only one standing committee, the Committee on Budget and Finance, which is asked to pronounce on issues on which it has limited expertise, like legal aid and the right of detainees to family visits. The temporary oversight committee in charge of construction of the court's permanent building in The Hague is expected to conclude its work later this year.

The assembly has not established an effective structure to deal with specific issues that are common to legislative bodies that work well. Instead, it uses temporary working groups, which are convened during the assembly sessions. In place of specific resolutions, it has adopted a practice of using omnibus resolutions, which result in vote trading and compromising on issues unrelated to each other. It has also not convened an advisory committee on nominations for elections, which was contemplated by the Rome Statute and would ensure that only the most qualified individuals are elected as judges and to other key posts.

Third, the assembly has not put together an independent oversight mechanism, as provided in the Rome Statute, for the inspection, evaluation and investigation of the court. This mechanism would help detect and prevent waste, fraud and abuse by the court as well as deter and address misconduct and criminal activity by its staff and agents. The mechanism would require an effective committee structure in the assembly to which it would report.

Although the court is a young and capable institution, it has yet to complete a trial or fully establish itself as a world institution. As the states parties take stock of the Rome Statute at the 2010 Review Conference and consider possible amendments, including defining the crime of aggression, they will have many challenges to consider. Those nations most committed to the ICC should take concrete steps to ensure that it can carry out its work and deliver justice. ∎

New Judges at the Helm

By Ana Gomez Rojo

Six judges were elected to the International Criminal Court in January 2009, as the Assembly of States Parties to the court met in a resumed session at United Nations headquarters in New York. The meeting was a continuation of the session that began at The Hague in November 2008.

The new judges are Sanji Monageng of Botswana, Fumiko Saiga of Japan, Mohamed Shahabuddeen of Guyana, Cuno Tarfusser of Italy, Christine Van Den Wyngaert of Belgium and Joyce Aluoch of Kenya. The judges serve nine-year terms and cannot be re-elected. In February 2009, however, Shahabuddeen resigned for health reasons, and a judge to replace him will be elected in June 2009.

The court seats 18 judges. Nominations for 21 candidates were received by the closing date, Nov. 24, 2008. The criteria considered are high moral character, impartiality and integrity, expertise in criminal or international law, possession of the qualifications required in the respective states for appointment to the highest judicial offices and an excellent knowledge of and fluency in at least one working language of the court. In addition, states parties making nominations are required to take into account the need to include judges with legal expertise on specific issues, including, but not limited to, violence against women or children.

The elections were conducted by secret ballot. The successful candidates were those who obtained the highest number of votes and a two-thirds majority of the states parties present and voting. When a sufficient number of judges were not elected on the first ballot, eight additional ballots were held until the remaining vacancies were filled. The American NGO Coalition for the ICC, a UNA-USA affiliate, monitored the elections as an accredited participant. ■

For more information, visit
www.icc-cpi.int/Menus/ASP/Elections/Judges/2009/Results/Final+Results.htm

At a meeting convened by the secretary-general, Ban Ki-Moon, and Miguel d'Escoto Brockmann, president of the 63rd General Assembly, world leaders, private-sector representatives and civil-society partners gathered in September 2008 in the General Assembly Hall at UN Headquarters in New York to discuss the Millennium Development Goals.

7

Adapting the United Nations to The 21st Century

Management and Secretariat Reform

Rosemary Banks

At the 2005 World Summit, which was meant to be a follow-up meeting to the United Nations' 2000 Millennium Summit, members reaffirmed a commitment to strengthen the organization through an efficient, effective and accountable Secretariat. Reform was seen as a means to make the UN better able to respond to rising expectations and growing demands. The secretary-general has spoken of a need to make the organization more modern—faster, more flexible and responsive. This can happen only when systems, resources and the management culture are better aligned.

The summit outcome document explicitly recognized all dimensions of effective management: human-resource reform; mandate review; accountability; and the budget process. Management reform in the UN is a continuing challenge, one that is viewed differently by members through the lens of their own national and regional experience. Whatever progress is made—and there have been major achievements—there is always more work ahead. What is needed in 2009 is renewed effort to sustain the drive for modernization.

Effective Management of Global Human Resources

The human-resource reforms put forward by the secretary-general after the World Summit were aimed at significantly improving the way the UN manages its enormous staff.

The operational needs of the UN have become increasingly complex over the years, with field operations playing a much larger role. The UN's human-resource systems, originally tailored to a UN staff serving out its careers in headquarters, have not kept up with the changing UN. As a result, problems have grown worse in recruitment, administratively burdensome practices, inconsistent terms and conditions, and high vacancy and turnover rates, especially in the field. At the same time, demands on the UN have continued to grow, along with expectations about what it should accomplish.

Achieving agreement on human-resource reforms has not been easy. Members' positions diverge over how much scope and authority the secretary-general should have to manage human resources, and issues like geographical representation require serious and sensitive treatment. The financial costs of reforms in this area have also been a huge obstacle, made worse by the difficulty of quantifying in dollar terms the return on investment for such reforms over the long term.

In 2008, the General Assembly agreed to streamline the UN's contractual framework. Three types of contracts—temporary, fixed and continuing—were brought under one set of staff rules, harmonizing (and for many staff members, improving) terms and conditions for serving in the field. The agreement reached on a new system of Administration of Justice was another important and complementary reform.

These steps and others over recent years, including the secretary-general's compacts with senior managers, will help to improve the UN's management of its most important asset, its people. Reviewing the managed mobility program, which is currently in abeyance, will also be an important exercise. The secretary-general has rightly emphasized the importance of staff mobility in an organization the size and scope of the UN. Much more remains to be done, including work on recruitment processes, performance management and other areas. This will need to continue in 2009 and beyond.

Accountability of Members and the Secretariat

The current global financial crisis has sharpened the focus on the accountability and governance of international organizations, particularly the UN. Leaders at the 2005 World Summit emphasized "the importance of establishing effective and efficient mechanisms for responsibility and accountability of the Secretariat." Since 2005, the secretary-general has been undertaking projects to strengthen accountability throughout the organization. Perhaps the largest barrier to date stems from a lack of shared understanding by all member states of the actual concept.

Most visible of the recent initiatives has been the introduction of senior management compacts. These are, in essence, performance contracts between the secretary-general and the senior management team, which seek to make managerial responsibilities more transparent to both staff and member states. These compacts were intended to complement the new "accountability architecture" proposal that the secretary-general presented to the General Assembly in the first quarter of 2008. The proposal comprised three pillars: performance, integrity and compliance and oversight; it seeks to carry out the concepts of enterprise risk management, internal control and results-based management.

While the current proposal addresses many of the accountability gaps in the organization, the secretary-general's report was widely viewed as not fully articulating a clear vision for the future. The assembly considered the secretary-general's report in the main part of its 63rd session, but member states neither endorsed nor rejected the proposal.

In March 2009, the assembly was scheduled to reconsider the secretary-general's proposal. A request for a more detailed report on a strategy and its components was a likely outcome.

Lessons Learned From Mandate Review

The World Summit agreed "to strengthen and update the program of work of the United Nations so that it responds to the contemporary requirements of member states." To this end, the assembly was directed to review all mandates originating in resolutions of the assembly and other UN bodies. This was the first such directive in UN history. While everyone agreed on the broad objective of renewal, there were sharply different views about what the exercise should produce and how. Some major donors focused on cost savings and resetting priorities, while developing countries were more interested in proof of implementation and adequate resources.

After more than two years of effort to turn the concept of mandate review into practice, members concluded that the painstaking process of checking the relevance of 9,000 individual mandates was not resulting in greater clarity or improved efficiency. In practice, the great majority of mandates, which had become redundant over time, were no longer attracting resources or the Secretariat's attention. In the two areas analyzed in the 2007-08 mandate review process—humanitarian assistance and African development—there were very few active mandates that members regarded as valuable.

In retrospect, the mandate review initiative might have been easier to carry out if it had been framed differently: for example, as a review of mandate implementation. As co-chair of the mandate review process in 2007-08, New Zealand found that members accepted that they were responsible for tighter management of mandates, though the framework for doing this was not obvious. The existing mechanism with the potential to be used more actively for this purpose is the Committee for Program and Coordination. This body of 32 representatives (with two seats to be filled from the Western European and Others group) is charged with recommending priorities; guiding the Secretariat on translating legislation into programs; advising on preventing duplication; and developing evaluation procedures.

Despite the frustrations of mandate review, on the positive side it has brought home to members their own responsibility to define tasks clearly and to direct the Secretariat. It has resulted in a permanent database on existing mandates, which can be accessed online. It has also laid a steppingstone, if member states choose to start down this path, for analyzing mandates from formation through implementation and for evaluating results and reporting back on them. Experience so far would suggest that such a revived initiative would be most likely to succeed if it were part of an agenda of wider management reform.

The United Nations Budget

It is widely acknowledged that the UN budget process does not serve members or the organization particularly well, but that it is also very difficult to change.

Concerns about the budget process are many and varied. It is complex, lengthy and not well understood; budget negotiations are susceptible to politicization and focus mainly on inputs rather than outcomes. The ever-increasing budget level is a big concern for many member states, especially the major contributors. Other members believe that new mandates are being established without enough new resources to pay for their execution.

The World Summit asked the secretary-general to provide an assessment and recommendations to ensure that budgetary and financial rules and regulations respond to the needs of the organization. The subsequent proposals put forward were highly controversial and were not agreed upon, although those discussions were colored by ill feelings about the spending cap put in place in the budget negotiations in late 2005.

Special political missions, especially those in Iraq and Afghanistan, account for much of the budget growth. In addition, a large number of new initiatives have been approved in recent years in the Secretariat, but their full costs often do not become apparent until several years later. These factors will continue to drive significant budget growth over the next few years.

Although most of the attention focuses on the regular budget, peacekeeping costs are much larger—nearly fourfold—and are rising even faster.

There has been widespread criticism of "add-on" budget proposals presented by the secretary-general outside the budget cycle. These have been described as "ad hoc" and a "piecemeal" approach to budgeting. Some of the proposals originated at the World Summit; others were initiated by the secretary-general.

Given this background, there are numerous areas where it should be possible to agree on improvements: for example, strengthening the links between planning, allocating resources and evaluating performance. Efforts at budget reform should involve full consultation, with an emphasis on identifying core problems and building consensus on appropriate solutions. ■

'Delivering as One' at the Country Level
Paul Kavanagh

The concept of "delivering as one" entails a root-and-branch renewal of the way the United Nations development system operates at the country level.

Steps toward this goal are being pursued at a crucial time for the international community. The world is facing a development emergency: nearly a billion people find themselves in extreme poverty, and progress toward achieving the Millennium Development Goals is hampered by myriad crises. The global challenges faced, like the food and financial crises, climate change and the HIV/AIDS pandemic, require collective solutions, but over the years the UN has become increasingly marginalized in the realm of international development. Although the UN is the only international organization with universal legitimacy and a comprehensive mandate, it remains fragmented and incoherent in the way it delivers development assistance.

Delivering as One is based on the premise that by delivering together the UN can deliver more. It aims to harness the resources and expertise of all the funds, programs and agencies in the UN system in a way that aligns the UN's work more closely with the national priorities of the country concerned. This improves coherence and coordination, eliminates fragmentation and duplication while capitalizing on efficiency and economies of scale.

Better Collaboration

The Delivering as One vision encompasses four "ones." These are: One Program, One Budget, One Office and One Leader, who would be the UN resident coordinator.

These four principles form the core of the concept, which would see the UN working together under one leader through a jointly produced unified program with a single budgetary framework, aligned with national priorities. In many cases the UN's in-country presence will be co-located in a single office, strengthening the collaborative relationships among all areas of the UN operating in that country.

While these reforms emphasize coherence, they must also recognize that one size does not fit all. Although the methods by which the UN is reorganizing itself at the country level are similar, the substantial problems facing developing countries, and thus the support that the UN provides, must be tailored to each country's needs. National ownership and leadership are central priorities of this reform and require the UN to become a more responsive partner for developing countries' governments.

Carrying out these reforms has widened the scope of expertise available to developing countries' governments, as nonresident agencies from the UN system have become more engaged in the planning process. While the UN reform process initially started in eight pilot countries—Albania, Cape Verde, Mozambique, Pakistan, Rwanda, Tanzania, Uruguay and Vietnam—they have now been joined by Malawi and, more recently, Botswana, Papua New Guinea and Zambia, among others.

Major progress has been made since these reforms began in 2006. In May 2008, the government of Mozambique held a conference in its capital, Maputo, which produced the Maputo Declaration, outlining an initial positive assessment of progress made and of challenges remaining on Delivering as One. The General Assembly also acknowledged this progress in a consensus resolution adopted at the end of the 62nd Session in 2008. Other countries are reporting an improved and better-performing UN system as a result of these reforms.

This progress is encouraging and will have wider benefits as common lessons learned are diffused across the system. However, while much valuable work has been done both at the national and global levels to advance reform, this needs to be deepened and broadened. While it is clear that this task is immense, it is ever more urgent and necessary, as we are now past the halfway mark in the timetable for achieving the Millennium Development Goals. ■

Revitalizing the General Assembly

Lydia Swart

On becoming president of the General Assembly in September 2008, the Reverend Miguel d'Escoto Brockmann of Nicaragua made revitalization and democratization top priorities.

"I believe we need to take radical steps to regain the authority of the GA so that it can perform its duties as the most democratic organ of the United Nations," he said in a speech on Nov. 20, 2008.

In January 2009, in a move to take such a "radical step," President d'Escoto called for an emergency special session of the General Assembly on the crisis in Gaza, reasserting the assembly's role on matters of peace and security and underscoring the fact that the UN Charter allows this as long as the issue is not under consideration by the Security Council. President d'Escoto called the special session in the assembly by using the Uniting for Peace resolution, which was adopted in 1950 and allows an alternative route when the council faces political gridlock. Use of the resolution requires a vote from any of the seven members of the council or a majority of member states. (In total, 10 emergency special sessions have been convened using the mechanism, which implores the assembly to consider matters immediately when the council cannot maintain international peace and there is a "threat to the peace, breach of the peace or act of aggression.")

Since 1945, the disparity of power between the assembly and the council has been a growing point of contention at the United Nations, especially for countries in the Southern Hemisphere, as their numbers and voting strength have grown over the last few decades. Some members believe that expansion of the council might ease some of that friction, but even as the council's membership expands, it will continue to be an exclusive group of veto-wielding countries with the biggest say on critical issues.

A Lasting Debate

On matters of reform, President d'Escoto has his work cut out for him. The revitalization debate has been lately divided into three areas: the role and authority of the assembly; selection of the secretary-general; and improvement of assembly working methods. Previous reform leaders have openly expressed their frustration about this process, which has undergone rather repetitive discussions and resolutions over the last 18 years. Apart from the Nonaligned Movement, there appears to be no great appetite in the assembly to continue discussions on democratization and revitalization. For many countries, the revitalization debate should be about practical improvements in the work of the assembly, while for others, the main value of the debate is to ensure that the assembly becomes the pre-eminent deliberative body in the UN. President d'Escoto belongs in the latter group.

His latest attempt at revitalization—to evoke a strong, independent message from the assembly on the Gaza conflict—failed. At the close of the special session, he expressed his disappointment, saying, "We will never make it if we don't act in a more decisive and affirmative manner."

Arguably, however, President d'Escoto's bold move in the special session to pass an assembly resolution on such a contentious issue as Gaza could be viewed as a success, given that it resulted in a outcome that a large majority of the assembly could live with. (The assembly resolution mirrored the Security Council's Resolution 1860, which included an urgent call for an "immediate, durable and fully respected cease-fire, leading to the full withdrawal of Israeli forces and unimpeded provision of humanitarian assistance.")

But, as the president, d'Escoto needs to be regarded as a neutral facilitator by all member states. The fact that many member states now view him as pushing his own agenda too much, aligning himself with some of the more extreme positions in the assembly, may turn out to be the biggest failure in the attempt to strengthen the assembly. ∎

Reforming the Security Council (Again)

Arnav Chakravarty and Simon Minching

The end of the 62nd General Assembly in 2008 brought a decision to begin negotiations on Security Council reform in an informal plenary of the assembly no later than the end of February 2009. Putting these negotiations into the assembly removes the consensus restriction, which has often hampered work in the Open-Ended Working Group, the entity that has sought to deal with the issue for years. In the assembly, any proposal or resolution regarding council reform can be debated in a forum that allows for majority decisions. However, the acceptance of any resolution or proposal still requires a two-thirds majority vote.

There is also a timeline on the working group's efforts. The chairman was directed to give the results of consultations to the assembly no later than Feb.1, 2009. On the basis of these recommendations, the informal plenary was to begin intergovernmental negotiations no later than Feb. 28.

These steps and deadlines have infused new life into the council reform process, yet larger concerns remain. Miguel d'Escoto Brockmann, the current assembly president, who is eager to set reform in motion, has expressed his wish to rectify the unequal distribution of power within the UN. His main proposals call for an expansion of both permanent and nonpermanent seats in the council. While proponents say that expanding the council will improve regional representation, any prospect for expansion is fraught with problems and raises doubts about the democratic nature of such a change.

Expansion, for example, requires a change in the Charter and therefore not only acceptance by two-thirds of the assembly but also the approval of all five permanent members of the council. Needless to say, such a plan would require a Herculean effort.

Seeking Support

Even if an expansion proposal were to clear the assembly, gaining support in the council would be nearly impossible. China has historically indicated that it will not uphold a Japanese bid for permanent membership, and it is increasingly clear that the current permanent members are quite satisfied with the size of their club.

Moreover, as middle-power countries like India, Germany, Japan and Brazil —the Group of Four, known sometimes as the G-4—ally to strengthen their bid for permanent seats, their opponents multiply. For example, India's primary opposition was initially Pakistan, but it now faces opposition from Argentina, Canada, Italy, Malta, Mexico, South Korea, Spain and Turkey, also known as the Uniting for Consensus faction.

In Africa, where regional rivalries dominate political proceedings, the competition among countries becomes even more intense.

Yet the dialogue by President d'Escoto's open-ended working group continued last fall and into the winter, albeit in a highly technical manner, focusing on the terms and forms of reform. Heated discussions that took place from November 2008 through January 2009 concentrated on the idea of consensus and its application in the informal plenary. In working groups, there is a common understanding that decisions should generally be reached by consensus. But the process of how to conduct intergovernmental negotiations within the informal plenary became unclear. The G-4 argued that the rules of the General Assembly, as defined in the Charter, should apply, thereby allowing the voting method to be used.

On the other hand, the Uniting for Consensus faction argued that decisions during the informal plenary should continue by consensus, just as decisions were determined in the working group. These differences parallel the two distinct positions the camps follow toward possible expansion. The G-4, which seek permanent seats for themselves, fear that use of consensus will continue to obstruct their ambitions. Conversely, the Uniting for Consensus group, which favors adding only nonpermanent members and ardently opposes its rivals' ambitions, worries that it may come up short in votes on reform.

The Transitional Approach

A compromise between the interests of the groups, which remain far apart, is the transitional approach. The idea behind this approach has been proposed in the working group since the mid-1990s but to no avail. Since then, the compromise has taken many forms, but its underlying feature—a test period of interim solutions followed by a review conference—remains its foundation.

The major obstacle to this approach is the power that the review conference would have: would interim reforms become void if not approved at the review conference, as some states prefer, or would there be an automatic renewal of them if a two-thirds majority cannot be achieved against the reforms? The skepticism behind the transitional approach may be rooted in a similar failure to assemble a review conference of the Charter.

A review of the Charter, provided for in Article 109, paragraph 3, was to be convened 10 years after the document's implementation, but it never occurred because of a lack of majority support. Therefore, doubts that a scheduled review conference would occur soon seem inevitable, and fears of de facto permanence of a transitional approach are understandable.

Making the Council More Accessible

There is also growing impetus to improve the council's transparency and accountability. Such reforms in its working methods are more feasible as they do not require amending the Charter. Over the last 15 years, the council has slowly been reforming itself under pressure from the 10 nonpermanent elected members. It now holds more effective public meetings, coordinates more quickly with noncouncil members on important issues and has become less ambiguous. For example, the council now publishes its program of work, which includes a daily schedule of all meetings. To this end, Security Council reform has been far more successful.

Much more needs to be done. Failure to achieve marked progress on the issue of expansion highlights the divisiveness among factions within the assembly. While the consensus is that the council must be changed, there are bitter differences on how and what should be instituted. To many, the reform should focus on its legitimacy and makeup in a world that is very different from the post World War II era in which it was conceived.

Expansion of council membership would help address such criticisms, but doing so creates a set of new issues concerning efficiency. Reform of its working methods could make the council more transparent, and agreeing to limit the use of the veto power in serious cases where peremptory norms of international law were breached, such as genocide or acts of aggression, would make the council more productive. Current members of the P-5, however, are unlikely to ever cede such exclusive power. And there are others who view reforming the council as a way to increase their state's power, which would result from acquiring the plum seat at the UN's most illustrious bargaining table. But competitiveness between regional groups and individual states bring about obstructionist tendencies in this regard.

Concerted pressure from the 63rd assembly on expansion and improving working methods of the council is expected to persist, although efforts to make the council as accountable and representative as possible will continue down a long, winding road. ■

Gender Architecture: Toward a Single, Stronger Agency for Women

Emily Davila

Gender equality has always been a priority of the United Nations, but its bodies currently charged with enhancing women's economic and decision-making power have overlapping and underfinanced mandates, rendering them less effective than envisioned. In the current system, many urgent issues, like programs for gender equality in the field, fall through the cracks. A reformed "gender architecture" at the UN could respond to immediate needs, as when rape is used as a weapon of war, or address crosscutting themes that are overlooked by other UN agencies, like the rise of HIV/AIDS among women, or the lack of financing for women's rights and development organizations in the global south.

Part of the reason for the fragmented structure is that as the UN's work for women has evolved, different offices were established at different times. Shortly after the UN's founding in 1945, the Commission on the Status of Women was created, reporting to the Economic and Social Council and served by the Division for the Advancement for Women. After the First World Conference on Women in 1975, members called for the creation of the UN Fund for Women and the International Research and Training Institute for the Advancement of Women. Finally, in 1997 the Office of the Special Adviser to the Secretary-General on Gender Issues and the Advancement of Women was given the task of bringing this issue to the fore across the UN, including the goal of gender parity within the Secretariat staff. In addition, UN bodies dealing with humanitarian emergencies, refugees, human rights, development and children have gender-related staff and strategies.

The current mishmash of mandates and underfinanced offices are not able to serve women worldwide, nor are they able to serve members who look to the UN to take the lead in setting norms, policy and programs. Responding to pressure from women's rights groups, in 2006 the secretary-general's High-Level Panel on Systemwide Coherence made this fragmented system a priority for reform.

After the panel's recommendation, UN members, rarely quick to join any agenda, eventually agreed to consider a new entity. "Member states strongly reaffirmed that gender equality is a central goal for member states and the UN system," said Rachel Mayanja, assistant-secretary-general and special adviser on gender issues and advancement of women, when she addressed the General Assembly in October 2007. Members "recognized gender equality as a crosscutting issue and agreed that the existing gender architecture was incoherent, fragmented and under-resourced," she added.

To help them proceed, members asked the deputy secretary-general, Dr. Asha-Rose Migiro, to outline various options for gender reform. Dr. Migiro presented this paper to the General Assembly in July 2008. It outlined four options: keeping the status quo; creating a fund or program; creating a department; or developing a composite or hybrid entity.

While it was broadly agreed by the membership that every development issue had a women's component, some still had reservations about plans for reform. For instance, members of the G-77, a coalition of 132 developing countries, saw it as a donor-driven agenda, while others were concerned that it would be viewed as a cost-cutting exercise aimed at reducing overhead expenses, not necessarily at delivering services for women on the ground. Still, after deliberations, members' concerns were assuaged enough so that in October 2008, the assembly adopted Resolution 62/277 on Systemwide Coherence asking the secretary-general to produce a second paper outlining further technical details on the four options.

This time, a team of three consultants led by Mayanja's office drafted a more detailed paper, with particular emphasis on the fourth option, the hybrid entity. This paper had contributions not only from women's groups but also from representatives from humanitarian and refugee offices, Unicef, the United Nations Development Program and civil society. The paper was presented to the assembly in early 2009. A new resolution on how to proceed is expected by the end of the 63rd session.

But outlining the specifics of combining all the gender work of the UN is just the beginning. Securing agreement in the assembly will be no easy task, nor will settling on governance and financing. Advocates expect the new entity to be led by an under-secretary-general, the highest ranking position possible. The new entity could report to a new or existing executive board or to the Commission on the Status of Women.

From the beginning, the recommendations of the high-level panel requested that the entity be "ambitiously resourced," but there is no guarantee that donors will come to the table. Financing will come from regular UN dues as well as from voluntary contributions. Details will be hammered out by the assembly's Fifth Committee, which deals with budgetary questions. It is expected that the new entity will have to scale-up gradually over time, but advocates are calling for a fixed clear goal—the bigger the number the better.

Speaking on behalf of the European Union in June 2007, the German representative said: "A new entity must deliver better. . . . It also has to be better resourced. In short, we have to go beyond a mere replication of the existing gender entities under a new umbrella."

Perhaps the most challenging task will be making the impact of gender equality reform felt at the field level, with mandates, staff and resources to make a difference.

No matter what happens, one thing is certain: civil society has been a major proponent in this process. Since the creation of the high-level panel, members of the Gender Equality Architecture Reform Campaign have forged a grassroots effort led by 275 member organizations. Their voices will continue to be heard, pushing the UN to meet high expectations. ■

Trouble Fixing the Internal Justice System
Shelley Walden

For years the United Nations, like other intergovernmental organizations, has faced harsh criticism for failing to reform itself and combat internal corruption. In 2008, the UN had an unprecedented opportunity to promote accountability and to protect the rights of staff members. Instead, the General Assembly opted for the status quo.

Because intergovernmental organizations have sovereign immunity, their employees cannot raise grievances in national courts. Their employees depend on internal justice systems when their rights are violated. But structural conflicts of interest are built in, as the institution is both defendant and judge. In 2006, an expert panel of independent jurists found that the UN justice system did not "meet many basic standards of due process established in international human rights instruments," lacked independence, had insufficient resources and was ineffective.

The jurists recommended the creation of a new system, since "effective reform of the United Nations cannot happen without an efficient, independent and well-resourced internal justice system that will safeguard the rights of staff members and ensure effective accountability of managers and staff members."

In 2007, the assembly committed to establishing a new system—with informal and formal components—by January 2009. But in December 2008, the launch of the formal system, consisting of both a Dispute and Appeals Tribunal, was postponed six months. Meanwhile, the General Assembly approved the statutes for both tribunals, as written by the secretary-general's office. But this step was at odds with the panel's recommendations, which suggested that an independent internal group should write the statutes.

The New System's Limits

In its proposed form, the justice system covers only "staff members" and thus excludes nonstaff personnel like interns, consultants and peacekeepers even though they are vulnerable to abuse. This exclusion ignores the expert panel's recommendations and does not guarantee everyone the right to equal recognition before the law, legal protection and a fair hearing by an impartial tribunal.

The jurisdiction of the new justice system would also be curtailed. The independent panel envisioned two tribunals that would hear diverse allegations, including claims by employees of violations of rights or breaches of staff rules. Instead, the secretary-general proposed limiting the tribunals' jurisdiction to appeals of certain administrative decisions, greatly limiting staff members' ability to contest discrimination, harassment and other forms of abuse. This limitation will prevent tribunals from ordering redress when human rights have been violated.

The statutes also do not allow staff associations to bring actions or to provide staff members with professional legal counsel. Rather than embrace the professionalized system proposed by the expert panel, this proposal seeks to use an old model, in which volunteers represented staff members. The institution and UN managers, on the other hand, can be represented by professional lawyers within the organization, paid for by the organization.

In its proposed form, the new UN justice system is fundamentally the same as the old discredited one. Member states should intervene to ensure that the new system complies with the panel's recommendations and honors human and labor rights. ■

The Democracy Fund, Committed to an Open Society

Simon Minching

When United Nations members gathered in September 2004 to hear President George W. Bush's staunch defense of Operation Iraqi Freedom at the 59th General Assembly, Bush proposed the creation of a "democracy fund" within the UN, saying that "the advance of liberty is the path to both a safer and better world."

The initiative was intended to provide money and technical support to countries lacking resources and expertise needed to establish democratic governance. Bush said it would help them "lay the foundations of democracy by instituting the rule of law and independent courts, a free press, political parties and trade unions."

Kofi Annan, the secretary-general at the time, announced the establishment of the United Nations Democracy Fund at the Summit of the African Union in July 2005, with the primary purpose of supporting democratization worldwide. Since then, according to the fund's latest figures, more than $91 million in voluntary contributions from 35 member countries has gone to projects that strengthen civil society, promote human rights and encourage the participation of all groups in the democratic process.

The secretary-general's advisory board is the fund's main governing mechanism. It is composed of 19 members who provide guidance on programming framework, financing guidelines and assessment of the merits of projects on a short list before sending them to the secretary-general for approval. The advisory board includes representatives of 13 member states, 4 personal representatives of the secretary-general and 2 nongovernmental organizations. Member states represented on the 2008 advisory board are the 7 biggest donors and 6 other countries chosen for proven commitment to democracy.

Seven Give the Most

As of Jan. 5, 2009, the seven donor countries were the United States, India, Japan, Qatar, Australia, Germany and France, which account for over $79 million, or 86.9 percent of all contributions. The six representing the balance of UN membership were Botswana, Lebanon, Mongolia, Panama, Slovenia and Trinidad and Tobago. This selection complies with the principle of equitable geographic representation. The two other main organs of the fund are the Office of the UN Democracy Fund and the Program Consultative Group. The funds' administration is handled by the Office of the UN Democracy Fund, led by Roland Rich. The office plays a subsidiary role, as does the Program Consultative Group, which provides technical assistance and support to the advisory board on program-financing criteria and project proposals.

Project proposals are assessed by the advisory board on the basis of their merits at supporting action-oriented projects for democracy and whose yields reinforce its foundations within civil society. They can be wide-ranging in scope, with global, regional and single-country projects considered, and differ significantly as to which area of democracy they seek to advance; for example, it supports grassroots empowerment, increased media transparency or women's rights development.

While applications from all countries are considered, the fund, under its guidelines, gives strong preference to applicants from countries and regions where "the challenges of democracy are more critical." These can be places emerging from conflict, new and restored democracies, the least developed countries, and low- and middle-income countries, as classified by the World Bank.

Global and regional projects are handled by international nongovernmental organizations, but the large majority of the fund's grants—75.9 percent in 2007—go to local NGOs, which typically handle single-country projects. "This flows from UNDEF's strategy to 'invest' in local civil society whenever possible," according to an approved-project report from the fund in September 2008.

Africa Gets the Largest Share

Submissions for help on projects are received from all over the world, with Africa usually applying for and receiving the largest amount of help. Grants are at least $50,000, but no more than $500,000. Sub-Saharan Africa submitted more than one-third of all applications—37.3 percent—and received 34 percent of all funds allocated in 2007, for a total of $8.1 million. Freedom House, a US-based NGO dedicated to the worldwide expansion of political and economic freedom, asserts that the concentration on Africa "is a positive development, given the relative dearth of democracy funding for this region."

In August 2006, when the fund first began disbursing grants, it selected 122 projects totaling $35 million out of 1,303 proposals. With a 44 percent jump in applications in the second round in 2007, the fund awarded less money to a smaller number of projects, choosing 83 proposals out of 1,873 applications for a total just under $24 million. According to the fund's new newsletter, there were 2,143 applications in the third round in 2008, and applicants on the short list should be notified by mid-2009.

Originally described by Bush in 2004 as "a great calling for this great organization," the fund's role in democracy promotion has been limited when measured against its early high expectations. Because it relies on voluntary contributions, underwriting has become a major issue. That only 35 countries have so far contributed is a signal that individual member states may not be persuaded of the efficiency or overall merit of the UN's efforts.

By No Means a Universal Plan

However, as Rich of the Office of the UN Democracy Fund notes, "Even the most generous analyst would concede that a significant number, and perhaps even a majority, of UN member states do not practice democracy." The paucity of democratic states, though, cannot be the sole cause for lack of funds. Despite the wealth and strength of democracy in Europe, Britain has contributed only $609,350, and as of December 2008, France had not provided 2.14 million of the 3.4 million euros pledged in early October 2007.

Even the US, the top contributor, has chosen itself to be the primary arbiter of how to distribute the majority of its allocations toward world democracy instead of yielding that role to the fund. The US State Department estimates that for the fiscal year 2006, just over $74 million was appropriated to the National Endowment for Democracy, a private non-profit organization created in 1983 to strengthen democratic institutions around the world through NGO efforts, and that $80 million was requested in the fiscal year 2007. By comparison, the US has contributed just under $26 million to the UN Democracy Fund in the nearly four years since its establishment in July 2005.

Yet, with a more with less attitude, the UN fund has made significant contributions complementing the work of the UN and its members in strengthening democratic governance around the world. In northern Iraq, Concordia, a local NGO aimed at increasing the knowledge and respect for human rights and fundamental freedoms, is carrying out seminars and workshops on gender equality and social change. Supporting a project of the National Union of Somali Journalists, the fund has provided financing for professional-training workshops for participants who aspire to pursue ethical journalism in Mogadishu despite considerable personal risk.

In Peru, the fund supports a pilot project called Innovative System for Citizens' Participation With Congressmen and Congresswomen, which seeks to provide Peruvian citizens with access to their representatives, in both Spanish and Quecha, from any telephone or Internet cafe.

Although the word does not appear in the UN Charter, there is a strong historical basis for a UN role in promoting democracy. The Universal Declaration of Human Rights clearly states that "the will of the people shall be the basis of the authority of government" and that this should be expressed through elections, with equal suffrage and a secret vote.

In 1996, Secretary-General Boutros Boutros-Ghali wrote "An Agenda for Democratization." This asserted that "the special power of democratization lies in its logic, which flows from the individual human person, the one irreducible entity in world affairs and the logical source of all human rights."

The creation of the Democracy Fund continues this trend. Recognizing that "there is no single model of democracy," and that it does not belong to any country or region, the UN is specially situated to midwife democracy in a nonthreatening manner, without conditionality, and while assuaging fears of political interference among indigenous populations. As states and broader institutions conclude that democracy is a critical ingredient for peace, prosperity and human rights, and as they reinforce their verbal pledges with money, the fund's efforts to finance the projects of a more open, democratic world will have greater effect. ■

Capital Master Plan: Time for a Facelift

Simon Minching

The mission of the office of the Capital Master Plan, headed by an American, Michael Adlerstein, is to supervise renovation of United Nations Headquarters in New York, ensuring its completion by 2013 and within its $1.97 billion budget.

Such improvements are long overdue: the original UN structures, built from 1950 to 1952, lack the safety and efficiency of a modern building. The UN is spending $19 million a year on maintenance and $6 million on maintenance staff; with operating systems that in some cases are 30 years past their life expectancy, renovating the complex makes sense in terms of dollars and safety. The headquarters, a historic and architectural symbol around the world, sits on 17 acres overlooking the East River and is made up of 6 buildings that total 2.6 million square feet.

In 1998, Arup, a multinational engineering firm, was first contracted to recommend repairs for the headquarters. The complexity of the planning and the inevitable political wrangling over appropriations slowed progress. But the appointment of Skanska USA as the construction manager in July 2007 and a resolution that December by the General Assembly approving the secretary-general's accelerated strategy gave renewed focus to the planning, design and procurement phases, which began 11 years ago.

Recent Events

Significant progress toward actual renovations has occurred in the last year. In February 2008, the UN rented 80,000 square feet in Long Island City, Queens, to use as swing space for 300 staff members. A month later, 423,000 square feet on Madison Avenue in Manhattan provided the UN all the additional space it needed for more than 1,800 staff members, completing its leasing plan. By early February 2009, construction workers were putting up the steel frame of the temporary North Lawn Conference Building, which will allow the functions of the current Conference Building and General Assembly to continue without delay when those buildings are renovated, beginning in mid-2009 and continuing through mid-2013. These steps will allow much needed upgrades to begin in earnest when most of the UN occupants move out by August 2009.

Instead of renovating the Secretariat in four phases, 10 floors at a time as originally planned, the accelerated strategy called for leasing office space elsewhere so that the project could be completed in one phase. The Conference Building and the General Assembly will also be refurbished in one sweep. Among the benefits of the strategy are to potentially shorten work time by two years, to five altogether, and reduce the risk of complications and delays that were possible if work went on in a partly occupied Secretariat building.

Besides making the complex safer and more current, the Capital Master Plan will result in a considerable greening of the UN, reducing energy consumption and operating costs, improving the aesthetic quality of the landscaping and lowering carbon emissions.

"We'll reduce energy consumption by a projected 44 percent," said Adlerstein, the executive director, who in the 1980s was the project director for the restoration of Ellis Island and the Statue of Liberty. This would be an improvement on top of the 40 percent reduction the UN reported making in energy use last year.

Specifically, sustainability measures will include automated interior blinds, which will maximize the use of natural light, a high-technology heating and air-conditioning system, new insulation and a double-glazed curtain wall so the "building envelope will leak less energy," according to Adlerstein.

Money for the plan is coming directly from UN members. These contributions are assessed using the scale for the 2007 regular budget, to be paid either as lump sums or over five years. In addition, a reserve fund was established to handle any cash shortfalls that occur. To ensure fiscal responsibility, the UN Office of Internal Oversight Services has two auditors working full time on the project, and the US Government Accountability Office has repeatedly reviewed the Capital Master Plan at the request of the UN.

By replacing antiquated systems, upgrading safety, security and accessibility for the disabled and improving its environmental performance, the Capital Master Plan will give UN Headquarters the makeover it badly needs. ■

UN Photo/Marco Dormino

A peacekeeping officer from Brazil distributes food rations as part of the UN Stabilization Mission in Haiti.

Appendices

Appendix A: 60 Important Dates in United Nations History

Compiled by Max McGowen

June 12, 1941 Inter-Allied Declaration signed in London, encouraging free people to work together in war and peace.

Jan. 1, 1942 Representatives of 26 Allied nations meet in Washington to sign Declaration of United Nations, in which US President Roosevelt coins the term "United Nations."

Sept. 21-Oct. 7 1944 US, Soviet Union, Britain and China agree on basic blueprint for a world organization at Dumbarton Oaks mansion near Washington.

Feb. 11, 1945 Roosevelt, Churchill and Stalin meet in Ukraine, resolving to establish "a general international organization to maintain peace and security."

June 25, 1945 United Nations Charter unanimously adopted by delegations of 50 nations in San Francisco.

Oct. 24, 1945 The five permanent members of the Security Council and a majority of other signers ratify Charter, creating the UN we know today.

Feb. 1, 1946 Trygve Lie of Norway becomes first secretary-general of United Nations.

Jan. 17, 1946 Security Council, in London, holds first meeting, establishing its procedural rules.

Jan. 24, 1946 General Assembly adopts first resolution, focused on peaceful uses of atomic energy and abolition of weapons of mass destruction.

Dec. 1946 United Nations International Children's Emergency Fund created to provide food, clothing and health care to children suffering famine and disease. Name is later changed to UN Children's Fund but acronym remains Unicef.

Dec. 10, 1948 General Assembly adopts Universal Declaration of Human Rights.

Aug. 21, 1950 Secretariat workers move into offices in the new headquarters complex in New York. Campus eventually comprises Secretariat, General Assembly, Conference Area and Library.

1954 Office of UN High Commissioner for Refugees wins first of two Nobel Peace Prizes, for European work.

Aug. 30, 1955 First United Nations Congress on the Prevention of Crime and the Treatment of Offenders adopts standard minimum rules for treatment of prisoners.

Nov. 7, 1956 General Assembly holds first emergency special session in Suez Canal crisis. Two days before, it established first UN peacekeeping force, called the UN Emergency Force.

Nov. 20, 1959 General Assembly adopts Declaration of the Rights of the Child.

Sept. 1960 Seventeen newly independent states, all but one in Africa, join UN. It marks biggest increase in membership in a single year.

Sept. 18, 1961 Secretary-General Dag Hammarskjold dies in plane crash on mission to the Congo. U Thant, Burmese diplomat, named to succeed him.

Dec. 21, 1965 General Assembly adopts International Covenant on Social, Economic and Cultural Rights along with counterpart, International Covenant and Civil and Political Rights.

Nov. 22, 1967 After Six-Day War in the Middle East, Security Council adopts Resolution 242, stipulating requirements for end of hostilities.

June 12, 1968 General Assembly approves Treaty on Nonproliferation of Nuclear Weapons.

Jan. 4, 1969 International Convention on the Elimination of All Forms of Racial Discrimination goes into effect.

Oct. 21, 1971 General Assembly admits representative from People's Republic of China, displacing Republic of China on Taiwan.

June 1972 First UN Environment Conference held in Stockholm, bringing establishment of the UN Environment Program.

Nov. 13, 1974 General Assembly recognizes Palestinian Liberation Organization as "the sole legitimate representative of the Palestinian people."

Nov. 5-16, 1974 UN conducts conference in Rome on food and agriculture, declaring freedom from hunger as a universal human right.

June-July 1975 UN holds first conference on women, in Mexico City, coinciding with International Women's Year.

May-June 1978 General Assembly holds first special session on disarmament.

May 8, 1980 World Health Organization declares smallpox eliminated.

1981 UN High Commissioner for Refugees receives second Nobel Peace Prize, this for work with Asians.

Nov. 25, 1981 General Assembly adopts Declaration on the Elimination of All Forms of Intolerance and Discrimination Based on Religion or Belief.

Dec. 10, 1982 A hundred and seventeen states and two entities sign UN Convention on the Law of the Sea, largest number of signatures affixed to a treaty in one day.

Dec. 10, 1984 Convention Against Torture and Other Cruel, Inhuman or Degrading Treatment or Punishment adopted by General Assembly.

Sept. 1987 Treaty on Protection of the Ozone Layer, also known as Montreal Protocol, signed.

1988 UN Peacekeeping receives Nobel Peace Prize.

Sept. 2, 1990 Convention on Rights of the Child enters into effect.

April 1991 UN Iraq-Kuwait Observation Mission established to carry out elimination of weapons of mass destruction in Iraq after the Gulf War.

Jan. 31, 1992 Leaders from all 15 members of the Security Council attend first Security Council Summit in New York. The meeting leads to Secretary-General Boutros Boutros-Ghali's report, "An Agenda for Peace."

June 1992 Rio de Janeiro is host to more than 100 countries at the UN Conference on Environment and Development, popularly known as the Earth Summit. Recognition of the importance of sustainable development is major outcome.

Feb. 22, 1993 Security Council establishes first international tribunal to examine human rights violations in the former Yugoslavia.

April 5, 1994 José Ayala-Lasso of Ecuador becomes first UN High Commissioner for Human Rights.

May 6, 1994 Secretary-General Boutros Boutros-Ghali issues Agenda for Development plan to improve human condition.

Nov. 8, 1994 Security Council establishes second international tribunal to investigate Rwandan genocide.

March 1995 World Summit for Social Development held in Copenhagen seeking new commitment to combat poverty, unemployment and social exclusion.

June 1996 Second UN Conference on Human Settlements convenes in Turkey.

Sept. 10, 1996 General Assembly adopts Comprehensive Test-Ban Treaty. It remains to be entered into force.

July 18, 1998 International Criminal Court is established by Rome Statute.

March 1, 1999 Ottawa Convention on antipersonnel mines enters into force.

Sept. 2000 General Assembly adopts Millennium Declaration starting the clock for eight Millennium Development Goals to reduce worldwide poverty by 2015.

Nov. 12, 2001 Security Council adopts Resolution 1377, eliminate "the scourge of international terrorism" in the aftermath of the Sept. 11 terrorist attacks in the US.

July 1, 2002 Rome Statue enters into force, and the International Criminal Court begins work.

Aug. 19, 2003 Twenty-two staff members and officials, including Ambassador Sergio Vieira de Mello, killed in a terrorist attack on UN headquarters in Iraq.

Jan. 27, 2006 Nearly 2,000 people gather in the General Assembly Hall for International Holocaust Remembrance Day.

Sept. 2005 Secretary General Kofi Annan presents his report, "In Larger Freedom: Toward Security, Development and Human Rights for All," to a special session of the General Assembly, where member states discuss significant reform of UN.

Feb. 27, 2006 The 50th session of the Commission on the Status of Women convenes to review the progress and chart new goals.

Jan. 1, 2007 Ban Ki-moon of South Korea succeeds Kofi Annan as the eighth Secretary-General.

Sept. 24, 2007 The Future in Our Hands, called to discuss leadership issues relating to climate change, brings together representatives of more than 150 member states.

Jan. 1, 2008 UN establishes Joint United Nations/African Union Mission in Darfur to assume responsibility for the war-torn region from the African Union. The peacekeeping operation was UN's largest.

May 30, 2008 A hundred and seven states adopt Convention on Cluster Munitions, first agreement to seek a ban on a particular class of weapons worldwide.

Dec. 10, 2008 A year of celebrations across the UN system culminates on the 60th anniversary of signing of the Universal Declaration of Human Rights, a key step in the founding of the United Nations and important in international law.

Sources:
www.unhchr.ch/chrono.htm
www.un.org/issues/gallery/history/index.html www.un.org/Overview/milesto4.htm
UNA-USA e-news updates

Appendix B: The United Nations System Today

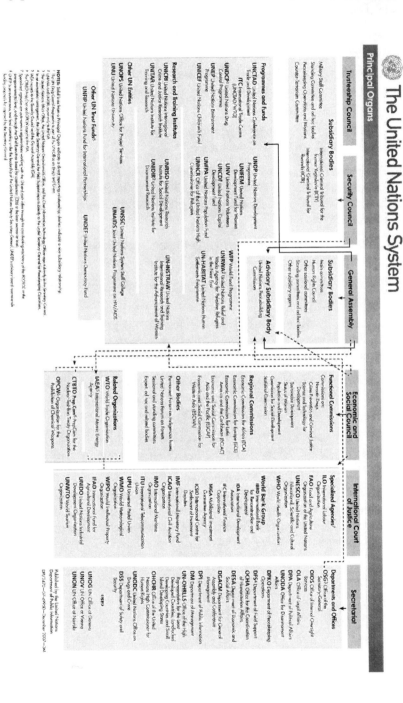

Appendix C: Composition of the Secretariat

Compiled by Max McGowen

These figures cover the period from July 1, 2007, to June 30, 2008, unless otherwise noted as a specific date.

39,503 is the worldwide total of staff members in the Secretariat. They are based as follows:

11,687 are at headquarters
2,564 at regional commissions
21,790 in peacekeeping missions
1,386 in other places in the field
2,076 in tribunals

As of June 30, 2008, they held posts at these levels:

Total, under-secretaries-general and assistant secretaries-general	124 (0.3%)
Total, director category	559 (1.4%)
Total, professional category	10,459 (26.5%)
Total, general category	28,361 (71.8%)

As of June 30, 2008, the distribution in posts was:

Post Level	Quantity in Post
Professional 1/2	1,363
P-3	3,190
P-4	2,762
P-5	1,281
Director 1	428
D-2	131
assistant secretaries-general	56
under-secretaries-general	68

The total in "professional or higher categories" is 9,279, which accounts for 28.2% of Secretariat personnel. The 71.8% remaining of the staff come under "General Service and related categories"

Geographical distribution, 2004-2008

Posts in nonlinguist, professional and senior categories financed by the regular budget are subject to requirements of geographical distribution. The formula reflects a country's membership, assessment rate and population.

Category of member states	June 2004	June 2008
Unrepresented	15	16
Underrepresented	10	24
Within range	145	131
Overrepresented	21	21

Source:
UN Resolution A/63/310 www.un.org/ga/fifth/63/aai/123.shtml

Appendix D: Operations & Budgets

Compiled by Max McGowen

TABLE 1: REGULAR BUDGET APPROPRIATIONS FOR 2008-2009

(estimated*, in US$ millions; extrabudgetary appropriations not included in total)

Expenditures:

Part I: Overall Policy Making, Direction and Coordination

1. Overall policy making, direction and coordination
Initial appropriation for 2006-07: **77.0**
Increase/(decrease): **.4**
2008-09 estimate: **77.4**
(Extrabudgetary appropriation, 2008-09 estimate: **31.5**)
Total: $77.4 million

2. General Assembly affairs and conference services
Initial appropriation for 2006-07: **602.5**
Increase/(decrease): **18.3**
2008-09 estimate: **620.8**
(Extrabudgetary appropriation, 2008-09 estimate: **24.2**)
Total: $620.8 million

Part II: Political Affairs

3. Political affairs
Initial appropriation for 2006-07: **686.9**
Increase/(decrease): **10.1**
2008-09 estimate: **697.0**
(Extrabudgetary appropriation, 2008-09 estimate: **6.7**)
Total: $697 million

4. Disarmament
Initial appropriation for 2006-07: **20.5**
Increase/(decrease): **1.2**
2008-09 estimate: **21.7**
(Extrabudgetary appropriation, 2008-09 estimate: **10.0**)
Total: $21.7 million

5. Peacekeeping operations
Initial appropriation for 2006-07: **96.7**
Increase/(decrease): **4.8**
2008-09 estimate: **101.5**
(Extrabudgetary appropriation, 2008-09 estimate: **484.9**)
Total: $101.5 million

6. Peaceful uses of outer space:

Initial appropriation for 2006-07: **6.2**
Increase/(decrease): **0.4**
2008-09 estimate: **6.6**
(Extrabudgetary appropriation, 2008-09 estimate: **0.7**)
Total: $6.6 million

Part III: International Justice and Law

7. International Court of Justice

Initial appropriation for 2006-07: **36.8**
Increase/(decrease): **3.4**
2008-09 estimate: **40.2**
(Extrabudgetary appropriation: **none**)
Total: $40.2 million

8. Legal affairs

Initial appropriation for 2006-07: **42.2**
Increase/(decrease): **2.6**
2008-09 estimate: **44.8**
(Extrabudgetary appropriation, 2008-09 estimate: **11.9**)
Total: $44.8 million

Part IV: International Cooperation for Development

9. Economic and social affairs

Initial appropriation for 2006-07: **154.9**
Increase/(decrease): **7.5**
2008-09 estimate: **162.4**
(Extrabudgetary appropriation, 2008-09 estimate: **122.5**)
Total: $162.4 million

10. Least-developed countries, landlocked developing countries and small island developing states

Initial appropriation for 2006-07: **5.1**
Increase/(decrease): **0.5**
2008-09 estimate: **5.6**
(Extrabudgetary appropriation, 2008-09 estimate: **1.1**)
Total: $5.6 million

11. UN support to the New Partnership for Africa's Development

Initial appropriation for 2006-07: **10.8**
Increase/(decrease): **0.4**
2008-09 estimate: **11.2**
(Extrabudgetary appropriation, 2008-09 estimate: **0.5**)
Total: $11.2 million

12. Trade and development
Initial appropriation for 2006-07: **117.2**
Increase/(decrease): **5.2**
2008-09 estimate: **122.4**
(Extrabudgetary appropriation, 2008-09 estimate: **61.4**)
Total: $122.4 million

13. International Trade Center, UNCTAD/WTO
Initial appropriation for 2006-07: **26.9**
Increase/(decrease): **0.1**
2008-09 estimate: **27.0**
(Extrabudgetary appropriation, 2008-09 estimate: **none**)
Total: $27 million

14. Environment
Initial appropriation for 2006-07: **12.3**
Increase/(decrease): **1.4**
2008-09 estimate: **13.7**
(Extrabudgetary appropriation, 2008-09 estimate: **277.1**)
Total: $13.7 million

15. Human Settlements
Initial appropriation for 2006-07: **18.3**
Increase/(decrease): **2.1**
2008-09 estimate: **20.4**
(Extrabudgetary appropriation, 2008-09 estimate: **242.1**)
Total: $20.4 million

16. International drug control, crime and terrorism prevention and criminal justice
Initial appropriation for 2006-07: **32.8**
Increase/(decrease): **2.7**
2008-09 estimate: **35.5**
(Extrabudgetary appropriation, 2008-09 estimate: **290.2**)
Total: $35.5 million

Part V: Regional cooperation for development

17. Economic and social development in Africa
Initial appropriation for 2006-07: **105.7**
Increase/(decrease): **12.3**
2008-09 estimate: **118.0**
(Extrabudgetary appropriation, 2008-09 estimate: **72.7**)
Total: $118 million

18. Economic and social development in Asia and the Pacific
Initial appropriation for 2006-07: **74.7**
Increase/(decrease): **6.5**
2008-09 estimate: **81.2**
(Extrabudgetary appropriation, 2008-09 estimate: **27.1**)
Total: $81.2 million

19. Economic and social development in Europe
Initial appropriation for 2006-07: **57.1**
Increase/(decrease): **2.5**
2008-09 estimate: **59.6**
(Extrabudgetary appropriation, 2008-09 estimate: **23.7**)
Total: $59.6 million

20. Economic and social development in Latin America and the Caribbean
Initial appropriation for 2006-07: **97.2**
Increase/(decrease): **6.3**
2008-09 estimate: **103.5**
(Extrabudgetary appropriation, 2008-09 estimate: **19.1**)
Total: $103.5 million

21. Economic and social development in Western Asia
Initial appropriation for 2006-07: 56.3
Increase/(decrease): **3.5**
2008-09 estimate: **59.8**
(Extrabudgetary appropriation, 2008-09 estimate: **9.0**)
Total: $59.8 million

22. Regular program of technical cooperation
Initial appropriation for 2006-07: **46.9**
Increase/(decrease): **3.4**
2008-09 estimate: **50.3**
(Extrabudgetary appropriation: **none**)
Total: $50.3 million

Part VI: Human rights and humanitarian affairs

23. Human rights
Initial appropriation for 2006-07: **90.6**
Increase/(decrease): **22.2**
2008-09 estimate: **112.8**
(Extrabudgetary appropriation, 2008-09 estimate: **196.5**)
Total: $112.8 million

24. Protection of and assistance to refugees
Initial appropriation for 2006-07: **67.0**
Increase/(decrease): **4.5**
2008-09 estimate: **71.5**
(Extrabudgetary appropriation, 2008-09 estimate: **2,765.0**)
Total: $71.5 million

25. Palestine refugees

Initial appropriation for 2006-07: **36.7**
Increase/(decrease): **2.7**
2008-09 estimate: **39.4**
(Extrabudgetary appropriation, 2008-09 estimate: **1,198.8**)
Total: $39.4 million

26. Humanitarian assistance

Initial appropriation for 2006-07: **26.6**
Increase/(decrease): **2.3**
2008-09 estimate: **28.9**
(Extrabudgetary appropriation, 2008-09 estimate: **368.9**)
Total: $28.9 million

Part VII: Public Information

27. Public information:

Initial appropriation for 2006-07: **178.9**
Increase/(decrease): **11.1**
2008-09 estimate: **190.0**
(Extrabudgetary appropriation, 2008-09 estimate: **7.1**)
Total: $190 million

Part VIII: Common support services

28. Management and central support services

Initial appropriation for 2006-07: **528.0**
Increase/(decrease): **42.1**
2008-09 estimate: **570.1**
(Extrabudgetary appropriation, 2008-09 estimate: **257.0**)
Total: $570.1 million

Part IX: Internal oversight

29. Internal oversight

Initial appropriation for 2006-07: **31.5**
Increase/(decrease): **9.5**
2008-09 estimate: **41.0**
(Extrabudgetary appropriation, 2008-09 estimate: **63.9**)
Total: $41 million

Part X: Jointly financed administrative activities and special expenses

30. Jointly financed administrative activities

UN's share of costs:
Initial appropriation for 2006-07: **7.8**
Increase/(decrease): **4.1**
2008-09 estimate: **11.9**

Other non-UN costs:
> Initial appropriation for 2006-07: **32.4**
> Increase/(decrease): **2.7**
> 2008-09 estimate: **35.1**

31. Special expenses
> Initial appropriation for 2006-07: **93.5**
> Increase/(decrease): **6.9**
> 2008-09 estimate: **100.4**
> (Extrabudgetary appropriation, 2008-09 estimate: **19.2**)
> **Total: $147.4 million**

Part XI: Jointly financed administrative activities and special expenses

32. Construction, alteration, improvement and major maintenance
> Initial appropriation for 2006-07: **78.5**
> Increase/(decrease): **(19.6)**
> 2008-09 estimate: **58.9**
> (Extrabudgetary appropriation, 2008-09 estimate: **none**)
> **Total: $58.9 million**

Part XII: Jointly financed administrative activities and special expenses

33. Safety and security
> Initial appropriation for 2006-07: **367.8**
> Increase/(decrease): **20.4**
> 2008-09 estimate: **388.2**
> (Extrabudgetary appropriation, 2008-09 estimate: **12.2**)
> **Total: $388.2 million**

Part XIII: Jointly financed administrative activities and special expenses

34. Development account
> Initial appropriation for 2006-07: **16.5**
> Increase/(decrease): **0.0**
> 2008-09 estimate: **16.5**
> **Total: $16.5 million**

Part XIV: Jointly financed administrative activities and special expenses

35. Staff assessment
> Initial appropriation for 2006-07: **436.3**
> Increase/(decrease): **25.5**
> 2008-09 estimate: **461.8**
> **Total: $461.8 million**

Total 2007-08 appropriation: $4.344 billion

Total increase: $227.3 million

Total 2008-09 Projected Expenditures: $4.572 billion
(excluding extrabudgetary appropriations)

Estimates of income

1.Income from staff assessment
Data not available

2.General income
2007-08 estimate: **41.6**

2008-09 estimate: **47.9**

Increase/(decrease): **6.3**

3.Services to the public
2007-08 estimate: **3.9**

2008-09 estimate: **1.1**

Increase/(decrease): **(2.8)**

Total income: $49 million

Sources: UN Resolution A/62/6, "Estimates of Expenditure," Sections 1-35,
"Estimates of Income," Sections 1-3 www.un.org/ga/61/fifth/ppb89sg.htm

TABLE 2: PEACEKEEPING OPERATIONS APPROPRIATIONS 2006-07 / APPROPRIATIONS 2007-08 / APPROPRIATIONS 2008-09
(figures from the Dept. of Peacekeeping Operations Web site)

Figures in US$ millions

UN Mission for the Referendum in Western Sahara (MINURSO)
7/1/06 – 6/30/07: **45.9**

7/1/07 – 6/30/08: **47.6**

08-09: **47.7**

UN Stabilization Mission in Haiti (MINUSTAH)
06-07: **489.2**

07-08: **535.4**

08-09: **601.6**

UN Organization Mission in the Democratic Republic of the Congo (MONUC)
06-07: **1,094.2**

07-08: **1,115.7**

08-09: **1,242.7**

UN Operation in Burundi (ONUB)
06-07: **128.5**

07-08: -

UN Mission in Sierra Leone (UNAMSIL)
06-07: -

07-08: -

African Union-United Nations Hybrid Operations in Darfur (UNAMID)
06-07: -

07-08: **1,264.3**

08-09: **1,569.3**

UN Disengagement Observer Force (UNDOF)
06-07: **39.9**
07-08: **39.7**
08-09: **47.9**

UN Peacekeeping Force in Cyprus (UNFICYP)
06-07: **46.3**
07-08: **48.1**
08-09: **57.4**

UN Interim Force in Lebanon (UNIFIL)
06-07: **350.9**
07-08: **713.6**
08-09: **680.9**

UN Mission in Ethiopia and Eritrea (UNMEE)
06-07: **137.4**
07-08: **113.5**

UN Interim Administration Mission in Kosovo (UNMIK)
06-07: **218.0**
07-08: **210.7**
08-09: **207.2**

UN Mission in Liberia (UNMIL)
06-07: **714.9**
07-08: **688.4**
08-09: **631.7**

UN Mission in the Sudan (UNMIS)
06-07: **1,079.5**
07-08: **846.3**
08-09: **858.8**

UN Mission of Support in East Timor (UNMISET)
06-07: -
07-08: -

UN Integrated Mission in Timor-Leste (UNMIT)
06-07: **170.2**
07-08: **153.2**
08-09: **180.8**

UN Operation in Cote d'Ivoire (UNOCI)
06-07: **472.9**
07-08: **470.9**
08-09: **497.5**

UN Observer Mission in Georgia (UNOMIG)
06-07: **33.4**
07-08: **35.0**
08-09: **36.1**

UN Mission in the Central African Republic and Chad (MINURCAT)
08-09: **315.1**

Subtotal of missions:
06-07: **5,021.2**
07-08: **6,475.9**
08-09: **to be determined**

UN Logistics Base at Brindisi (UNLB)
06-07: **35.5**
07-08: **40.4**

Support account:
06-07: **189.0**
07-08: **230.5**

TOTAL:

06-07: **5,245.7**
07-08: **6,746.8**

*Figures come from the 61st session of the General Assembly, the last date for which comprehensive numbers are available. The 2008-09 are estimates; updates to the actual figures have been made. Part IV, Section 13 comes from a resolution in the 62nd session of the General Assembly – this figure was not available in resolutions of previous sessions.

Figures also do not reflect a General Assembly approved increase of nearly 17 percent in the current UN budget for the 2008/2009 period.

Sources:

06-07 appropriations: UN Resolution A/C.5/61/18
daccessdds.un.org/doc/UNDOC/GEN/N07/209/37/PDF/N0720937.pdf?OpenElement

07-08 appropriations: UN Resolution A/C.5/62/63
daccessdds.un.org/doc/UNDOC/GEN/N08/223/16/PDF/N0822316.pdf?OpenElement < 07-08 appropriations

08-09 appropriations:
www.un.org/Depts/dpko/dpko/bnote.htm

www.un.org/ga/61/fifth/hr.htm
www.un.org/Depts/dpko/dpko/contributors/financing.html

TABLE 3: INTERNATIONAL WAR CRIMES TRIBUNALS APPROPRIATIONS
(in US$ millions)

International Criminal Tribunal for Rwanda
Initial appropriation for 2006-07: **246.9 million**
Increase: **7.9 million**
Revised appropriation for 2006-07: **254.8 million**
Increase: **27.8 million**
Appropriation for 2008-09: 282.6 million

Source: UN Resolution A/Res/61/241
http:// daccessdds.un.org/doc/UNDOC/GEN/N06/508/83/PDF/N0650883.pdf?OpenElement
2008-09 source: http://www.un.org/News/Press/docs//2008/ga10804.doc.htm

International Tribunal for former Yugoslavia
Initial appropriation for 2006-07: **278.6 million**
Increase: **18.6 million**
Revised appropriation for 2006-07: **297.1 million**
Increase: **45.2 million**
Appropriation for 2008-09: 342.3 million

Source: UN Resolution A/Res/61/242
http:// daccessdds.un.org/doc/UNDOC/GEN/N06/508/89/PDF/N0650889.pdf?OpenElement
2008 09 source: http://www.un.org/News/Press/docs//2008/ga10804.doc.htm

The Special Court for Sierra Leone
(Financed by voluntary contributions)
Projected budget: **104 million (from 2002 to the end of 2006)**,
annual budget: **~25 million**

Source: "The Special Court for Sierra Leone Under Scrutiny," Tom Perriello, Marieka Wierda,
`International Center for Transitional Justice

Total budget: $89 million (approximately)
(In June 2007, the court appealed for an additional 60 million)

"The SCSL will exhaust its current funding by approximately November 2007 and still needs $89 million to conclude its operations – $36 million for 2007, $33 million for 2008, and $20 million for 2009."

Source: http://www.un.org/News/Press/docs/2007/sc9037.doc.htm

Source: "Special Court of Sierra Leone Briefing: The Taylor Trial and Lessons from Capacity-Building Outreach," Scott Worden and Emily Wann, US Institute of Peace

http://www.usip.org/pubs/usipeace_briefings/2007/0821_special_court.html

Extraordinary Chambers in the Courts of Cambodia:
Original estimate of pledges: **13.3 million**
New funds requirement from Cambodian component: **5.8 million**
Revised estimate for the budget contribution: **18.7 million**

Original estimate of pledges: **43.0 million**
New funds requirement from UN: **38.3 million (increase)**
Revised estimate for the budget contribution: **78.7 million**

Source: http://www.unakrt-online.org/Docs/Other/2005-2009%20ECCC%20Approved%20Budget.pdf, Revised Budget Estimates 2005-09, UNAKRT Online (UN Assistance to the Khmer Rouge Trials)

Total requirement (shortfall)of new funds from Cambodia and UN : 44.1 million

TABLE 4: PERCENT OF BUDGET CONTRIBUTIONS BY MEMBER STATE (as assessed by UN)

Member State	Regular Budget for 09 (by %)	DPKO 08/09 (by %)
US*	22.0000	26.2240
Japan	16.624	16.624
Germany	8.577	8.577
Britain*	6.642	7.9173
France*	6.301	7.5108
Canada	2.977	2.977
Spain	2.968	2.968
China*	2.667	3.2375
Mexico	2.257	2.257
Republic of Korea	2.173	2.173

* Security Council members

Source for top 10 list: http://www.un.org/ga/president/60/summitfollowup/060202sgb.pdf

Regular budget source: UN Resolution A/Res/61/237
http://daccessdds.un.org/doc/UNDOC/GEN/N06/508/59/PDF/N0650859.pdf?OpenElement

Peacekeeping source: UN Resolution A/61/139
http://daccessdds.un.org/doc/UNDOC/GEN/N06/430/08/PDF/N0643008.pdf?OpenElement

http://daccessdds.un.org/doc/UNDOC/GEN/N06/508/83/PDF/N0650883.pdf?OpenElement

http://www.un.org/Depts/dpko/factsheet.pdf

TABLE 5: TOP MEMBER STATE ARREARS TO THE UN ($US MILLIONS) AS OF MAY 31, 2008*

	Regular Budget	Tribunals	DPKO	Total
United States	846.0	52.7	486.3	1,385.0
Japan	210.7	48.0	374.7	633.4
Britain	-	-	12.5	12.5
Germany	78.4	-	-	78.4
Italy	-	-	0.6	0.6
France	-	-	11.7	11.7
Canada	-	-	4.7	4.7
China	24.8	8.9	133.8	167.5
Netherlands	-	-	6.6	6.6
Russian Federation	-	-	20.1	20.1

Source: UN Resolution ST/ADM/SER.B/733

http://www.un.org/ga/search/view_doc.asp?symbol=ST/ADM/SER.B/733

*Figures were calculated from the debts owed toward missions outlined in Table 2 and UN Logistics Base but not political/peacekeeping missions. Debts toward the peacekeeping support account are not included.

Top 10 Member States Contributions to the UN regular budget for the year 2009

(Millions of US$)

United States	598.3
Japan	405.0
Britain	161.8
Germany	209.0
Italy	123.7
France	153.5
Canada	72.5
China	65.0
Netherlands	45.6
Russian Federation	29.2

UN Resolution ST/ADM/SER.B/755
Source: http://www.un.org/ga/search/view_doc.asp?symbol=ST/ADM/SER.B/755

Appendix E: Acronyms and Abbreviations

Compiled by Arnav Chakravarty

ACABQ Advisory Committee on Administrative and Budgetary Questions

ACC Administrative Committee on Coordination

ACPR Advisory Committee of Permanent Representatives

ADB Asian Development Bank

ADN European Agreement Concerning the International Carriage of Dangerous Goods by Inland Waterways

ADR European Agreement Concerning the International Carriage of Dangerous Goods by Road

AFDB African Development Bank

ALADI Asociación Latino Americana de Integración

AMAP Arctic Monitoring and Assessment Programme

AMIS African Union-led Mission in the Sudan

APCAEM Asian and Pacific Centre for Agricultural Engineering and Machinery

APCC Asian and Pacific Coconut Community

APCICT Asian and Pacific Training Center for Information and Communications Technology for Development

APCTT Asian and Pacific Center for Transfer of Technology

APEC Asia-Pacific Economic Cooperation

APO Asian Productivity Organization

ASEAN Association of South East Asian Nations

AU African Union

BCEAO Central Bank of West African States

BCIE Central American Bank for Economic Integration

BINUBUN Integrated Office in Burundi

BIPM International Bureau of Weights and Measures

BIS Bank for International Settlements

BONUCA UN Peacebuilding Office in the Central African Republic

CAAC Working Group on Children and Armed Conflict

CABI CAB International

CAPSA Centre for Alleviation of Poverty through Secondary Crops Development in Asia and the Pacific

CARICOM Caribbean Community and Common Market

CAT Committee Against Torture

CBD Convention on Biological Diversity

CBF Committee on Budget and Finance

CBSS Council of the Baltic States

CCAMLR Commission for the Conservation of Antartic Living Marine Resources

CCE Committee on Central American Economic Cooperation

CCPCJ Commission on Crime Prevention and Criminal Justice

CD Conference on Disarmament

CDB Caribbean Development Bank

CDCC Caribbean Development and Cooperation Committee

CEBUN System's Chief Executives Board for Coordination

CEC Commission for Environmental Cooperation (North America)

CEDAW Convention on the Elimination of All Forms of Discrimination Against Women

CEGAN Committee of High-Level Government Experts

CERD Committee on the Elimination of Racial Discrimination

CERN European Organization for Nuclear Research

CESCR Committee on Economic, Social and Cultural Rights

CFA Committee on Food Aid Policies and Programmes

CFF Compensatory Financing Facility

CGAP Consultative Group to Assist the Poorest

CGIAR Consultative Group on International Agricultural Research

CHR Commission on Human Rights

CIRDAP Center on Integrated Rural Development for Asia and the Pacific

CIS Commonwealth of Independent States

CITES Convention on International Trade in Endangered Species of Wild Fauna and Flora

CMS Convention on the Conservation of Migratory Species of Wild Animals

CMW Committee on the Protection of the Rights of All Migrant Workers and Members of their Families

CND Commission on Narcotic Drugs

CNGO Committee on Nongovernmental Organizations

COE Council of Europe

COMESA Common Market for Eastern and Southern Africa

COPUOS Committee on the Peaceful Uses of Outer Space

CPA Comprehensive Peace Agreement

CPC Committee for Program and Coordination

CPF Collaborative Partnership on Forests

CPLP Community of Portuguese Speaking Nations

CPR Committee of Permanent Representatives

CRC Committee on the Rights of the Child

CRIC Committee for the Review of the Implementation of the Convention (to Combat Desertification in Countries Experiencing Serious Drought and/or Desertification. especially in Africa)

CSD Commission on Sustainable Development

CSocD Commission for Social Development

CST Committee on Science and Technology

CSTD Commission on Science and Technology for Development

CSW Commission on the Status of Women

CTBTO Comprehensive Nuclear Test Ban Treaty Organization

CTC Counter-Terrorism Committee

CTED Counter-Terrorism Committee Executive Directorate

CWC Convention on the Prohibition of the Development, Production, Stockpiling and Use of Chemical Weapons

DESA Department of Economic and Social Affairs

DFS Department of Field Support

DGACM Department for General Assembly and Conference Management

DM Department of Management

DPA Department of Political Affairs

DPI Department of Public Information

DPKO Department of Peacekeeping Operations

DRC Democratic Republic of the Congo

DSS Department of Safety and Security

EBRD European Bank for Reconstruction and Development

ECA Economic Commission for Africa

ECB European Central Bank

ECE Economic Commission for Europe

ECHR European Court of Human Rights

ECLAC Economic Commission for Latin America and the Caribbean

ECOWAS Economic Community of West African States

EFTA European Free Trade Association

EPO European Patent Office

EPTA Expanded Program of Technical Assistance (UN)

ESCAP Economic and Social Commission for Asia and the Pacific

ESCWA Economic and Social Commission for Western Asia

EU European Union

EUTELSAT European Telecommunications Satellite Organization

FAO Food and Agriculture Organization of the United Nations

GATT General Agreement on Tariffs and Trade

GEF Global Environment Facility

GHS Globally Harmonized System of Classification and Labeling of Chemicals

HELCOM Helsinki Commission- Baltic Marine Environment Protection Commission

HIPCs Heavily Indebted Poor Countries

HLCM High Level Committee on Management

HLCP High Level Committee on Programs

HONLEA Heads of National Drug Law Enforcement Agencies

HRC Human Rights Campaign

IADB Inter-American Development Bank

IAEA International Atomic Energy Agency

IATTC Inter-American Tropical Tuna Commission

IBE International Bureau of Education

IBRD International Bank for Reconstruction and Development

IBSFC International Baltic Sea Fishery Commission

ICAO International Civil Aviation Organization

ICCAT International Commission for the Conservation of Atlantic Tunas

ICCROM International Center for the Study of the Preservation and Restoration of Cultural Property

ICES International Council for the Exploration of the Sea

ICO International Coffee Organization

ICOM International Council of Museums

ICOMOS International Council on Monuments and Sites

ICSG International Copper Study Group

ICSID International Center for Settlement of Investment Disputes

ICC International Criminal Court

ICTR International Criminal Tribunal for Rwanda

ICTY International Criminal Tribunal for the former Yugoslavia

IDA International Development Association

IDC International Data Center

IEFR International Emergency Food Reserve

IFAD International Fund for Agricultural Development

IFC International Finance Corporation

IGCP International Geoscience Program

IHO International Hydrographic Organization

IIC InterAmerican Investment Corporation

ILO International Labor Organization

ILPES Latin American and Caribbean Institute for Economic and Social Planning

IMF International Monetary Fund

IMFC International Monetary and Financial Committee

IMO International Maritime Organization

INCB International Narcotics Control Board

INDES Inter-American Institute for Social Development

INSTRAW International Research and Training Institute for the Advancement of Women

INTAL Institute for the Integration of Latin America and the Caribbean

INTERPOL International Criminal Police Organization

IOM International Organization for Migration

IOTC Indian Ocean Tuna Commission

IPCC Intergovernmental Panel on Climate Change

IPHC International Pacific Halibut Commission

ISA International Seabed Authority

ISDB Islamic Development Bank

ITC International Trade Center

ITU International Telecommunication Union

IWC International Whaling Commission

JAG Joint Advisory Group (of the ITC)

JIU Joint Inspection Unit

LDCs Least Developed Countries

MAB International Coordinating Council of the Program on Man and the Biosphere

MAC Military Armistice Commission

MDGs Millennium Development Goals

MIF Multilateral Investment Fund

MIF Multinational Interim Force (Haiti)

MIGA Multilateral Investment Guarantee Agency

MINURCAT United Nations Mission in the Central African Republic and Chad

MINURSO United Nations Mission for the Referendum in Western Sahara

MINUSTAH United Nations Stabilization Mission in Haiti

MONUC United Nations Organization Mission in the Democratic Republic of the Congo

NAALC Commission for Labor Cooperation (North America)

NEPAD New Partnership for Africa's Development

NPT Nuclear Non-Proliferation Treaty

OAU Organization of African Unity

OCHA Office for the Coordination of Humanitarian Affairs

ODA Office for Disarmament Affairs

OECD Organization for Economic Cooperation and Development

OHCHR Office of the UN High Commissioner for Human Rights

OIOS Office of Internal Oversight Services

OLA Office of Legal Affairs

ONUB United Nations Operation in Burundi

OPCW Organization for the Prohibition of Chemical Weapons

OPEC Organization of Petroleum Exporting Countries

OSG Office of the Secretary-General

PBC Peacebuilding Commission

POC Postal Operations Council

SBC Secretariat of the Basel Convention on the Control of Transboundary Movements of Hazardous Wastes and their Disposal

SBSTTA Subsidiary Body on Scientific, Technical and Technological Advice

SDRs Special Drawing Rights (IMF and Asian Development Bank)

SIAP Statistical Institute for Asia and the Pacific

STAP Scientific and Technical Advisory Panel

STRP Scientific and Technical Review Panel

TDB Trade and Development Board (of UNCTAD)

TSAG Telecommunication Standardization Bureau

UNAIDS Joint UN Program on HIV/AIDS

UNAMI UN Assistance Mission for Iraq

UNAMID UN/African Union Hybrid Operation in Darfur

UNAMIS UN Advance Mission in Sudan

UNAMSIL UN Assistance Mission in Sierra Leone

UNAT UN Administrative Tribunal

UNC UN Command-Korea

UNCC UN Compensation Commission

UNCCD UN Convention to Combat Desertification

UNCDF UN Capital Development Fund

UNCIP UN Commission for India and Pakistan

UNCITRAL UN Commission on International Trade Law

UNCLOS UN Convention on the Law of the Sea

UNCTAD UN Conference on Trade and Development

UNDC UN Disarmament Commission

UNDCP UN International Drug Control Program

UNDEF UN Democracy Fund

UNDG UN Development Group

UNDOF UN Disengagement Observer Force

UNDP UN Development Program

UNECE UN Economic Commission for Europe

UNEP UN Environment Program

UNESCO UN Educational, Scientific and Cultural Organization

UNFCCC UN Framework Convention on Climate Change

UNFF UN Forum on Forests

UNFICYP UN Peacekeeping Force in Cyprus

UNFIP UN Fund for International Partnerships

UNFPA UN Population Fund

UNGEGN UN Group of Experts on Geographical Names

UN-HABITAT UN Human Settlements Program

UNHCR UN High Commissioner for Refugees

UNICEF UN Children's Fund

UNICRI UN Interregional Crime and Justice Research Institute

UNIDIR UN Institute for Disarmament Research

UNIDO UN Industrial Development Organization

UNIDROIT International Institute for the Unification of Private Law

UNIFEM UN Development Fund for Women

UNIFIL UN Interim Force in Lebanon

UNIOSIL UN Integrated Office in Sierra Leone

UNIPOM UN India-Pakistan Observation Mission

UNITAR UN Institute for Training and Research

UNMEE UN Mission in Ethiopia and Eritrea

UNMIK UN Interim Administration Mission in Kosovo

UNMIL UN Mission in Liberia

UNMIN UN Mission in Nepal

UNMIS UN Mission in Sudan

UNMIT UN Integrated Mission in Timor-Leste

UNMOGIP UN Military Observer Group in India and Pakistan

UNMOT UN Mission of Observers in Tajikistan

UNMOVIC UN Monitoring, Verification and Inspection Commission

UNOCI UN Operation in Côte d'Ivoire

UNODA UN Office for Disarmament Affairs

UNODC UN Office on Drugs and Crime

UNOG UN Office at Geneva

UNOGBIS UN Peacebuilding Support Office in Guinea-Bissau

UNOHRLLS Office of the High Representative for the Least Developed Countries, Landlocked Developing Countries, and Small Island Developing States

UNOL UN Peacebuilding Support Office in Liberia

UNOMIG UN Observer Mission in Georgia

UNON UN Office at Nairobi

UNOPS UN Office for Project Services

UNOSAT UN Institute for Training and Research (UNITAR) Operational Satellite Applications Program

UNOTIL UN Office in Timor-Leste

UNOV UN Office at Vienna

UNPOS UN Political Office for Somalia

UNRISD UN Research Institute for Social Development

UNRISD UN Research Institute for Social Development

UNRWA UN Relief and Works Agency for Palestine Refugees in the Near East

UNSCEAR UN Scientific Committee on the Effects of Atomic Radiation

UNSCO Office of the United Nations Special Coordinator for the Middle East Peace Process

UNSCOM UN Special Commission (Iraq)

UNSDRI UN Social Defense Research Institute

UNSMA UN Special Mission to Afghanistan

UNSSC UN Systems Staff College

UNTOP UN Tajikistan Office of Peacebuilding

UNTSO UN Truce Supervision Organization

UNU UN University

UNV UN Volunteers

UNWTO World Tourism Organization

UPOV International Union for the Protection of New Varieties of Plants

UPU Universal Postal Union

WEOG Western European and Others Group

WHC World Heritage Committee

WHO World Health Organization

WFP World Food Programme

WIPO World Intellectual Property Organization

WMDs Weapons of Mass Destruction

WMO World Meterological Organization

WSIS World Summit on the Information Society

WSSD World Summit on Sustainable Development

WTO World Trade Organization

Appendix F: Glossary

Compiled by Christopher J. Tangney

absolutism A theory of government vesting unrestrained power in a person, a dynasty, a party or an administration.

acclamation An overwhelmingly affirmative vote. If no opposition is indicated, an item of business is declared adopted "by acclamation."

accord A diplomatic agreement that stipulates action on the part of the signers. It does not have the force of a treaty but is often treated similarly (e.g., the Camp David Accords signed by Israel and Egypt in 1978).

act of state The actions of a government for which no individual can be held accountable.

ad hoc Latin phrase meaning "to this." For a specific or temporary purpose. An ad hoc committee is not a standing committee.

ad litem Latin phrase meaning "for the litigation."

aegis Greek for a "shield," thus a power or influence that organizes, protects or shields. Nations join in peacekeeping under the aegis of the United Nations.

African Development Bank Established in 1964, it provides loans for and invests in its African member states, offers technical assistance for development, promotes investment for development and helps coordinate regional policies and plans. Its members, or shareholders, consist of 53 African countries and 14 non-African countries.

African Union Created in July 2002 to replace the Organization of African Unity. Promotes democracy, human rights and development across the continent and works to increase foreign investment through the New Partnership for Africa's Development.

aggression An act of force; a belligerent action by one state against another.

allegiance Loyalty to a principle, leader or country.

alliance A union of powers or countries created to undertake joint action.

ambassador The highest ranking diplomat who can be sent by one government to another or to an international organization.

amicus or amici curiae In Latin, "friend or friends of the court." Someone who is not party to a legal proceeding. Often identified as "third parties."

amnesty A pardon given by a government to a group or class of people, usually for political reasons.

anarchy Absence of government; a state of lawlessness or political disorder.

annexation An act in which a country proclaims sovereignty over territory beyond its domain. Unlike secession, whereby territory is given or sold by a treaty, annexation is a unilateral act made effective by actual possession and legitimized by general recognition.

appeasement The policy of giving in to the demands of another.

Arab League Established on March 22, 1945. Formed to consider cultural cooperation among the Arab states. Its headquarters are in Cairo.

arbitration A way to settle disputes outside ordinary court procedures by giving an agreed-upon third party authority to make a legally binding decision.

area of operation The portion of an arena of conflict necessary for the conduct of a peacekeeping operation.

area of separation The area between the forces of parties in a conflict where they have agreed not to deploy troops. Sometimes called a demilitarized zone.

aristocracy Government by a small privileged class; power is vested in a minority considered to be those best qualified.

arrears The unpaid portion of an assessment for a given financial period.

appropriations Funds set aside for a specific use.

assessment The amount a member state must pay toward the expenses of the UN in a financial period, as specified in the relevant budget adopted by the General Assembly.

asylum Protection granted by a country to the citizen of another (usually a political refugee).

atrocities Acts of unusual cruelty or brutality, usually inflicted on large groups of defenseless people.

authoritarianism A system of government with a concentration of power in a leader or small elite not constitutionally responsible to the people.

autonomy The right of self-government.

back-channel diplomacy Secret lines of communication, often through an informal intermediary.

barter system The exchange of goods or services without use of money or other medium of exchange, either based on established rates of exchange or bargaining.

Beijing Declaration An international agreement signed at the Fourth World Conference on Women in Beijing in 1995 affirming the equal rights of men and women and calling upon nations to promote gender equality and the empowerment of women.

bilateral A two-way agreement or exchange.

biological warfare Use of disease-producing agents, like bacteria and viruses, on humans, animals or plants.

bloc An informal grouping of countries.

blockade A maneuver to prevent ships or other carriers from getting goods into a port or region.

Bonn Agreement An agreement on Dec. 5, 2001, creating an interim administration to lead Afghanistan for two years until a representative government could be elected. Elections were held in October 2004.

breach A failure to observe agreed-upon terms; a break or interruption in friendly relations.

Bretton Woods institutions Financial bodies, including the World Bank and International Monetary Fund, which were set up at a meeting of 43 countries in Bretton Woods, N.H., in July 1944 to help rebuild postwar economies and promote economic cooperation.

buffer zone Also known as an area of separation, a neutral space between hostile parties; as a demilitarized zone, an area in which the parties have agreed not to deploy military forces.

bureaucracy An administrative structure usually composed of officials in a hierarchy.

Bush Doctrine Also known as the new National Security Strategy of the US, adopted in September 2002, providing for the pre-emptive use of force.

cease-fire An end or pause in hostilities.

censorship The suppression or prohibition of material considered harmful by those in control.

Central American Free Trade Agreement This US-proposed agreement, modeled after the North American Free Trade Agreement, promotes trade liberalization between the US and Costa Rica, the Dominican Republic, El Salvador, Guatemala, Honduras and Nicaragua.

chemical warfare Hostile use of chemical compounds, usually toxic agents.

civil disobedience The refusal to obey the demands or commands of a government or occupying power; violence or active measures of opposition are not used.

civil society The institutions, organizations and behaviors among the government, business world and family. Civil society includes voluntary and nonprofit organizations, philanthropic institutions and social and political movements.

coalition A temporary alliance between two or more political units for the purpose of joint action. In the 2003 Iraq war, the "coalition of the willing" involved primarily the US, Britain, Australia and Poland.

Coalition Provisional Authority A temporary administration set up in Iraq by the US and its allies in May 2003 to maintain stability, security and institutional structures until an interim government was established in June 2004.

coercion Forced compliance through fear and intimidation.

cold war The rivalry after World War II between the US and the Soviet Union and their respective allies.

collective security A concept that seeks to ensure peace through enforcement by the community of nations.

commission A body created to perform a function, administrative, legislative or judicial.

Commonwealth of Independent States A union of 12 of the 15 former Soviet republics, created in December 1991 to promote common policies.

communiqué An official document, usually an announcement to the public or press.

Comprehensive Nuclear Test-Ban Treaty Opened for signatures on Sept. 10, 1996, it established a global verification mechanism for nuclear weapons. The treaty says that signers agree not to carry out explosions of nuclear weapons and to prohibit and prevent such explosions anyplace under its jurisdiction or control.

conciliation The process of bringing two sides in a dispute to agree to a compromise.

conservatism An ideology generally characterized by a belief in individualism, with minimal government intervention in the economy and society.

consolidated appeals process A mechanism used by aid organizations to plan, carry out and monitor their activities; they use this data to produce a Common Humanitarian Action Plan and appeal to be presented to the international community yearly.

constituency A body of citizens that elects a representative to a public body.

constitution The fundamental rules and principles under which a state is organized.

constitutionalism The belief that governments will defer to the rules and principles of their constitutions and uphold the rule of law.

convention A practice or custom followed by nations. Some international laws are called conventions, like the Convention on the Rights of the Child.

Convention on the Elimination of All Forms of Discrimination Against Women Adopted by the General Assembly in 1979 as an international bill of rights for women, defining what constitutes discrimination and setting up an agenda for national action to end such differentiation.

coup d'état French for "blow to the state": a sudden overthrow of a government.

cross-borrowing Borrowing from one account to meet the needs of another.

Dayton Peace Accords An agreement among Bosnia, Herzegovina, Croatia and the Federal Republic of Yugoslavia in 1995 to respect one another's sovereignty and to settle future disputes peacefully.

delegate A representative.

delegation A group of representatives.

demilitarized zone The area between parties in a conflict where they have agreed not to deploy military forces. It may be placed under control of peacekeepers.

democracy A form of government in which political decisions are made by all citizens. In direct democracy, citizens exercise their control directly through the process of majority rule. In representative democracy, citizens exercise the same right through representatives chosen by election.

Department of Peacekeeping Operations The main UN office dealing with peacekeeping and peace-building.

developed countries Those with more fully industrialized economies, more productive agriculture and a relatively high standard of living.

developing countries Those not fully industrialized, with limited specialization and financial savings. These countries are identified by a population that is outgrowing its resources and who have a low standard of living.

diplomacy The conduct of relations between nations, often through representatives empowered to seek agreements.

diplomatic immunity Special rights for official representatives of foreign governments, including immunity from laws in the country to which they are assigned.

directive A communication in which policy is established or a specific action is ordered concerning conduct or procedure.

disarmament The reduction or removal of armed forces and armaments.

displaced person Someone left homeless as a result of war or disaster. A person fleeing war or disaster who crosses a national border is considered a refugee. People who take flight but never leave their country are considered internally displaced persons.

draft resolution A document prepared for formal debate; it is written in the form of a resolution but has not been adopted by the committee.

dumping In relation to trade, the selling of goods in a foreign market below the cost of production, or for less than they are sold in the home market.

Economic and Social Council A 54-member body elected by the General Assembly to three-year terms. It is responsible for coordinating and overseeing UN economic and social work.

economic growth An increase in a nation's production of goods and services, often measured by gross national product.

embargo A government order prohibiting entry or departure of foreign commercial carriers, especially as a war measure. Also refers to a restriction imposed on commerce by law.

embassy A body of diplomatic representatives, specifically one headed by an ambassador.

eminent domain Also called condemnation or expropriation, this describes the power of government to take private property for public use without the owner's consent.

envoy A diplomatic agent of any rank.

epidemic An infectious disease widespread among the population of a community or region.

ethnic cleansing The expulsion, imprisonment or killing of members of one ethnic group by another seeking ethnic homogeneity.

ethnocentrism Belief in the inherent superiority of one's own cultural or ethnic group.

European Union With its headquarters in Brussels, this organization of 25 countries seeks economic and social progress for a strong European presence in the world and a free and secure citizenship.

exile A prolonged stay away from one's country or community, usually forced. The term can also refer to banishment but is sometimes self-imposed.

extort To get money or other items of value through violence, threats or misuse of authority.

extremist One who supports ideas, doctrines or policies beyond the norm, usually in politics or religion.

facilitator In diplomacy, a neutral person or country bringing warring parties to a meeting with the goal of exchanging views and, possibly, finding preliminary agreement. The facilitator's role is less formal than that of a mediator or a broker in a treaty negotiation.

faction An association of people hoping to influence a government toward actions favorable to their interests; known also as an interest group.

famine An acute general shortage of food.

federalism A system of government in which sovereignty is distributed among a central government and provincial or state governments.

Food and Agriculture Organization Headquartered in Rome, FAO was founded in 1945 with a mandate to raise levels of nutrition and standards of living, to improve agricultural productivity and to better the condition of rural populations.

free trade Trade carried on without governmental regulations, especially international trade conducted without protective tariffs and customs duties.

Group of Seven (G7) First made up of the seven most industrialized nations--Britain, Canada, France, Germany, Italy, Japan and the US--the group now includes Russia and is more often referred to as the Group of Eight (G8).

Group of Eight (G8) See G7.

Group of 20 (G20) A group of nations created in 1999 that includes the world's leading industrialized countries (G8), the European Union, the International Monetary Fund and the World Bank. The G20 is a forum to promote dialogue between developed and developing countries on key issues of economic growth and the financial system.

Group of 77 (G77) A group established in 1964 by 77 developing countries that now has 130 members. As the largest coalition in the UN, it provides a way for the developing world to promote its collective economic interests and enhance its negotiating strength.

General Agreement on Tariffs and Trade, or GATT. This 1948 agreement was incorporated into and superseded by the World Trade Organization in January 1995. The 100-plus members of GATT established rules for international trade, with the aim of reducing trade barriers. The World Trade Organization offers a dispute-settlement system to enforce those rules.

General Assembly The central deliberative organ of the UN. Each of the 192 member states is represented equally and has a vote.

genocide Systematic killing to eliminate a whole people or nation

Global Fund The Global Fund for HIV/AIDS, Tuberculosis and Malaria is a non-UN body initiated by Secretary-General Kofi Annan to raise money to fight deadly diseases in developing nations.

grassroots Originating among ordinary citizens.

gross domestic product An economic measure embracing the total value of all products manufactured and goods provided within a territory (often, per year). Like the gross national product (see below) it is used to assess a nation's economy.

gross national product The value of all goods and services produced by a country's nationals.

guerrilla A member of an irregular force of soldiers, usually volunteers.

habeas corpus Latin for "you have the body." A legal action demanding that a prisoner be brought before the court.

The Hague Home to many international courts and tribunals, particularly the International Criminal Court.

head of government The person in effective charge of the executive branch of a government. In a parliamentary system, the prime minister.

head of state The person who represents the state but may not exercise political power. In a parliamentary system, it may be a president or a monarch.

human rights law Obligations regulating government behavior toward groups and individuals in political, civil, economic, social and cultural spheres.

ideology A system of beliefs and values.

immunity Exemption from the application of a rule or jurisdiction.

indictment A formal written statement by a court or other authority calling upon a prosecutor to start a trial on specified charges.

indigenous Born, growing or produced naturally in a region or country; native.

inter alia Latin term for "among other things."

interdependence Dependence on each other or one another; mutual dependence.

intergovernmental organization Any body with two or more member states.

International Atomic Energy Agency Established in 1957. With headquarters in Vienna, this agency serves as the world center for nuclear information and cooperation. It is also the chief inspector of the world's nuclear facilities.

International Court of Justice Also known as the World Court, this is the main judicial organ of the UN for settling disputes between member countries and giving advisory opinions to the UN and its agencies. It does not hear cases brought by or against individual people or private organizations nor does it hear criminal cases.

International Criminal Court A permanent court established in 1998 with jurisdiction over individual people accused of war crimes, crimes against humanity or genocide.

international criminal law This involves violations of international law that point to individual criminal accountability. It provides a legal basis for trying heads of state and the like on charges of genocide, war crimes and crimes against humanity.

International Criminal Police Organization or Interpol Established in 1956, it promotes international cooperation among police authorities. Interpol has 181 members.

International Criminal Tribunal for the former Yugoslavia Established by the Security Council in 1993, this organization was created to prosecute those responsible for serious violations of international humanitarian law since 1991 in the territory that was formerly Yugoslavia.

International Criminal Tribunal for Rwanda Established by the Security Council in 1994, this organization was created to prosecute those responsible for genocide and other serious violations of international humanitarian law committed in the year 1994 in Rwanda, or by Rwandans in neighbor states.

International Development Association Created in 1960, it provides interest-free loans to the world's poorest countries. It is part of the World Bank group.

International Finance Corporation A member of the World Bank Group, this corporation was founded in 1956. It is currently the largest multilateral source of financing for private-sector projects in the developing world.

international humanitarian law Also called the law of war or armed conflict law, this aims to protect those who are not taking part in hostilities and restricts the methods of fighting between countries or other combatants.

International Labor Organization Set up in 1919, it became a specialized agency of the UN in 1946. It seeks to improve working and living conditions by establishing standards that reduce social injustice in areas like employment, pay, health, job safety and freedom of association among workers.

international law Traditionally defined as the agreements and principles governing relations between countries; increasingly it regulates state behavior toward nonstate actors.

International Law Commission Established in 1947 with a membership of 15 people competent in international law, it encourages progressive development of international law and its codification.

internally displaced person See displaced person.

International Monetary Fund Established at the Bretton Woods Conference in 1944, it provides financial advice and financing to countries having trouble with their balance of payments.

interstate Actions between two or more states or countries.

Intifada The word has come to symbolize the Palestinian uprising against Israeli occupation.

intrastate Actions within a state or country.

Joint United Nations Program on HIV/AIDS This body began work in 1995 as the main advocate for global action on HIV/AIDS under the sponsorship of the UN Children's Fund, the UN Development Program, the UN Population Fund, the UN Educational, Scientific and Cultural Organization, the World Health Organization and the World Bank. Today, the UN Office on Drugs and Crime, the International Labor Organization and the World Food Program also sponsor it.

junta A Spanish word for a group or council holding governmental power. After a revolution or coup d'état, frequently a group of military officers.

Kyoto Protocol 1997 A treaty resulting from the UN Framework Convention on Climate Change, this agreement outlines goals to limit greenhouse gas emissions and honor commitments to reduce greenhouse gas by the signing nations.

League of Arab States See Arab League.

League of Nations Organization created after World War I to achieve international peace and security.

least-developed country A country characterized by a low standard of living, limited industrial capacity and long-term barriers to economic growth.

Loya Jirga A Pashtun phrase meaning "grand council." For centuries, leaders in Afghanistan have convened Loya Jirgas to choose new kings, adopt constitutions and decide important political matters. The most recent such process was set in motion by the Bonn Agreement of Dec. 5, 2001.

mandate As it applies to the UN, it is an authoritative command given by the Security Council or General Assembly to a UN mission or representative.

maquiladora Assembly production of products in Mexico using US resources.

member state One of the 191 countries now belonging to the UN.

microcredit The lending of small amounts of money to people unable to provide traditional collateral or security. Microcredit has emerged in places like Bangladesh as a way for people to set up a business and escape poverty.

Millennium Development Goals Eight benchmarks and accompanying targets agreed upon at the Millennium Summit of 2000. It set goals to be reached by 2015 for poverty eradication and developmental progress worldwide.

Millennium Summit Conference A meeting on Sept. 6-8, 2000, at UN headquarters. It gathered 150 heads of state and government to tackle global challenges. The Millennium Declaration outlines the eight Millennium Development Goals.

Montreal Protocol Signed in 1987 and amended in 1990 and 1992, this pact aims to protect the stratospheric ozone layer.

most-favored nation The clause in a treaty by which one party or both agree to grant to the other all privileges granted to any third party.

multilateral Involving or participated in by more than two nations or parties.

nation Individuals in a specific geographical area who share a strong historical continuity, common culture and language and are under the rule of one government.

nation-state A sovereign state whose citizens or subjects are relatively homogeneous in factors like language or common descent.

nationalism Loyalty and devotion to a nation, especially a sense of national consciousness exalting one nation above all others and placing primary emphasis on promotion of its culture and interests.

national interest Interests specific to a nation-state, especially including survival and maintenance of power.

nationalize To take over ownership, performed by a national government.

Nonaligned Countries An alliance of third-world nations seeking to promote the political and economic interests of developing countries. At the UN, this alliance is referred to as the nonaligned movement.

nongovernmental organization A nonprofit organization that contributes to development through cooperative projects, financial and material aid, education and the dispatch of personnel. Some NGOs are accredited by the UN system and can represent their interests before the Economic and Social Council.

North American Free Trade Agreement An agreement that became effective in January 1994 among Canada, the US and Mexico.

North Atlantic Treaty Organization or NATO A military alliance formed in 1949 when 12 democratic nations signed the treaty. NATO now has 26 members.

Nuclear Nonproliferation Treaty Taking effect in 1970, this treaty was intended to limit the number of countries with nuclear weapons to five: the US, Soviet Union, Britain, France and China. Since then, more than 140 countries have pledged not to acquire nuclear weapons and to accept the safeguards of the International Atomic Energy Agency.

observer mission Unarmed officers sent to observation posts to monitor cease-fires and armistices.

Official Development Assistance Loans, grants, technical assistance and other forms of cooperation extended by governments to developing nations to promote progress.

Organization of American States A regional organization created in 1948 to promote Latin American development. It has 35 members. Cuba remains a member but has been excluded from participation since 1962.

Organization of the Islamic Conference An association of 57 countries and three observer Islamic countries seeking Muslim cohesion in social, economic and political matters.

pandemic An infectious disease affecting a large part of the population in a wide geographical area, often on a global scale.

peace enforcement Also known as third-generation peacekeeping. This does not require consent from the conflicting parties and is undertaken to protect the populace from an aggressor or a civil war.

peacekeeper A person assigned to help maintain peace where conflict has just ended. Peacekeepers can include civilian staff; "peacekeeping soldiers" do not.

peacekeeping operation This involves military personnel operating under the precepts of impartiality and neutrality, undertaken by the UN to help maintain or restore international peace and security. Second-generation peacekeeping, which includes preventive diplomacy and post-conflict peacebuilding, is based on the consent of the parties involved and incorporates a multi-faceted UN role.

peacebuilding mission A project aimed at development activities in post-conflict regions to ensure that conflicts do not resume and that reconstruction efforts are fair.

peacemaking A diplomatic process of brokering an end to conflict, principally through mediation and negotiation. Military activities contributing to peacemaking include military-to-military contacts, security assistance, shows of force and preventive deployments.

permanent five The five permanent members of the UN Security Council, now the US, Britain, Russia, China and France.

political asylum Protection granted to a person by a foreign government when the applicant demonstrates that he or she would be persecuted or harmed if returned to the country of origin.

political office UN political offices work to support the peace missions through reconciliation and negotiation.

preventive deployment The interposition of a military force to deter violence in a zone of potential conflict.

preventive diplomacy Also known as conflict prevention, this form of diplomacy is geared to prevent disputes from arising.

protectionism The practice of protecting domestic products from foreign competition by placing tariffs and quotas on imports.

protocol A document that records basic agreements reached in negotiations before the formal document is ready for signing.

quorum The number of members of an organization required to be present for conduct of business.

recosting A UN budgetary practice providing for adjustment of foreign exchange rates and inflation assumptions in a budgetary cycle.

referendum The practice of submitting to popular vote a measure proposed by a legislative body or sought by part of the public; a referendum is a direct vote in which an entire electorate is asked to accept or reject a proposal.

refugee See displaced person.

regular budget At the UN, includes costs of the Secretariat in New York, the UN offices in Geneva, Vienna and Nairobi, the regional commissions, the International Court of Justice and the Center for Human Rights. More than 70 percent of the UN regular budget is earmarked for staff costs. The scale of assessment (how much each country owes) is based on the principle of capacity to pay.

repatriate To restore or return to the country of origin, allegiance or citizenship.

resolution A document adopted by a committee or body that expresses the opinions and decisions of the UN.

rule of law The principle that authority is legitimately exercised only in accordance with written, publicly disclosed laws adopted and enforced in accordance with established procedural steps.

sanction An economic or military measure, usually by several nations in concert, to force a nation violating international law to desist.

Security Council The UN organ responsible for maintaining peace and security. It is composed of five permanent member—Britain, China, France, Russia and the US—and 10 rotating members elected to two-year terms by the General Assembly to represent equitable geographic distribution.

Secretariat The UN organ that runs the daily affairs of the organization. It consists of international civil servants and is led by the secretary-general.

Secretary-General Defined in the UN Charter as the chief administrative officer of the UN and head of the Secretariat. The secretary-general acts as the primary spokesperson and de facto leader of the UN.

self-determination The choice of a people in a given area to select their own political status or independence.

sovereign Supreme power, especially over a body politic; political authority free from external control.

sovereignty Autonomy; the right to control a government, a country, a people or oneself.

state-building (nation-building) The concept of rebuilding a post-conflict country, most often so that its sovereignty is recognized by the international community.

state party Countries that are party to—or have joined as a member—a particular group or have signed a particular protocol or other document.

sustainable development A term for economic progress that meets the needs of the present without compromising the potential of future generations.

terrorism The systematic use of unpredictable violence against governments or people to attain a political objective.

treaty A formal, binding international agreement. In the US, treaties proposed by the executive branch that have been negotiated with a foreign country or international organization must be approved by a two-thirds majority in the Senate and then signed by the president.

tribunal A committee or board appointed to judge a particular matter.

truce A suspension of fighting by agreement.

Trusteeship Council A principal organ of the UN, it was established to help ensure that nonself-governing territories were administered in the best interests of the inhabitants, peace and security. The council suspended operation in 1994 after the independence of Palau, the last remaining UN trust territory.

United Nations Charter It established the UN and its method of operating and was drawn up and signed by representatives of 50 countries in 1945.

United Nations Children's Fund or Unicef Founded in 1946 as the UN International Children's Emergency Fund. With headquarters in Paris, it is the only UN organization devoted solely to children and their rights.

United Nations Development Fund for Women Created in 1976, the fund fosters the empowerment of women and gender equity.

United Nations Development Program The main body for UN development work and the largest provider of developmental grant assistance in the UN system.

Universal Declaration of Human Rights A proclamation of the basic rights and freedoms of all people, adopted by the General Assembly on Dec.10, 1948, and commemorated every year on Human Rights Day.

United Nations Educational, Scientific and Cultural Organization (Unesco) A specialized agency working for world peace and security by promoting collaboration in education, science, culture and communication.

United Nations Environment Program Headquartered in Nairobi, Kenya, this project provides leadership and encourages partnerships to protect the environment.

United Nations Framework Convention on Climate Change To counter global warming, this agency seeks to stabilize greenhouse-gas concentrations in the atmosphere and to disseminate technology and information to help developing countries adapt to climate change.

United Nations High Commissioner for Human Rights A UN office established in 1993 to protect human rights.

United Nations High Commissioner for Refugees A UN office created by the General Assembly in 1951 to help refugees.

United Nations Population Fund The largest internationally financed source of population assistance for developing countries. It began its work in 1967.

United Nations University An international educational institution engaged in scholarly work on pressing global problems. Its two main goals are to strengthen research and educational abilities of institutions in developing countries and make policy-relevant contributions to the UN's work. It was established in 1972 and has its headquarters in Tokyo.

war crime A crime that breaches the laws of international armed conflict as defined by the Geneva Conventions, Hague Conventions and, most recently, the Rome Statute. War crimes include, but are not limited to, willful killing, torture or inhumane treatment, unlawful deportation, various abuses against prisoners of war, taking of hostages and extensive destruction and appropriation of property not justified by military necessity and carried out unlawfully and wantonly.

weapons of mass destruction Weapons, biological, chemical and nuclear, designed to kill large numbers of people at once.

World Bank Established at the Bretton Woods Conference in 1944. As a multilateral lending agency, it seeks to reduce poverty by promoting sustainable growth.

World Food Program The frontline UN organization fighting to eradicate hunger. Its headquarters are in Rome and it began work in 1963.

World Health Organization Founded in 1948 with headquarters in Geneva, this organization promotes technical health cooperation among nations, carries out programs to control and eradicate disease and works to improve the quality of life.

World Trade Organization An international organization meant to liberalize trade. It is a forum for governments to negotiate trade agreements and settle disputes.

Zionism Zionist ideology holds that Jews are a people or nation and should gather in a single homeland. Zionism evolved into an international movement for the establishment of a Jewish community in Palestine and later for the support of modern Israel.

Appendix G: And the Prize Goes to . . .

Compiled by Tendai Musakwa

The selection of Martti Ahtisaari, a former UN under-secretary-general, for the 2008 Nobel Peace prizes, brings the total to three prizes in the last five years that have been awarded to people directly related or affiliated with the UN. These accomplishments underscore the organization's role as the world's foremost peacekeeper.

2008: Ahtisaari joined the UN in 1976 in the UN Institute for Namibia, when it was established as the first university in southwest Africa. (It is now called the University of Namibia.) Ahtissari then rose through UN ranks, ultimately becoming under-secretary-general for administration and management in 1987 under Secretary-General Javier Pérez de Cuéllar. Ahtisaari won the Peace Prize in recognition of his mediation efforts in Asia, Africa and Europe.

2007: The UN's Intergovernmental Panel on Climate Change and former US vice president Al Gore were jointly awarded the prize for their work on global warming. The panel was honored for bringing thousands of scientists and officials together to establish certainty on climate change.

2005: The International Atomic Energy Agency (IAEA) and its director general, Mohamed ElBaradei, were honored for their work on nuclear nonproliferation. ElBaradei was a diplomat at Egypt's permanent mission to the UN in New York and worked as senior fellow in charge of the international law program at the UN Institute for Training and Research before heading the IAEA.

2001: The UN and Kofi Annan, the secretary-general at the time, were both awarded the prize "for their work for a better organized and more peaceful world," the Nobel Committee said. Annan was cited for rejuvenating the UN, particularly in working on peace, security and human rights as well as the challenges of HIV/AIDS and terrorism. The committee citation proclaimed that "the only negotiable route to global peace and cooperation goes by way of the United Nations."

1988: UN peacekeeping forces were recipients for operating "under extremely difficult conditions" while contributing to "reducing tensions where an armistice has been negotiated but a peace treaty has yet to be established" and therefore making a decisive effort towards "the initiation of actual peace negotiations."

1981: The Office of the UN High Commissioner for Refugees "carried out work of major importance to assist refugees, despite the many political difficulties with which it has had to contend," namely coping with increasing numbers of refugees flowing from Vietnam and the exodus from Afghanistan and Ethiopia.

1969: On its 50th anniversary, the International Labor Organization, a specialized agency, was honored for succeeding in "translating into action the fundamental moral idea on which it was based"—that is, "if you desire peace, cultivate justice."

1965: Unicef, for acting as a "peace factor of great importance" and for forging a link of solidarity between rich and poor countries and the caring for children.

1961: Dag Hammarskjold, the second secretary-general of the UN, from 1953 until his death in 1961, was the only person to receive the Nobel Peace Prize posthumously (though he had been nominated before he died). He was instrumental in establishing the first UN peacekeeping force and became deeply involved in the Congo war in the early 1960s and died in a plane crash while on a UN mission in the region.

1954: To the UN High Commissioner for Refugees for its work helping refugees and displaced people in Europe in the aftermath of World War II.

1950: Ralph Bunche, UN mediator in Palestine, received the prize for his mediation of the 1949 armistice between Israel and seven Arab countries. By carrying out these difficult talks, the committee stated, and "by exercising infinite patience," Bunche "finally succeeded in persuading all parties to accept an armistice."

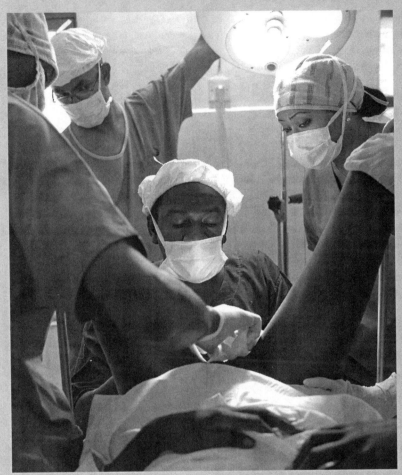

Repairing and ending obstetric fistula among poor women is a major project of the UN Population Fund. Here, a fistula medical team examines a patient in Zalingei, Sudan.

Charts and Tables

Ongoing UN Peacekeeping Operations, as of September 2008

The United Nations deployed approximately 109,000 personnel to 16 UN peacekeeping operations as of September 2008. This table indicates the location, personnel distribution, and mandate type and size of each operation. (Dollars in millions)

Name of operation/ location/ start date	2008–2009 budget	Troops and military observers	Police	Civilians (international, local, and UN volunteers)	Total	Mandate type and number of mandated tasks
UN Organization Mission in the Democratic Republic of the Congo (MONUC) November 1999	1,242.73	17,369	1,065	3,657	22,091	Multidimensional 12
UN Mission in Liberia (UNMIL) September 2003	631.69	11,671	1,037	1,688	14,396	Multidimensional 10
UN Mission in Côte d'Ivoire (UNOCI) April 2004	497.46	8,017	1,136	1,305	10,458	Multidimensional 9
UN Stabilization Mission in Haiti (MINUSTAH) June 2004	601.58	7,012	1,868	1,900	10,780	Multidimensional 11
UN Mission in the Sudan (UNMIS) March 2005	858.77	9,333	600	3,457	13,390	Multidimensional 14
UN Integrated Mission in Timor L'este (UNMIT) August 2006	180.84	33	1,542	1,377	2,952	Multidimensional 10
African Union/United Nations Hybrid Operation in Darfur (UNAMID) Sudan Authorized July 31, 2007; started December 31, 2007	1569.26	8,422	2,039	2,244	12,705	Multidimensional 13
African Republic and Chad (MINURCAT) September 2007	315.08	45	226	481	752	Multidimensional 7
TOTAL	**$7,057.75**	**76,900**	**11,515**	**20,692**	**109,107**	

Source: GAO analysis of UN data.

[a]Figures are rounded to nearest $10,000.

[b]UNTSO and UNMOGIP are funded from the United Nations regular biennial budget. Costs to the United Nations of the other current operations are financed from their own separate accounts on the basis of legally binding assessments on all member states. For these missions, budget figures are for July 2008—June 2009 unless otherwise specified.

[c]A UN document notes that the total peacekeeping budget is about $7,080 million, as it includes $105.01 million funded for the United Nations Mission in Ethiopia and Eritrea (UNMEE) operation that ended in July 2008, and requirements for the support account for peacekeeping operations and the UN Logistics Base in Brindisi (Italy). Pg. 56 GAO-09-142 UN peacekeeping.

Name of operation/ location/ start date	2008-2009 budget	Troops and military observers	Police	Civilians (international, local, and UN volunteers)	Total	Mandate type and number of mandated tasks
UN Truce Supervision Organization in Palestine (UNTSO) Middle East 1948-	66.22[b]	142	0	235	377	Traditional 2
UN Military Observer Group in India and Pakistan (UNMOGIP) Jammu, Kashmir and Pakistan 1949-	16.96[b]	44	0	71	115	Traditional 1
UN Peacekeeping Force in Cyprus (UNFICYP) 1964	57.39	846	69	146	1,061	Traditional 3
U.N. Disengagement Observer Force (UNDOF) Israel-Syria: Golan Heights 1974	47.86	1,043	0	144	1,187	Traditional 2
UN Force for Southern Lebanon (UNIFIL) 1978 augmented 2006	680.93	12,543	0	963	13,506	Multidimensional 6
UN Mission for the Referendum in Western Sahara (MINURSO) Apr. 1991	47.70	21[c]	6	270	495	Multidimensional 2
UN Observer Mission in Georgia (UNOMIG) Aug. 1993	36.08	132	17	273	422	Traditional 3
UN Interim Administration Mission in Kosovo (UNMIK) June 1999	207.20	29	1,910	2,481	4,420	Multidimensional 10

Global Summary of the AIDS Pandemic

Compiled by Max McGowen

Number of people living with HIV in 2007	**Total**	**~33.2 million**
	Adults	~30.8 million
	Women	~15.4 million
	Under 15	~2.5 million
People newly infected with HIV in 2007	**Total**	**~2.5 million**
	Adults	~2.1 million
	Under 15	~420,000
AIDS deaths in 2007	**Total**	**~2.1 million**
	Adults	~1.7 million
	Under 15	~330,000

Source: 2007 AIDS Epidemic Update, Global Overview, UNAIDS & WHO
Note: The ~ symbol represents an approximation

Consolidated Appeals

Compiled by Max McGowen

The consolidated appeals process is a tool used by worldwide aid organizations to plan, carry out and monitor their activities together as well as request money. The appeals are presented to the international community and donors once a year in New York and Geneva and in countries where aid groups work. The UN Office for the Coordination of Human Affairs manages the appeals process. Here is a snapshot of recent years' financial requests.

(#'s in millions of US$)

2009
Original requirements: $7,015
Revised requirements: $7,100
Commitments, contributions and carryover: $50.4
Amount covered: 1%
Unmet requirement: $7,050
Uncommitted pledges: $3.8

2008
Original requirements: $5,674
Revised requirements: $7,163
Commitments, contributions and carryover: $5,009
Amount covered: 70%
Unmet requirement: $2,154
Uncommitted pledges: $181.1

2007
Original requirements: $4,455
Revised requirements: $5,142
Commitments, contributions and carryover: $3,724
Amount covered: 72%
Unmet requirement: $1,148
Uncommitted pledges: $21.7

2006
Original requirements: $4,351
Revised requirements: $5,061
Commitments, contributions and carryover: $3,364
Amount covered: 66%
Unmet requirements: $1,697
Uncommitted pledges: $59.3

Source: ReliefWeb Financial Tracking Service

Charts compiled by the UN Office for the Coordination of Humanitarian Affairs (OCHA)

Millennium Development Goals and Targets

Compiled by Max McGowen

GOAL 1: ERADICATE EXTREME HUNGER AND POVERTY

Target 1. By 2015, halve the proportion of people whose income is less than $1 a day.

Target 2. By 2015, halve the proportion of people who suffer from hunger.

GOAL 2: ACHIEVE UNIVERSAL PRIMARY EDUCATION

Target 3. Ensure that by 2015, boys and girls everywhere will be able to complete a full course of primary schooling.

GOAL 3: PROMOTE GENDER EQUALITY AND EMPOWER WOMEN

Target 4. Eliminate gender disparity in primary and secondary education, preferably by 2005, and in all levels of education no later than 2015.

GOAL 4: REDUCE CHILD MORTALITY

Target 5. By 2015, reduce the under-five mortality rate by two-thirds.

GOAL 5: IMPROVE MATERNAL HEALTH

Target 6. By 2015, reduce the maternal mortality ratio by three-quarters.

GOAL 6: COMBAT HIV/AIDS, MALARIA AND OTHER DISEASES

Target 7. By 2015, have stopped and begun to reverse the spread of HIV/AIDS.

Target 8. By 2015, have stopped and begun to reverse the incidence of malaria and other major diseases.

GOAL 7: ENSURE ENVIRONMENTAL SUSTAINABILITY

Target 9. Integrate the principles of sustainable development into country policies and programs and reverse the loss of environmental resources.

Target 10. By 2015, halve the proportion of people without sustainable access to safe drinking water and basic sanitation.

Target 11. By 2020, achieve a major improvement in the lives of at least 100 million slum dwellers.

GOAL 8: DEVELOP A GLOBAL PARTNERSHIP FOR DEVELOPMENT

Target 12. Develop further an open, rule-based, predictable, nondiscriminatory trading and financial system (includes a commitment to good governance, development and poverty reduction, both nationally and internationally).

Target 13. Address the special needs of least-developed countries (includes tariff- and quota-free access for least-developed countries' exports, enhanced program of debt relief for heavily indebted poor countries and cancellation of official bilateral debt and more generous official development assistance for countries committed to poverty reduction).

Target 14. Address the special needs of landlocked developing countries and small island developing states (through the Program of Action for the Sustainable Development of Small Island Developing States and 22nd General Assembly provisions).

Target 15. Deal comprehensively with the debt problems of developing countries through national and international measures to make debt sustainable in the long term.

Target 16. In cooperation with developing countries, develop and carry out strategies for decent and productive work for youth.

Target 17. In cooperation with pharmaceutical companies, provide access to affordable essential drugs in developing countries.

Target 18. In cooperation with the private sector, make available the benefits of new technologies, especially information and communications technology.

Source: UN Millennium Project, 2006

"A Global Agenda" Index

Membership Application

Join UNA-USA today and become part of a nationwide movement for a more effective United Nations:

The United Nations Association of the United States of America (UNA-USA) is the nation's largest grassroots foreign policy organization and a leading center of policy research on the UN and global issues. UNA-USA offers Americans the opportunity to connect with issues confronted by the UN and encourages public support for strong US leadership in the UN. UNA-USA is a member of the World Federation of United Nations Associations.

For more information on the organization or how to join, visit www.unausa.org.

To join UNA-USA by mail, please return this form with your payment to:

UNA-USA MEMBERSHIP SERVICES
801 Second Avenue, New York, NY 10017

☐ $1,000 Lifetime (one-time dues payment)

☐ $500 Patron

☐ $100 Sponsor

☐ $40 Member

☐ $25 Introductory (first year only)

☐ $25 Limited Income

NAME

ADDRESS

CITY, STATE AND ZIP

HOME PHONE / CELLPHONE   BUSINESS PHONE

E-MAIL

CHECK ONE: ☐ AMEX ☐ MASTERCARD ☐ VISA ☐ DISCOVER

CREDIT CARD NUMBER

EXPIRATION DATE

SIGNATURE

Membership in UNA-USA is open to any citizen or resident of the US who is committed to the purposes of UNA-USA, a 501(c)3 nonprofit organization.

Breinigsville, PA USA
09 January 2010
230455BV00005B/54/P